Legal Issues in Cultural Heritage Management

Lex et Res Publica
Polish Legal and Political Studies
Edited by Anna Jaroń

Volume 5

Zur Qualitätssicherung und Peer Review der vorliegenden Publikation

Die Qualität der in dieser Reihe erscheinenden Arbeiten wird vor der Publikation durch die Herausgeberin der Reihe geprüft.

Notes on the quality assurance and peer review of this publication

Prior to publication, the quality of the work published in this series is reviewed by the editor of the series.

Alicja Jagielska-Burduk / Wojciech Szafrański

Legal Issues in Cultural Heritage Management

A Polish Perspective

PL ACADEMIC RESEARCH

Bibliographic Information published by the Deutsche Nationalbibliothek
The Deutsche Nationalbibliothek lists this publication in the Deutsche Nationalbibliografie; detailed bibliographic data is available in the internet at http://dnb.d-nb.de.

Project financed with the resources from the National Science Centre.
Decision number: DEC-2012/05/D/HS5/02822.
Reviewer: Kamil Zeidler

Translation and proof-reading:
Iwona Grenda, Maria Ingham, Piotr Tomasz Żebrowski, John Ingham, Ryszard J. Reisner

NATIONAL SCIENCE CENTRE
POLAND

ISBN 978-3-631-67033-0 (Print)
E-ISBN 978-3-653-06247-2 (E-Book)
DOI 10.3726/ 978-3-653-06247-2

PL Academic Research is an Imprint of Peter Lang GmbH.

Peter Lang – Frankfurt am Main · Bern · Bruxelles · New York ·
Oxford · Warszawa · Wien

This publication has been peer reviewed

www.peterlang.com

Contents

I. "The economics of cultural heritage protection law" or the Loch Ness Monster

It happens very rarely that arguments related with law, economics or cultural heritage arouse the interest among those who are not professionally involved in them. The creation of economic models or the refining of legal concepts can be as boring to the average reader or listener as the fourth hour of a guided tour in a museum. Each of these disciplines not only uses its own hermetic language but also implies a starting point which is not accepted by other disciplines that assume different points of view. Each discipline is quite sensitive about its assumptions and keen to point out mistakes made by researchers from other disciplines. For example, economists sharpen their knives and become quite sensitive about the use of terms such as economy and the economics of culture.[1] Lawyers, in turn, are sensitive about the conceptual ranges of terms such as monument, cultural property or heritage. There are numerous recurring questions e.g. what is heritage management? Can it be distinguished from culture management and, if so, how, etc.?

The situation gets even worse when one tries to combine the three elements and create something in the nature of "the economics of cultural heritage protection law", a kind of hybrid in which both the assumptions, arguments and conclusions ought to take into consideration the fact that all these elements permeate each other. The hybrid could be compared to the Loch Ness Monster, because everyone denies its existence and at the same time would like to believe that they would be the one to prove its existence, just as they would 'discover' an exceptional model of heritage management. Furthermore, even if many researchers claim there is nothing to discover, it is still worthwhile to research, analyse and spend time on it. Just as the very image of the Loch Ness Monster is useful for the tourists and local people making a living from the legend, so is "the economics of cultural heritage protection law" useful for political decision-makers or directors of cultural institutions

1 If the economics of culture, as a branch of economics, deals with the cultural sector or, as claimed nowadays, with creative industries and analyses phenomena and economic patterns in culture among which there are cultural industries, then the study of the cultural economy deals with the way culture influences national economic management and the national economy and thereby the wellbeing of individuals and society. See D. Ilczuk, *Ekonomika kultury*, Warszawa 2012, pp. 21–28; M. Noga, *Kultura a ekonomia*, Warszawa 2014, pp. 83–97.

for implementing and explaining changes (or stopping them) or for the critics of the current model of heritage protection. Every researcher has his own idea of the importance of law and economics in relation to cultural heritage just as everyone imagines the Loch Ness Monster in their own way and no one really knows which one is the absolutely true and final one. There is only agreement as to its general image and to the general assumptions about the way economics, law and cultural heritage influence each other. The only difference between the Loch Ness Monster and the hybrid of "the economics of cultural heritage protection laws" is the amount of data available, in the former case rather minimal and in the latter in an overabundance which prevents the uniform tracking of the influences of individual factors. Despite the extreme differences the results are the same in both cases as one can never completely recreate reality (you cannot analyse data either too limited or overabundant) but that does not mean that there is no point in studying these issues. On the contrary, each new study in this field allows us to accumulate arguments in favour of the importance of the particular disciplines of economics, law and cultural heritage and the need to fill the gaps that have appeared in the process of their development or their isolation.

It is worth noting here that the Loch Ness Monster as such also belongs to cultural heritage, most definitely to world heritage, which is also confirmed by law (intangible heritage protection law) and by economics (the supremacy of the benefits over the costs of its supposed existence).

In the case of a hybrid such as "the economics of cultural heritage protection law" every researcher representing one of these disciplines will strive to prove the superiority of his or her discipline over the other two as, broadly speaking, law, economics and cultural heritage have always existed as distinct spheres of human interest. Their combination can be accidental (or intentional) but is not of the greatest importance for either of them. A very particular type of personification, which helps to spark the imagination, has been proposed by David Throsby, an economist who specialises mainly in the economics of culture. In his argument, economics could be represented by a not terribly attractive man with a tendency to verbosity, while culture could be personified by a wise and unpredictable woman. These two meet at a party. David Throsby posed a number of questions. To what extent would they be interested in each other? Would they start seeing each other? What kind of relationship would there be between them?[2] Throsby's idea is so original and imaginative, even to people not connected with these disciplines, that it is worth further expansion, with the help of personification to demonstrate

2 See D. Thorsby, *Ekonomia i kultura*, Warszawa 2010, p. 1.

the relations between economics, law and cultural heritage. Such an experiment was carried out during a lecture on cultural heritage protection at the Faculty of Law and Administration of Adam Mickiewicz University in Poznań. Following Throsby's idea, economics would be personified by the not so attractive, slightly dishevelled and talkative man, with a tendency to hypochondria, cultural heritage by the aforementioned interesting woman and law was by a self-confident man, overdressed and probably over the top in other respects too. These three people meet at a party. Which of these two men would the woman choose to talk to first? Which of the two men would approach her first? The students unanimously chose the attractive man, i.e. law. They did not seem to realise that the rightness of this answer cannot only be explained by the personal relationship but could also be translated by the direct ties between law and heritage. It may sound rather paradoxical but it is law that creates cultural heritage by its choice of objects, as well as the scope and subject of protection. The lack of precision in the terminology in statements made by representatives of disciplines such as the history of art, sociology, cultural studies or architecture makes it untranslatable into legislative acts and gives law the dominant position in setting the framework of heritage protection.[3] Historically, this relationship is the older one, although not necessarily the more stable, and is still evolving. It is only in the next phases that economics has become interested in cultural heritage.[4] It was as late as the 90s of the 20th century that such institutions as the World Bank mentioned culture in their documents as well as cultural heritage as basic elements of economic development.

The woman might flirt with both men as she would find each one interesting and, moreover, useful.

a) She would consider economics as the justification of her existence and an unverifiable form of GDP creation through culture, including cultural heritage. In addition, it is axiomatic in economics that cultural heritage and its most precious monuments can only be viewed in relation to costs; benefits are considered guaranteed because of their practical and also non-practical value (existential, optional and inherited) and other external factors.[5]

3 Cf. J. P. Pruszyński, *Dziedzictwo kultury i ochrona zabytków w Polsce. Perspektywa na najbliższe dziesięciolecie*, in: *Spotkania w Willi Struvego 2001–2003. Wykłady o dziedzictwie kultury*, (eds.) D. Królak-Merska, K. J. Kwiecińska, Warszawa 2004, p. 148.

4 Despite the search for its source in the 18th century works of Adam Smith, it is only in the second half of the 20th century that there has been a growth of interest in research on the relationship of culture (including cultural heritage) and economics.

5 Cf. D. Throsby, op. cit., pp. 77–79.

Additionally, economics would work as a type of barrier against the law, which ought to reckon with economics. Sometimes the ideas of political decision-makers to increase standards of heritage protection can lead to catastrophic results for heritage[6] especially when the financial consequences of protecting too many monuments and direct and indirect costs are incorrectly calculated.

b) She would find law attractive as a way of advertising her own existence but also as protection against economy, which, with easy access to cultural heritage resources without any legal constraints, would try to measure and improve it on the basis of its own criteria of cost effectiveness. Thus the 'flirting' of heritage with economy and law would be profitable for the former but could also turn out dangerous if one of these disciplines were to gain total dominance in cultural heritage. We can find examples of this in the modern world.

Thus in cases of the pre-eminence of economy we have witnessed closures of public museums in the German Lands because of excessive costs and a lack of interest on the part of the general public which favours private museums (offering more interesting museum architecture or art narrative)[7], or the idea of selling museum exhibits by the Detroit Institute of Art (DIA) as a result of the bankruptcy of the city itself.

In the scenario where law is pre-eminent we have seen a new form of heritage protection in Poland, known as the List of National Treasures, with no definition of heritage treasure as such and with violations of the principle of proportionality between heritage protection and private ownership, which allows for an ex officio entry on the List of a movable monument despite the owner's objections or, in special circumstances, the takeover of a movable monument by the State.[8]

---

6 For example the functioning of heritage monuments (mainly palaces and stately homes) within the framework of the Agencja Nieruchomości Rolnych (Agency of Agricultural Property) or Agencja Mienia Wojskowego (Military Property Agency), which, as representatives of the State, are treated differently from the private owners of similar monuments. In practice this means that many of the monuments under the control of the two Agencies are allowed to fall into a state of complete disrepair and devastation with impunity.

7 Decision makers 'slept' through the moment of symbiosis in the work of publicly and privately owned collections.

8 A proposal for an amendment to the Act on the Protection and Guardianship of Monuments has been sent by the President of the Republic of Poland to the Constitutional Tribunal Court. See more in the chapter on the forms of protection.

It can thus be said that relationships and processes in the field of heritage protection exist also in the economic and legal spheres and are interpreted accordingly in their respective categories. This is why it is so important to prevent, on the one hand, heritage being turned too much into a commodity (a tendency of economists who like to ask about the economic value of heritage) and, on the other, the process of "tethering" by law practised by lawyers who invent more and more new forms of protection or who introduce new concepts without establishing their relations with existing ones or who overinterpret heritage protection in view of a lack of clarity in legislative acts.

At this point it is worth noting another process which has been intensifying along with the 'heating up' of the discussion on the economic importance of culture and the systematisation of the cultural and creative industries. Owing to the conventionality and ambiguity of the term 'heritage', many researchers like to create new cultural spheres and a hierarchisation of this sector in their search for ever stronger ties between culture and economy. These studies are based on the research carried out by KEA European Affairs for the European Commission and show how culture and the creative sector significantly influence information and communication technology as well as tourism and related sectors. Thus cultural heritage seems to be embedded in the cultural and creative industries and makes full use of the economic benefits of the culture sector.[9] Although the hierarchisation of the sector might raise some objections, in practice it is beneficial for cultural heritage as it implies an imperative to:

- finance heritage as if it were a type of kernel of the creative industries and consequently to have to draft heritage protection finance policies;
- justify the need for state intervention in this sector;
- create and sustain public awareness of the importance of culture in its broadest sense but also of cultural heritage as essential not only for future generations but also for contemporary generations because of their ability to create symbolic, historical, and also economic added value.

The observations made at the 'party' attended by cultural heritage, economics and law allow us to see the role of law as constitutionalising heritage by defining its protection and its importance in relation to the economy. It is worth noting here that law wears two types of suits at the same time when meeting heritage. The first is made for all sectors of the economy, including cultural heritage, the

9 Cf. more in KEA among others *The Impact of Culture on Creativity* of 2009 http://www.keanet.eu/docs/execsum_creativity_english%20.pdf?4f4eb7 (accessed: 10.07.2015).

second has been cut specifically for heritage itself. That is why law often looks ridiculous wearing two suits between which there are certain inconsistencies, which might have adverse consequences for heritage. Such a situation has occurred in Poland with respect to the purchase of a work of art (cultural property) from an unentitled vendor. Under Art. 169 § 2 of the Polish Civil Code purchasing an object of art from a vendor who is not its legal owner (unentitled vendor) may be deemed legal and result in the purchaser acquiring ownership of the object if the following conditions determining the validity of the sale have been fulfilled: i.e. the transfer of the object and good faith on the part of the buyer. Until 1990 these regulations had not been used in the evaluation of the disposal of state-owned properties. At that time Article 171 of the Polish Civil Code covering these situations was waived and now Article 169 of the Polish Civil Code applies to any type of ownership, including the trading of cultural property. No specific regulations similar to the Italian or French ones were introduced at that time either. Neither the amendment of the existing Act on the Protection of Cultural Property from 1990 nor the new Act of 2003 (APGM) or the very new regulations on museums have interfered to any degree in the principles of acquisition of cultural property based on the civil law regulations. The numerous problems that have appeared as a result of applying these articles and the unfavourable situations for the 'primary' owners have been pointed out and criticised in studies of this subject.[10] Changes in this legislation were introduced only in 2015 in connection with the introduction of the new legislation on unclaimed property and with the establishment of the National Register of Lost Cultural Property.

The dominant position of economics in the modern world has turned the economic type of reasoning into an indicator of rational thinking which is why it is possible to talk about the culture of 'economic self-confidence'. However, the 'culture of self-confidence' is not alien to law and, in my opinion, is more and more reinforced, not by the strength of the argument (the 'rational employer' which seems to be the only assumption first year law students have drummed into them has been turning into a myth) but by the force of the 'legislative authority' of the

10 Cf. Among others W. Kowalski, *Prawna ochrona zabytków w świetle aktualnych problemów zachowania dziedzictwa kulturowego Polski*, in: *Prawna ochrona dziedzictwa kulturowego. Wokół problematyki prawnej zabytków i dzieł sztuki*, Vol. 3, (eds.) W. Szafrański, K. Zalasińska, Poznań 2009, pp. 73–91; W. Kowalski, *Problematyka prawa obrotu dobrami kultury*, in: *Rynek sztuki. Aspekty prawne*, (eds.) W. Kowalski, K. Zalasińska, Warszawa 2011, pp. 38–42; A. Jagielska-Burduk, *Nabycie własności dobra kultury od nieuprawnionego. Wybrane zagadnienia*, "Santander Art and Culture Law Review" 2015, No. 1, pp. 118–133.

state, represented in the first place by political decision-makers and less so by the lawyers. The culture of the 'self-confidence' of law creates a mental barrier preventing full understanding of the consequences of cultural heritage protection law. One could quote here the system of export permits of cultural property which operated in Poland between 2003 and 2010 and certificates stating that no permit is required to export an object. The simultaneous existence of a high fee payable to obtain an individual export licence and the inability to control the export of cultural property in practice via the southern and western borders of Poland since 2007 has created a discrepancy between the legislative aims (i.e. increased heritage protection by restricting export) and reality. The number of export permits has gone down but the rate of smuggling out of cultural heritage property has gone up. Already at the stage of formulating these regulations many experts pointed out their 'paper' value; nevertheless political decision-makers paid no heed to those objections when passing the new laws.

A similar mental barrier is created by the culture of 'self-confidence' in the economy, which uses the arguments of economic rationality to create fear in cultural heritage institutions (it was especially noticeable in Poland at the beginning of the 1990s when institutions such as museums and the status of museum employees and the culture sector were being transformed by economic pressure and a reduction in state sponsorship. The question arises as to which type of fear is the stronger for cultural heritage: is it the fear of law or the fear of the economy? In the authors' opinion (W. SZ.) the stronger is the fear of the economic pressure rather than legal pressure because the free market economy within which culture is embedded has created its own culture based on efficiency and economic profitability.[11] This is always more terrifying than law because its external appearance is much more easily associated with the LACK OF MONEY for cultural heritage and for the salaries of those employed in its protection. Thus 'fear of the law' is often substituted by 'hope in the law', which for people employed in cultural heritage protection is to function as a kind of slider whose aim is to defend it against the economic rationality. In this respect no one should be surprised by the attempts of heritage protection sector employees, e.g. museologists to fight not only for economic but also for 'legal' guarantees of its existence by giving it a separate status. For example in the Act on museums of 1996, a great number of regulations (very specific ones) refer to museologists and not to museums or exhibits, and the stormy public consultations focused especially on the former and not the latter. The structural pressures (on the institutions) or the existential

11 See also P. Bendixen, *Wprowadzenie do ekonomiki kultury i sztuki*, Kraków 2001, pp. 20–26.

pressures (on the employees) are in the main of an economic nature and to a lesser degree of a legal character, because they are the consequence of limited resources and national or local budget deficits. You can only measure the efficiency of the legal process by its results and they are related not only to legislative correctness and the appropriate matching of methods to objectives, but also to adequate financing. What is the role of the law in the conflict between cultural heritage and economy?

Diag. 1. Conflict between cultural heritage and economy.

Source: author's description (W. Sz.), designed M. Danaj

In their internal confrontation law may at the same time function as a shield for cultural heritage or as a sword in the hands of economy. The shield is supposed to limit the extent to which market forces can permeate the system of cultural heritage. The sword in economy's hands allows for the changes resulting from the rationalisation of expenses which would never have been initiated by the heritage protection institutions themselves.

The confrontation between heritage protection and economy is the outcome of the diversity of the two disciplines. However, there is no doubt that a process of constant permeation is taking place between the two which is not so easily observable as the financial flow can only be seen happening in one direction. Although it is the economy that maintains cultural heritage, its survival also depends on culture and heritage and its development is closely related to cultural creativity. Economy is thus immersed in culture. Such a role of culture and of cultural heritage is more and more frequently proposed by researchers who try to emphasise its considerable merits in the creation of GDP. We believe this is just an unverifiable myth (see below) used in the basic aim of heritage protection, i.e. to preserve it for future generations, but which carries a rational justification equal to that used in economics.

Diag. 2. Chain of relationships in the confrontation between heritage and economy.

Source: author's description (W. Sz.), designed M. Danaj

The confrontation between heritage protection and economy does not take place in a void and its outcome is only superficially of no interest to the national budget, to local Government or to the employees of the cultural heritage sector. It happens that the main spectator of this duel is society, including those who are consumers of heritage and those who could not care less about it and whose awareness of it is that of a fly. They are spectators irrespective of their presence at it or not. The voices of a person in the fourth row and that of a person who has never bothered to witness the duel will become especially important at times of economic slow-down and of lack of state and international funds for the public financing of heritage. This is the situation that we have been condemned to in Poland (at least at present) owing to the lack of effective mechanisms for encouraging (but not forcing) the private funding of cultural heritage. Political decision-makers will listen to the voices of all these people. In situations like this it is the law that should safeguard heritage against the question of whether the financing of cultural heritage protection is unproductive and should be stopped." It would appear that in the view of the constitutional framework and the legal regulations of cultural heritage protection cultural heritage cannot be defeated in its confrontation with economy but it might suffer more or less serious wounds. This follows from the following observations.

Diag. 3. The duel of heritage and economy from the perspective of spectators.

Source: author's description (W. Sz.), designed M. Danaj

We believe that the financial objectives within the cultural framework are not determined by the State (a minister, etc.) nor are they the outcome of social agreement (the spectators) but instead by a kind of hierarchy in the mind set carried over into the funding of specific elements of culture, with cultural heritage in the first position on that ladder. This is related to, on the one hand, ideas of heritage and its typical examples and, on the other, its dilution not only by specialists but also by ordinary people.

In 2014 I asked my students to carry out a simple street survey and record definitions of cultural heritage by random passers-by. They were specifically asked to interview the public in a variety of settings such as supermarkets, housing estates or cultural institutions. The majority of answers were not really attempts at defining heritage but rather examples of it in Poland deeply embedded in Polish awareness, e.g. "Wawel Castle", "The Royal Castle in Warsaw", "various monuments", "The Old Market Square" (without specifying where), "Kórnik Castle", " Malbork Castle", "Matejko", "Battle of Grunwald" or "I do not know". When the question of financing heritage appears, the majority of people in the audience do not see some doubtful items which require a decision whether they constitute monuments in themselves or nor, but rather ready-made solutions and those monuments as to whose status 100% of respondents are certain that they are monuments of heritage so vital and important that they require public financing. This is not the same as to claim that it will always be like this and no changes will ever happen and if they do, they will not be sufficiently great as to let the financing of heritage drop 10 or 15 rungs down the ladder. It means that the State cannot ever afford to give up the public financing of cultural heritage (or at least its underwriting) or the financing of certain elements of cultural activities. This does not ensure so-called 'peace-of mind' for heritage as its financing can be in danger at times of either economic down-turn or growth. It is a consequence of the low status of culture as such (and cultural heritage as an element of it) in the priorities of political decision-makers and of the strength of opinion of the electorate. Among the political priorities there are numerous spheres higher in importance than culture, e.g. social benefits, support for the economy, internal and external security, health care and education.[12] Political priorities are translated into economic priorities, i.e. the funding allocated to particular spheres among which culture seems to be the lowest priority. Consequently there will never be sufficient funding for cultural heritage despite its prominent place on the cultural ladder. As it is within parliament's generally accepted prerogative to be able to

12 Ibid. pp. 183–187.

allocate funds, law thus becomes an easy means (in the form of legislative acts) of violation of the principle of equal public funding. This often happens when political decision-makers move funding as a reaction to public pressure or as a result of surveys. If we were to use the analogy of an audience watching a competition between heritage and economy and then confront that with watching a confrontation of public funding versus economy or health care expenditure versus economy, the first will appear rather hollow, while the second and third will arouse interest. This illustrates how little chance of acquiring sufficient funding cultural heritage has in relation to other public spheres higher up the hierarchy of priorities.

Is there a way in which cultural heritage can improve its position on the list of economic priorities? The answer is by 'cheating'. Culture and cultural heritage ought to 'cheat' by assigning to themselves the tourism element of GDP, even at the cost of double accounting and emphasising hard- core elements such as job creation in the heritage area or soft elements like innovation, citizenship, or human capital. In order not to disappear from political priorities and help it climb the ladder it needs to provide arguments of an economic and quasi-economic type. In an ideal model heritage ought to win public funds as a result of a narrative that its consumer wants and is willing to accept and this should be a decisive factor in public funding. In practice, however, the extent to which cultural heritage is used is so low in relation to its capital expenditure that to use this criterion would be dangerous for its future and its main objective, i.e. preserving it for future generations. Even though a proper understanding of cultural heritage and its use has a decisive influence on the acceptance of the need to fund it, if not privately then at least publicly, this is not to say that heritage will be able to survive in such an economic model. We need to ask the question whether in the modern world the need for cultural heritage is getting weaker or stronger and whether more or fewer people participate in it.

Leaving aside any doubt as to how to measure public cultural participation (also in using heritage), it is worth having a closer look at the ever changing social structure of the more and more prevalent neoliberal model and market competition, i.e. the function of market forces in all aspects of life. We have to accept as a fact the existence of a precariat in most European societies. The ever growing group of people working harder and harder just to make ends meet has less and less time for relaxation. In this group free time is usually spent on passive entertainment like the computer or watching television. Cultural activity as a form of relaxation is more demanding and related to what is known as *quality time,* i.e. using time when we are focused and not insecure or worrying about a lack of financial security.[13] No wonder that cultural participation is high at school level because, to a large extent, it is compulsory, and after that it is not. At the post school stage it demands continuous education and the sacrifice of time. The more you enjoy painting, the more you know about it and the more keenly you visit museums and art galleries. The growing precariat group will exclude itself from participation in cultural heritage not for lack of funds but for lack of *quality time*. Initiatives like 'one zloty museum entry' will not help much if the precariat group is only ostensibly in control of its time. Those who participate in cultural heritage and other users of culture are usually better educated in this area and better reception of culture demands more time.

Despite that decisions on the subsidising of culture are related to the opinion of the average taxpayer who never or hardly ever uses cultural heritage consciously (e.g. the flagship institutions such as museums, monuments). This *status quo* could become a pitfall for political decision-makers and cultural heritage protections institutions. On the one hand, the funding will mainly flow to the flagship sites and institutions as new ones might pose a risk in themselves. This kind of case, although in itself a consequence of ownership and of world view problems, is that of the funding for the John Paul II Museum by the Ministry of Culture and National Heritage in the Church of Holy Providence in Warsaw. On the other hand, there are some institutions so dependent on funding that eventually they apply only for funding for safe projects, as it is easier to get used to being funded than be creative.[14] It would be appropriate to note another problem here of whether state intervention in the form of public funding is the consequence of the withdrawal of private resources or the effect of certification and thus a guarantee of good quality and a way of attracting private resources. Funding in the latter case is supposed to help in obtaining resources for co-funding. In the cultural heritage area public funding is justified not only by constitutional heritage protection obligations but also because of the need to assure access to heritage. It appears that the attraction effect (certification) is an even better idea although much depends here on the way the state programme is thought out. The effect of certification could be applied to the National Culture Programme "Signs of the Times" ("Znaki Czasu") for the 2004–2013 period, the aim of which is the creation and development of regional civic institutions responsible for the purchase, recording and publicising of modern art works.[15]

---

13 G. Standing, *Prekariat. Nowa niebezpieczna klasa*, Warszawa 2014, pp. 258–260.

14 R. Towse, *Ekonomia kultury. Kompendium*, Warszawa 2011, p. 291.

15 The purchase of works of art was financed by ministerial and European funding. Some ownership problems that appeared as a result of the dual type of funding are a problem of ownership rights with respect to the purchased objects.

The dark clouds over cultural heritage come neither from the law nor even from the economics of culture but from changes in society and attempts to answer the question of how to reverse the unhelpful trend of failure to benefit from heritage and lack of interest in it.

Cultural Heritage Management – some obvious pitfalls

In cultural heritage management it is essential to have a good combination of heritage, legal and economic knowledge. Its interdisciplinary or transdisciplinary character excludes any balance between the three, which in turn will affect the actual practice of management more visible on the macro rather than the micro scale. For obvious reasons and because of their educational background and expertise they will place greater emphasis on one of those elements while treating the remaining two as only supplementary albeit necessary.

When reading publications on cultural heritage management one almost always comes across problems of models of management of either a governed, participatory or mixed type and the pros and cons of particular solutions. Nobody has yet proposed a universal model of heritage management which can be explained not only by the complexity of phenomena but also by the evolution of approaches to heritage, its aims and ways of achieving them. For years the essential aim has been the preservation and guardianship of heritage in its unaltered state, while only latterly a new approach, to preserve the value of heritage (understood in different ways), has been adopted in theory and practice. Current discussions have taken a new turn, focusing on the central point of the continuity of heritage in a given society, with more emphasis placed on intangible expressions of it, even at the cost of material ones.[16] Although this construction is not applicable in all cases, it opens up a new perspective in cultural heritage management by being so much at odds with previous approaches. Thus all the time cultural management is perceived as a practical activity which really ought to be reinforced by essential foundations, i.e. a specialist knowledge of the true nature of

16 So-called *concept of living heritage.* See more: G. Wijesuriya, *The past is in the present: perspectives in caring for Buddhist heritage sites in Sri Lanka,* in: *Conservation of Living Religious Heritage: Papers from the ICCROM 2003 Forum on Living Religious Heritage: Conserving the Sacred,* (eds.) H. Stovel, N. Stanley-Price, R. Killick, ICCROM, Rome 2005, pp. 31–43; I. Poulios, *Is every heritage site a 'living' one?: linking conservation to communities' association with sites,* "The Historic Environment: Policy and Practice" 2011, Vol. 2, No. 2, pp. 144–156; I. Poulios, *Discussing strategy in heritage conservation: Living heritage approach as an example of strategic innovation,* "Journal of Cultural Heritage Management and Sustainable Development" 2011, Vol. 4, No. 1, pp. 16–34.

cultural heritage (with respect to history of art, archaeology, architecture, monument conservation, specialist knowledge of antiquities), knowledge of cultural heritage law and knowledge of economics as a branch of classical management as well as marketing and public relations.[17] It would also seem that the evaluation of the legal forms of its management is easier to grasp and its principles specified than with an independent economic model. This is the consequence of, firstly, the enormous variety of the entities, subjects and phenomena within the broadly understood concept of heritage and secondly, the amount of information and the inability to confront it and read the correct relationships within it and thirdly, the natural pitfalls in heritage management which specifically relate to the entities and are very specific owing to the nature of the subject:

- the pitfall of heritage management domination;
- the pitfall of 'changes management' with the law pre-eminent;
- the pitfall of apparent efficiency;
- the pitfall of image;
- the pitfall of the preferences of future generations.

The pitfall of heritage management domination should be considered as natural since having assumed that cultural management has been isolated from cultural heritage management, it is a type of social exercise.[18] If so, then we could claim that practice has always dominated the discipline because the latter must draw on experiences so far, separating and evaluating them into 'good' and 'bad' from the point of view of the merit of specific activities or their effectiveness measured mostly by results (achieving certain goals by using specific means). The rules of management will either be weighted by their general scope because of the above- mentioned differentiation of heritage subjects and situations, or their detail as they would apply to very specific cases. This is not to claim that to formulate them within a new scientific discipline is unnecessary and that their strength lies in accepting an analogy which is much more acceptable within the rules of heritage management than in classic cultural property protection. Such rules will often be similar to economic rules because of a reliance on data available so far, i.e. historic data. In the eyes of many academics economics is a fusion

17 See K. Gutowska, Z. Kobyliński, *Zarządzanie dziedzictwem kulturowym – nowa dziedzina nauczania akademickiego i badań naukowych*, "Mazowsze. Studia Regionalne" 2011, No. 6, pp. 53–55.

18 K. Gutowska, Z. Kobyliński, J. Wysocki, *Nauczanie zarządzania dziedzictwem kulturowym w ramach różnych kierunków studiów wyższych*, in: *Nauczanie i popularyzacja ochrony dziedzictwa*, (ed.) B. Szmygin, Warszawa 2014, p. 125 and following.

of historical and futurological studies since solutions and conclusions are formulated on the basis of the past and hence are very difficult to forecast. In a similar way in heritage management past historical experiences (practical) have a decisive influence on the formulation of rules and regulations which may but do not have to work out in the future. There are two reasons why we can talk of the concept of 'pitfall' in relation to the domination of practice:

- we can never imagine the situation in reverse, whereby practical heritage management will be 'defeated' by the rules formulated by this discipline. In the case of their discrepancy we would have to deal with a pretence of following the rules or with attempts by decision-makers to claim that the status quo to which a given rule applies is different. Thus heritage management will always be tainted by the feature of improvisation. This situation will not change much as with the development of the concept of common participation in management, especially within the scope of the above-mentioned *concept of living heritage*, the role of experts will alter from a dominant one to an advisory and auxiliary one for a given social group as the main entity. At present improvised actions and their direction (both right and wrong) are often the consequence of the need to make quick decisions without a chance to refer to earlier established principles, plans, etc. In the future they might rather become the consequence of an excess of regulations, principles and plans, which, even if they do not contradict each other (which might in itself be considered a success), might become worthless and ignored owing to the very fact of their overproduction.[19]
- heritage management bodies in the main do not really practice management but rather, in the course of their work, they educate. This is not to claim that at present those bodies are 'undereducated' or lacking in educated experts.[20] This is a consequence of the differentiation of phenomena in a field so specific as for which the effectiveness method can be very varied and considerably postponed. It is very rare that the evaluation of the effectiveness of protection, its

---

19 Although such excessive regulation can be seen in other disciplines, there is an ongoing process of attempting to regulate and describe in detail different spheres of human life. In the field of heritage protection it is most visible in the example of regulations that, on the one hand, tend to 'cloud situations' contributing to a lack of clear rules, and on the other hand, are so complicated that there is no room for easy decision making or no allowance for exceptional cases.

20 Teaching heritage management has become quite common abroad and is only now becoming popular in Poland. See K. Gutowska, Z. Kobyliński, J. Wysocki, op. cit., pp. 129–132.

continuity in relation to tourism or the needs of balanced development can happen in the short or medium term. However, the criticism of the activities of such bodies at almost every level will happen independently of the planning perspective because of its strong ties with the interests of the moment.

The pitfall of managing change with the primacy of the law is natural in character. Heritage management has come into being as a result of accepting the concept of 'managing change', an extension of cultural property protection the aim of which in principle was meant to prevent or stop change happening.[21] The justification for the changes in heritage management is the idea of using all the heritage values for the public benefit. Hence all actions aimed at 'conserving' and 'development' are not contradictory and it is the aim of heritage management to reconcile such 'contrasting' interests for the benefit of public objectives. Managing change does not happen in the modern world in a void and does not rely on the freedom of the managing body to make decisions. It is to a large extent constricted by legal regulations not only of its own sphere of competence, but predominantly by those of the heritage protection area, i.e. the essential compulsory element to consider in its own management. Heritage protection law in the national and international dimension is increasingly enshrining protection itself in law, by extending its scope step by step. This is happening owing to ineffectiveness or lack of resources but also to its own inability to admit to its excessive extension of protection over all its' antiquities'. The intensification of this process is related to the recurring discussion of restitution and supranational problems (hence the creation of more and more comprehensive catalogues and categories of e.g. national cultural goods – a result of the new 2014/60 EU directive or of the much more rigorous legal regimes, e.g. *res extra commercium*) but also to the ongoing process of revering heritage as an essential prestigious element of the State. Although in public no country would admit to a return to the concept of national cultural property, one can still detect that kind of perception if only in attempts to hide them as part of world or European cultural heritage. The increase of interest in heritage protection on the part of political decision-makers and in consequence of legislators can also be seen in present day Poland. Awaiting their turn are an amendment to the Act on the Protection and Guardianship of Monuments, implementation in the Polish system of the ratified Conventions and directives (among others the UNIDROIT Convention of 1995 or the above mentioned directive of 2014/10 EU) and the new form of entry on the List of National Treasures. The primacy of law (including heritage protection law) over

21 Concept of B. M. Feilden, see K. Gutowska, Z. Kobyliński, op. cit., p. 52.

heritage management is moving on and in many cases has displaced solutions whose implementation would appear justified but are impossible to carry out because of their limitations. Unfortunately law can also be used to undertake actions which are in contradiction to rational heritage management change as advantage is taken of the fact that subsequent spheres of activity have been included in legislation, that there may be inaccuracies at the legislative stage and that apparent contradictions between regulations are used for personal aims (e.g. investor activity in the field of spatial planning). Frequently there have been cases of creating special legislation in a given sphere or waiting for the introduction of a specific solution.[22] Where is the pitfall of 'change management' with the primacy of law? It is to be found in the limiting of room for flexibility of management which will be shrinking not only because of legislation and directives but also because of other acts of local law and internal recommendations or instructions. At the same time nobody in practice carries the costs of such indirect actions, i.e. of creating, implementing and monitoring legal regulations.

The pitfall of 'apparent efficiency' in heritage management is related to the impossibility of establishing not just the unequivocal criteria of efficiency but most of all measures to achieve it. What can be considered as a criterion of successful management in this area? Would it be possible to use what is known as economic modelling for this purpose or at least as a constituent criterion of heritage management success? If so, we would be dealing with the apparent professionalism of management. This is due to the fact that although formal economic indicators can partly be used in non-economic spheres of activity, including heritage management, even a lay person would be able to spot the fault with such a course of action, because what should matter in heritage management and in its evaluation are the rather unmeasurable 'successes' like protection of heritage, its skilful use, its preservation for future generations, the building up of public awareness, etc.[23] Even if the judgement were up to the 'stakeholders'(direct and indirect ones as well as cultural and economic ones), the majority of them would consider it obvious that in their estimation greater emphasis would be placed on social benefits rather than social costs. Non-market benefits resulting from specific heritage management practically always (with the exception of borderline cases or obvious mishaps) absolve the managing bodies. It is thus possible to talk of the fortunate failure of market forces in heritage management.

22 Cf. The case of the 'gold train' in the locality of Wałbrzych and the legislation on found objects and the appropriate ministerial directive on notification so that the cost burden is carried by the State Treasury.

23 Cf. P. Bendixen, op. cit., p. 168.

Does this failure to evaluate specific heritage management actions along with the initial impossibility of putting a value on its benefits create a safe haven for heritage managers? This is the crux of the pitfall. The impossibility of measuring efficiency (hence the use of the term 'apparent') is the reason why it is easy to include in the evaluation of heritage management nonessential factors that affect the negative image of the managing entity and of its actions. This is why we often see heritage managing bodies giving in to pressure or even *quasi-blackmail* not only from entities outside the heritage area (which might be interested in certain 'management changes'[24]), but also from other heritage management bodies. An example of this would be attempts by major institutions (museums) to checkmate a Minister of Culture along the lines of: "well known and respected institutions should never lack funding because when the problem is blown up in the media the voters will tend to think that this is the result of incompetence at the central government level rather than at the museum". Thus if heritage management belongs to an area of practical activity of whose effectiveness is indefinable and whose tasks can only be accounted for in the long term, then it is easy to give the impression to the public of making both right and wrong management decisions depending on current interests.

The pitfall of image is the consequence of the impossibility of separating management from the state. Even in a situation when management is based on maintaining its multiple values whilst carrying out change on a tangible level and appears to be close to the participatory model of engaging the community though with managers (and experts) having a deciding voice then this kind of grass-roots approach does end in a top-down one. As heritage is used more and more for the purposes of creating the image of the State it cannot then disappear from the orbit of political interests and consequently of financing. What matters in the practice of heritage management is also who benefits from certain decisions. Heritage as such rarely attracts interest in the media and usually features in news items in the event of 'destruction' or 'openings'. Good heritage management aims to attract public interest and the subject of *public relations* also features in the course of studies in this field. It is very rare that legislative changes to do with heritage protection and indirectly with its management, are ever commented on publicly in the media as only a limited number of listeners or viewers show any interest in them. In terms of image the direction of heritage management can win few votes for political decision-makers even though they create its legislative

24 For example investors, municipal government in relation to the Voivodeship Inspector of Monuments, political decision-makers.

framework and often are the leaders of its structures. In this case what matters more than vote-winning is the presentation of the fact that something is actually happening in heritage management. There is a hidden meaning in this because along with such actions political decision-makers in management are trying to extend their power in the administration. On top of that, this area of management, i.e. the experts' participation, increases in time. The role of the expert mentioned in the previous subchapter becomes more visible in management support. The number of programmes in different spheres initiated by the Minister of Culture is increasing and although this is happening as a result of political initiative these programmes are implemented or evaluated by experts specially employed for that purpose. Work at arm's length, i.e. when the government indicates direction and ways and means but implementation or division of tasks is carried out by other bodies is growing in popularity, which can be clearly noted looking at heritage management courses. In other words it is possible to point out here elements of the participatory model but also the extension of the positive image onto the 'major' heritage manager in the country. The pitfall of image will always apply to the State, because, in the final analysis, it is the State that is responsible for heritage, irrespective of the individual managing bodies, and despite the fact, that formally, there has been a departure from "super patronage" and "super heritage management" by the state. The pitfall of image boils down to the fact that the benefits of successful heritage management are not transferred in practice onto the State while the failures in this area always are.[25]

The pitfall of the 'preferences' of future generations is the consequence of the popularisation in doctrine and over time in the public sphere of one of the aims of cultural heritage protection, i.e. that of preserving heritage for future generations. It originated in what is known as the integrated perspective and the compatibility of property such as monuments or endangered species as well as the need for their protection and conservation (cultural heritage) in undamaged condition for future generations.[26] Leaving aside considerations of whether it aims to protect the interests of successors or to achieve one of the aims of heritage protection, the transfer of heritage to future generations must be and is taken into consideration as one of the priorities in the process of heritage management. A heritage manager is thus faced with the problem of foreseeing future generations' preferences as to its use, which also envisages the prognostic and virtually

25 In this case mistakes are pointed out as early as the legislative stage, e.g. in the export system of cultural property in Poland between 2003–2010.

26 See A. Jagielska-Burduk, *Zabytek ruchomy*, Warszawa 2011, pp. 281–286.

futurological aspect of management. It would seem that the problems related to the correct reading of the future generations' preferences carry such a great risk that they may impede the balanced judgement of a manager. It appears that in practice things look quite different because both the preferences and benefits of heritage for future generations are unknown and unmeasurable at the same time, which results in two positive outcomes for a manager:

- they justify his choices as to the direction of 'management change' because even the lack of clear premises for undertaking certain actions can always be explained using the future generations argument. It is easier to counter attacks with arguments about future generations and thus avoid taking decisions that would 'interfere' too much in the heritage;
- they result in easier chances of obtaining funding because it is the state that carries responsibility for the wellbeing of the present and future generations.

Which 'elements' of heritage will future generations use and how? Are we perhaps at the present stage unaware of making mistakes that 'eliminate' irrelevant things which in the future might turn out essential for our successors? The current generation is not able to imagine the future generations and their preferences and as a consequence automatically assumes that unique objects with their wide-ranging values ought to be preserved and left for the use of future generations. A kind of 'precious crust' is thus forming which is ageing with time and is then imposed on future generations. They may maintain it further, possibly assuming a different point of view of conservation of the heritage of ancestors who had decided which elements of that heritage were the most important.

The pitfall of future generations' preferences lies in the conservatism of the heritage managers that is so deeply rooted that any doubts are decided in favour of preserving a given element of heritage. This principle of caution is significant in so far that it refers not just to the subject but also to the possible loopholes which might appear as a result of a loss and its replacement value and costs. In this way the pitfall of future generations' preferences encapsulates if not cultural heritage property itself then certainly our understanding of it, leaving the management decisions in the hands of experts and not to a specific social group (e.g. living in a certain locality) and also obstructing the fully participatory model of heritage management of the *living heritage* type.

„Let us imagine a painting cut into small quite monochrome pieces intended as the pieces of a puzzle. Even a less monochrome element cannot represent a shape but is simply a flat coloured stain. Only in conjunction with other pieces does it become a piece of sky, a shade or bright light, transparent or not and so on. Do these individual pieces show us the *true colours* of the fragment in this painting?"[27] This question, posed by Ludwig Wittgenstein in *Uwagi o barwach* (*Remarks on colour*), can be fully applied to heritage management. In principle it is impossible to discern all the individual elements of management, but only when they are assembled can we perceive and come to a value judgement of new directions in cultural heritage management.

27 L. Wittgenstein, *Uwagi o barwach*, Warszawa 2014, p. 23.

II. Law in cultural heritage management

II.1 Private- and public-law aspects of cultural heritage

II.1.1 Ownership of cultural heritage

The perception of ownership of cultural heritage follows two models in Poland. The first is based solely on findings concerning ownership and the entity that enjoys it. The second model, approaching a negotiating one, is taken advantage of when there is a problem with identifying the owner of a cultural heritage object. In the latter case, a willingness emerges to work out solutions satisfying for both the public and private entity. Claims filed with museums by the successors of owners have forced this model on public sector entities, who being merely possessors in the eyes of law, were restricted in what they could do. This model has been successfully used with respect to objects seized by museums from private collections pursuant to inapplicable nationalization laws. In such cases, the willingness to take up negotiations on the ownership of, and rights to, cultural heritage objects is greatly boosted by the desire to keep the objects available to the public, make them safe in their place, or to continue to use an immovable monument, housing an institution of culture.

The most frequently considered solutions have included entering into a contract of loan for use, setting up a foundation by those entitled to the objects, or even making a deed of gift to the possessors.[28] A departure from this practice will certainly be made in the wake of the judgment in the case of the Sanguszko family's objects. Under it, a museum, although it is not their owner, is under no obligation to restore the objects to their owners by reason of the limitation of actions for the delivery of the objects. No doubt, the potential new models of conduct following from this judgment will not help cooperation between the private and public sectors.

The ownership structure of cultural heritage is not entirely without an impact on the legal mechanisms of its management. Moreover, public and private owners will differ in their motives for efficiently managing heritage components under their control. For public entities or even private non-governmental organisations, the chief motive will be to attain their fundamental objectives set out in statutes (in the case of local government units) or charters (in the case of foundations or

28 P. Kosiewski, *Własność a zbiory publiczne*, in: *Własność a dobra kultury*, (eds.) G. Czubek, P. Kosiewski, Warszawa 2006, pp. 11–12.

associations). In each case, the proper treatment of a monument will show that a given entity is accomplishing its mission. Some jurists argue that exercising control over cultural heritage objects by private entities being their owners or lawful possessors cannot be considered management.[29] For their activity lacks any long-term perspective and is often aimed at concrete and relatively quickly attainable profits. This follows from the fact that such entities will act not only to preserve the heritage but will also try to pursue their private interest, not infrequently seen in the set financial objective.[30]

A private entity having control over a monument will be guided by the provisions of the Act on Protection and Guardianship of Monuments (APGM) in its treatment of the object. The conception of an entity consciously exercising control over monuments follows from the distinction between protection and care visible already in the title of the Act. The legislator assumes that some knowledge of the legal norms laid down in the Act is shared by their addressee exercising control over a monument. The assumption applies not only to owners, but also to possessors, usufructuaries and entities vested with a title to the monument under a civil-law agreement.[31] The legislator leaves out, however, components of cultural heritage other than monuments. Thus, only in relation to a segment of cultural heritage does the legislator assume that the entity exercising control over an object has the cognizance in question. To some extent, the fact that entities possessing objects are insensitive to their value when the objects are created and exist until they achieve the status of monuments may prove to be ultimately harmful and reduce the group of objects protected by the Act as monuments.

Restrictions on the ownership of monuments can be observed at the level of both constitutional norms and specific statutes.[32] Without attempting to analyse ownership restrictions, it must be stressed that:

> Legislation should attempt to make society compensate the owner for the duties borne by him or her relative to the ownership of monuments. The ownership is subject to restrictions for the sake of society's interest and so it is only fair that the preservation of a

---

29 For the museum mission see K. Zalasińska, *Muzea publiczne. Studium administracyjno-prawne*, Warszawa 2013, pp. 106 et seq.

30 D. Worthing, S. Bond, *Managing Built Heritage. The role if cultural significance*, Oxford 2008, p. 43.

31 For a broader treatment see A. Jagielska-Burduk, *Koncepcja świadomego dysponenta zabytków w polskim prawie ochrony zabytków*, in: *Prawo ochrony zabytków*, (ed.) K. Zeidler, Warszawa – Gdańsk 2014, pp. 311–318.

32 M. Drela, *Własność zabytku*, in: *Leksykon prawa ochrony zabytków. 100 podstawowych pojęć*, (ed.) K. Zeidler, Warszawa 2010, p. 387.

monument in a very good physical condition and making it available to third parties at fixed times be in the private interest of the owner concerned[33].

This suggestion is as much valuable as it indicates other interest groups; it is the belief of the present author that a stake in the assumed restrictions of an owner's rights is held by not only contemporary society but also future societies.

To some extent, the discussion how to compensate private entities for their share in the protection of heritage has already begun. This can be seen in publications on the practice of collecting heritage items and studies of encouragements addressed to the private sector. One of the purposes of the discussion is making the legislator begin work on bills related to the protection of cultural heritage and creating a network of supporting instruments.[34] It is important to raise the awareness of the significance of heritage for the development of societies. Owing to information campaigns, private entities will see their role differently: not through the prism of an obligation but rather as a necessary mission on behalf of monuments. Private persons, fulfilling specific roles in legal persons, will translate the knowledge thus obtained into the activity of the latter.[35]

The distinguishing of private interest in the protection of heritage components calls for a broader discussion. Private interest is understood in principle as the interest of only a given individual. This interest can be manifested in the advantages of both an economic and non-economic nature.[36] Economic advantages are moreover, related to the so-called natural economic value of monuments. Hence, the practice of private collecting ever more often attracts criticism, denouncing the prevalence of investments with respect to cultural property. Yet, even in this case, protection and care are only natural – every person would protect their own investment. Non-economic advantages, in turn, include any aspects of an individual's activity gratifying to the private entity such as acceptance by others, an increase in prestige, or an enhancement of the social status. Of course, it is not possible to make an absolutely sharp distinction between private

33 Ibid. p. 390.

34 W. Szafrański, *Publiczne aspekty prywatnych kolekcji*, in: *Kultura w praktyce. Zagadnienia prawne*, Vol. 1, (eds.) A. Jagielska-Burduk, W. Szafrański, Poznań 2012.

35 See *Kolekcjonerstwo – nauka i upowszechnianie*, a seminar held in the Staszic Palace, Warsaw, on 20 November 2015 by the History Encounter House, Polish Academy of Sciences Archives, and a group of collectors in cooperation with the National Institute of Museology and Heritage Protection.

36 For balancing public and private interests in heritage management see P. Howard, G. J. Ashworth, *European Heritage, Planning and Management*, Intellect, Exeter 1999, pp. 51–52.

interest defined inexactly in this way and public interest itself, because in some areas there will always be (regardless of the type of activity undertaken) some impact of private activity (collections, foundations) on the public sphere.[37] In the age of the commercialization of culture, the use of cultural property, including monuments, to achieve economic objectives is highly tempting for both private and public (State) owners. While working to achieve such measurable objectives, one must not forget about the question of constant care for cultural heritage. This should always remain in the centre of activities constituting in common heritage management.

The ownership of cultural heritage is also undergoing constant change, including one of law, with respect to the definition of what it encompasses. These changes are brought about by the new areas of regulation distinguished in the last twenty years. Besides tangible objects, quite naturally, cultural heritage is held to embrace intangible heritage, meaning a new approach to tradition, crafts and acceptance of folk culture. A very important aspect of the discussion of cultural heritage, the right to this kind of heritage, has taken on the status of one of the fundamental human and civil rights.[38] National legislation, laying down the basic principles for shaping the right to heritage, is only one of the (basic) levels in the network of norms applicable to heritage. While a reference to the question of ownership is left to national legislation on every occasion, international and EU law may exert influence on how ownership is exercised. Repeatedly, rights accorded to an individual by the acts of international law or the duties of member or signatory states make the legal situation of the owner of a cultural heritage object change. What is more, notice taken of the interest of cultural heritage protection or of access to heritage induces a new approach, on the one hand, open to heritage and, on the other, one that weighs up the interest of entities exercising control over a given cultural heritage object. Such an approach is not always consistent when considering various tiers of heritage management (regional, national and international).[39]

In the context of cultural heritage, which seems to be more permanent than entities entitled to its components under ownership, it can be ventured that ownership as a right to this kind of objects, does not sufficiently emphasise the factual

---

37 W. Szafrański, *Publiczne aspekty…*, pp. 43–58.

38 F. F. Francioni, *The evolving Framework for the Protection of Cultural Heritage in International Law*, in: *Cultural Heritage, Cultural Rights, Cultural Diversity. New Developments in International Law*, (eds.) S. Borelli, F. Lenzerini, Leiden – Boston 2012, pp. 3–4.

39 T. Scovazii, *The definition of Intangible Cultural Heritage*, in: *Cultural Heritage, Cultural Rights…*, pp. 157ff.; A. F. Vrdoljak, *Human rights and Illicit Trade in Cultural Objects*, in: *Cultural Heritage, Cultural Rights…*, p. 107 et.seq.

elements inside the real legal relationship. While the construction of the right in cultural property has not been effectively introduced yet into legal systems, research on the heritage or art market, lays a special emphasis now on the relationship between an entity and an object. In 1976, Richard Crewdson posed the question about the place of ownership of monuments in the legal system.[40] A debate ensued on whether the concepts of *cultural property* and *cultural heritage* were correct. Some believed that the former concept unnecessarily emphasized the word 'property', which carried some unfavourable consequences. The debate attracted pioneers of the study of heritage protection law on a global scale such as Lyndel V. Prott and Patrick O'Keefe,[41] John H. Merryman,[42] Joseph L. Sax[43] and Sarah A. Williams.[44] In this context, it should be mentioned that already in 1969, the elements of the conception of common heritage, admittedly in relation to the socialist system of government, were referred to by Andrzej Koppf, who considered entities owning a cultural heritage object from time to time as depositaries of communal good.[45] Astonishingly, under different theories of law and in contrasting social systems, authors discussing the legal questions of cultural heritage arrived at similar positions concerning the ownership of objects of historic interest, regardless of the place held by it in the system of the State.

In the discussions of socialist law, only in respect of 'inherited memorabilia' did the authors of authoritative juristic publications recognise the 'special attachment' of the owner to a thing. The satisfaction of culture-related needs within personal property was distinguished from the satisfaction of personal needs by using the components of national property.[46] A mystical attachment or spiritual ownership were not pivots on which socialist ownership revolved, nevertheless

---

40 R. Crewdson, *Cultural Property – a Fourth Estate?*, "The Law Society Gazette" 1984, No. 18, p. 126.

41 L. V. Prott, P. O'Keefe, *Law and Cultural Heritage*, Vol. 1: *Discovery and Excavation*, London 1984; *Law and Cultural Heritage*, Vol. 3: *Movement*, London 1989; *Cultural Heritage or Cultural Property*, "International Journal of Cultural Property" 1992, No. 1.

42 J. H. Merryman, *Thinking about Elgin Marbles: Critical Essays on Cultural Property. Art and Law*, The Hague – London – Boston 2000; *The Nation and the Object*, "International Journal of Cultural Property" 1994, Vol. 3, Issue 1.

43 L. Sax, *Playing Darts with Rembrandt. Public and Private Rights in Cultural Treasures*, Ann Arbor 2001.

44 S. Williams, *The International and National Protection of Movable Cultural Property. A Comparative Study*, Dobbs Ferry – New York 1978.

45 A. Kopff, *Własność dóbr kultury*, "Studia Cywilistyczne" 1969, Vol. XIII–XIV (published to honour the academic work of Jan Gwiazdomorski on his seventieth birthday), p. 183.

46 J. Wasilkowski, *Pojęcie własności we współczesnym prawie polskim*, Warszawa 1972, p. 196.

they accorded with things – objects of personal property. A mystical attachment (*Seelisches Eigentum* theory of Vinding Kruse[47]), a separation of property from its economic values and concentration, instead (in its psychological and sociological aspects) may be significant for the ownership of cultural property. This theory, however, was not developed with cultural heritage in mind but was a suggestion to expand the property that can be owned to cover intangible assets. Economic questions, although very important (for instance, the amending bill gives the amount of funds earmarked for the creation and maintenance of the Heritage Treasure List in the budget of the Ministry of Culture and National Heritage), remain a secondary issue when identifying heritage. The cost aspect gains prominence in the context of the upkeep of heritage and its economic attractiveness for potential investors. In the case of movable heritage, the cost aspect comes into play when the commercial value of its components, as objects of transactions, is assessed.

The construction of a special agreement concerning a monument was mentioned incidentally and later abandoned by Jan Piotr Pruszyński.[48] In the context of expropriation, a special legal regime for the most valuable collections was devised by Andrzej Grabowski.[49] In this context Wojciech Kowalski argued in the Polish professional literature in favour of the special nature of this object of legislation[50]. Writing on the ownership of monuments, reviewing the current real rights in cultural heritage components and being aware of the state our civilization is in and of the place of heritage in legal systems, authors begin to doubt if ownership actually befits cultural property. Wojciech Kowalski, actively participating in an international discussion on this question, wrote:

> An alternative for the modification of solutions used so far is a search for entirely new legal constructs which could be used in their place. The mostly conservative jurist community will be initially reluctant to accept this, but such a search in itself poses a fascinating challenge. After all, what indeed can replace ownership of a cultural property?[51]

---

47 Ibid. pp. 38–39.

48 J. P. Pruszyński, *Regulacja ustawowa ochrony zabytków*, "Ochrona Zabytków" 1985, No. 1, p. 30.

49 J. Grabowski, *Wywłaszczenie jako środek ochrony zabytków*, "Państwo i Prawo" 1967, Vol. 3, p. 492. For more on the statements by A. Kopff, J. P. Pruszyński, J. Grabowski see A. Jagielska-Burduk, *Zabytek ruchomy*, Warszawa 2011, pp. 231–232, 234–235.

50 W. Kowalski, *Nabycie własności dzieła sztuki od nieuprawnionego*, Kraków 2004, p. 144 det seq.

51 Ibid. p. 147.

In his opinion, Kowalski favoured the formulas similar to a trust or bailment. The work he inspired Polish jurists to undertake is not only a challenge for those who set out on the study of the questions of cultural heritage, but above all fundamental research, prerequisite to any efforts centred exclusively on the practical application of developed solutions. Perhaps, the diagnosis of ownership 'failure'[52] and research aimed at finding new solutions will help gradually abandon ones hitherto prevailing in the legal system. The current evolutionary approach to cultural heritage is seen in continual attempts to find new forms of protection.

The construction of civil-law ownership can be said to underpin property law. Ownership has changed historically; continual changes have determined how it is seen by society and expressed in the legal system. The construction of material resources therefore is based on the structure of ownership. Any transactions involving ownership based on its transferability are consequently an element contributing to social development. Studying the legal aspect of ownership, one must, in addition, never forget about its economic context.[53] Under Article 140 of the Polish Civil Code, within the limits set by statutes and the public policy, an owner may, to the exclusion of other persons, use a thing in accordance with the social and economic purpose of his right, and may, in particular, collect the profits and other revenues from the said thing. Within the same limits, he may dispose of the thing. This provision does not give an exhaustive catalogue of powers but makes a reference to the Roman triad of ownership: *ius possidendi, ius utendi, fruendi et abutendi*. A power following from the triad, but left out from the provision, is possession. No doubt, an owner will enjoy far more powers. The Polish Civil Code definition of ownership is based on the powers of an owner and the passive behaviour of third parties with respect to these powers. The legislator has positively listed the powers of the owner, while the legal situation of third parties has been negatively defined by the scope of powers enjoyed by the owner.[54]

The powers, defining a comprehensive situation of the owner, make up a single right. Some jurists maintain that the duties of the owner will not be part of ownership. However, they ought to be founded in it.[55] In relation to the management of cultural heritage, the discussion of the significance of individual powers

52 A. Jagielska-Burduk, W. Szafrański, M. A. Górska, *Wirtualna Galeria im. Mielżyńskich. Historia – idea – prawo*, Poznań 2013, p. 73.

53 E. Gniewek, in: *Prawo rzeczowe. System Prawa* Prywatnego, Vol. 3, (ed.) T. Dybowski, Warszawa 2013, pp. 338–340.

54 W. Szydło, in: *Kodeks cywilny. Komentarz*, (eds.) E. Gniewek, P. Machnikowski, Warszawa 2014, p. 303.

55 E. Gniewek, in: *Prawo rzeczowe...*, p. 379.

and their independent or dependent nature takes on a new tone. In the case of cultural property, the powers will be of various intensity and number, depending on the characteristics of the thing in question. The phrase 'within the limits set by statutes', which defines the owner's scope of freedom, calls for some discussion. It follows from it that only a statute, as far as legislation is concerned, may be the source of changes in the sphere of owner's rights. This is consistent with the constitutional principles of the protection of ownership and its limitations allowed by law. The limits set by statutes may have various motives and functions. The statutes mentioned in Article 140 of the Polish Civil Code, may be in the national interest, as well as in that of particular entities.[56] In the discussion centred on whether the duties of an owner are limitations of ownership or rather define it, examples referring to cultural heritage components have many a time been used.

Arising from the lack of any rightful civil-law claims, doubts as to the legal-administrative character of the owner's duties appeared also in the study of ownership in the socialist system of government. External entities such as the representatives of society have no claims against the owner of a monument. They are represented by an administrative agency, which may demand that the owner of a monument fulfil specific duties. In this case, protection, although provided for the sake of society as a whole and enforcing specific duties on the part of the owner, is not connected with any civil-law relationship between the owner and other entities. The determination of the existence of any civil-law relationships is absolutely independent of that of any relationships between contemporary and future generations. According to the conception of successor interest protection, the group of future generations are beginning to be reckoned with.[57]

The interest of future generations was also the reason for expanding Menach Mautner's Eternal Triangle into the Eternal Rhombus.[58] The questions of the rise and resolution of the conflict caused by the theft of a movable thing and its successive purchase in good faith were encapsulated by Menach Mautner in his conception of the Eternal Triangles of the Law, which consists of three parties: an owner, a thief and a *bone fide* purchaser (Fig. 1).[59] The conception resolves the conflict, taking into account the legal and economic situation of the entities involved. However, the position of the thief, who created the conflict of interest

56 Ibid. p. 401.

57 A. Jagielska-Burduk, *Zabytek ruchomy*, p. 281.

58 W. Szafrański, *Mity i patologie obrotu dziełami sztuki*, "Santander Art and Culture Law Review" 2015, No. 1, p. 161ff.

59 See M. Mautner, *"The Eternal Triangles of the Law": Toward a Theory of Priorities in Conflicts Involving Remote Parties*, "Michigan Law Review" 1991, No. 10, pp. 95–154.

between the owner and *bona fide* purchaser, in the triangle is not significant. In resolving the conflict, Mautner accepted that it was necessary to take into account elements of effectiveness and justice. Studying the relationships between the entities, we wondered why each movable thing was given a similar treatment. Consequently, Mautner's conception was expanded to take note of the new information concerning the object, for instance, a cultural property object. The conception of the Eternal Rhombus of the Law is a result of an overall change in the perception of the ownership of monuments.

Fig. 1. Eternal Rhombus of the Law – A. Jagielska-Burduk, W. Szafrański. A. J.-B., W. Sz.

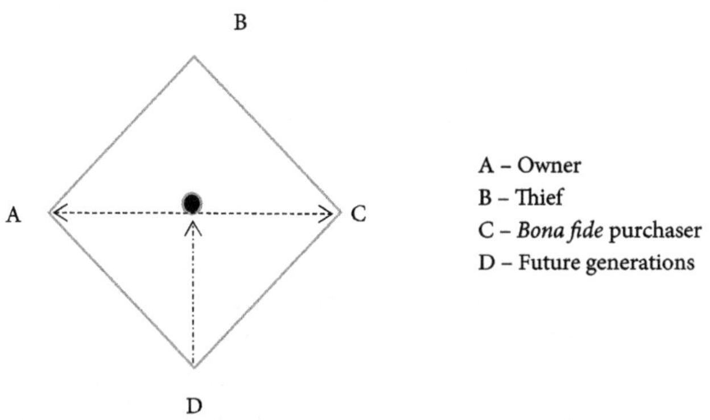

Source: "Santander Art and Culture Law Review" 2015, No. 1, p. 164.

In the Eternal Rhombus of the Law, the object of the conflict, a cultural property object, is a new variable. In this way, a private-law relationship between the owner and the *bona fide* purchaser takes on a public-law complexion – sufficiently important for the resolution of the conflict as to justify the addition of the new point D, standing for future successors. The model of Eternal Triangles, by adapting it to the plane on which cultural heritage components are traded and change hands, was modified into the Eternal Rhombus. On apex D of the Eternal Rhombus of the Law

> Future generations can be inscribed as the representatives of the interest in the protection of movable heritage components and later – in exclusion of objects from private-law transactions or imposition of certain conditions on such transactions. The emergence of new stakeholders and a fourth entity, so to speak, results in the rearrangement of interests and the building of a model centred on the object.[60]

60 W. Szafrański, *Mity i patologie...*, pp. 163–164.

The question remains whether *D* can also lay claim to this asset. We are convinced that such claims may have an institutionalised form or be a major signpost in the line of reasoning. Leaving *D* open, helps continue research in this area and search for entities – attorneys or even conservators for *D*'s heritage. *D*, creating a new extra-economic factor, is a singular regulator of the overall principles of effectiveness and justice proposed by Mautner.

The Model of the Eternal Rhombus of the Law may be considered not only a voice in the discussion on the trade in works of art, but also an opinion in a broader discussion on special legal regimes constructed on cultural property.[61] On each occasion, the reason for a change, or rather a departure from the set standard, is an object – a piece of cultural property. In this sense, it is worth considering whether future generations as beneficiaries of the efforts to protect heritage undertaken by present generations enjoy the status of an entity, which could be a party to a civil-law relationship. Future generations as a collective entity, not carrying any rights at present, cannot be a party to any legal relationship now in existence. With each successive generation, new communities will function and consequently there will arise successive particular relationships, creating together a general relationship based on relations between contemporary and future generations. The duty of the present generations, consisting in the care for heritage and its transmission to successive generations is matched by the duty to inherit the transmitted heritage by the latter. The future generations, being 'indebted' to contemporary generations long gone, will deliver a performance for the benefit of successive generations.

Having regard to changes in the perception of cultural heritage in Poland and the evolution of legislation towards greater deference to the rights of private entities, it is worthwhile to cite the decisions of the Constitutional Tribunal Court[62] and the European Court of Human Rights[63] concerning heritage. Both decisions analysed the legal situation of private persons as owners of monuments and other objects covered by a special legal regime, and the heritage protection legislation currently in force. The opinion given by the Constitutional Tribunal Court analyzed also the role of the State in the protection of cultural heritage in the context of its obligation to bear the costs of the upkeep of monuments. The professional literature has canvassed various views on this opinion but in

---

61 Ibid. p. 165ff.

62 Verdict by the Constitutional Tribunal Court dated 8 October 2007, K 20/07, OTK-A 2007/9/102, Dz.U.2007/192/1394.

63 Verdict by the ECHR dated 29 March 2011, 33949/05 *Potomska i Potomski v. Polska*, LEX 784737.

principle there was widespread agreement as to the co-participation of the State in the protection of cultural heritage.[64]

Co-participation therefore is to take the form of diverse support for entities exercising control over monuments and mechanisms favourable to heritage held by public and private entities. This task is specified in the Constitution. The crucial and purposeful verb 'safeguard' used in it should set the course of the State in relation to relevant legislation and administration. In its opinion, the Constitutional Tribunal Court emphasised that the limitations of the ownership of monuments were necessary for their proper protection.[65] When an owner is being determined, it is only of secondary importance if they are private or public, i.e. the State Treasury and its *statio fisci*. The judgment of the Constitutional Tribunal Court thus upholds the limitations of ownership in relation to monuments, resumes the research into the constitutionality of such limitations and is yet another voice in the discussion on the congruence of ownership and monuments whose safeguarding is one of the constitutional duties of the State.

In the study of the ownership of an object – a component of heritage – and the burdens borne on account of it, one can hardly ignore two questions, which are crucial for any owner, related to the end of the relationship between the entity and object or the renouncement or destruction of property. This is a situation when the owner no longer wishes to own a monument and intends to sever his or her ties with it by annihilating the property in question or disposing of it. In some situations, which shall be discussed below, a monument cannot function as a regular object of transactions. This question is regulated by both heritage protection laws and copyright law. The preservation of privately-owned works of art and monuments for the sake of society has been discussed in the culture sector for years. Rather graphic examples of destroying paintings by world-famous

64 M. Drela, *Z orzecznictwa Trybunału Konstytucyjnego (obowiązek finansowania prac archeologicznych przez inwestora), Glosa do wyroku z 8 X 2007, K 20/07*, "Państwo i Prawo" 2008, Issue 11, pp. 139 et seq.; K. Zalasińska, *Glosa do wyroku Trybunału Konstytucyjnego z dnia 8 października 2007 r., K 20/07*, "Przegląd Orzecznictwa" 2008, No. 2, pp. 3ff; M. Trzciński, *Glosa do wyroku TK (sygn. akt K 20/07)*, "Zeszyty Naukowe Sądownictwa Administracyjnego" 2008, No. 2, p. 173; A. Jagielska-Burduk, *Własność zabytków w świetle wyroku Trybunału Konstytucyjnego z dnia 8 października 2007 r.*, in: *Prawo wobec wyzwań współczesności*, Vol. 6, (eds.) B. Guzik, N. Buchowska, P. Wiliński, Poznań 2010, pp. 57 et.seq.

65 For more on this point see A. Jagielska-Burduk, *Własność zabytków…*, pp. 57 et seq.

masters with an axe[66], using pictures as targets in the game of darts[67] or cremating one's body together with masterpieces of painting[68] left most of the public in shock. It is only when outraged by such vivid examples that the public focuses on the problem and its imperfect legal setting. It must be added that even protective laws cannot always ensure preservation of an object. Therefore, the problem lies, besides deficient legislation, in the enforcement of laws and a failure to make a complete inventory of heritage, due to the shortage of heritage protection personnel. In the case of this kind of cultural property, practice is of the essence and the destruction of an object is usually irreversible.

Maintaining balance between the universal interest and the interest of ownership protection, in the context of Article 1 of Protocol No. 1 to the Convention,[69] was studied by the ECHR. In the case of *Potomska & Potomski v. Poland*,[70] a property, which once had been a Jewish cemetery, was entered into the register of monuments already after it was purchased by private persons. It must be observed that according to the findings of fact presented in the judgment, at the time of purchasing the property, the potential purchasers were not aware of its value and significance for history, culture and the cult of the dead. When attempts to use the property for residential and commercial purposes failed because heritage protection agencies refused their approval, the owners asked to have the property exchanged for another. Unfortunately, this attempt was not successful, either. It must be stressed that the findings of fact analyzed by the ECHR included many elements related to the changing perception or even realization of Jewish heritage as an object of protection. Already earlier, the professional literature discussed the problem of old cemeteries and the historical reasons lying behind their poor state of preservation.[71] This, however, does not alter the contemporary assessment of the situation which has arisen and put the persons exercising control over the property in an unfavourable position.

---

66 D. Gillman, *The Idea of Cultural Heritage*, Cambridge University Press, Cambrigde 2011, p. 171.

67 The example is given in the controversial title of the publication itself: J. L. Sax, op. cit.

68 W. Kowalski, *Nabycie własności…*, pp. 144–145.

69 Protocol no. 1 to the Convention for the Protection of Human Rights and Fundamental Freedoms of 11 November 1950. Dz. U. 1995, No. 36, item 175; Poland ratified Protocol no. 1 on 10 October 1994.

70 Verdict by the ECHR dated 29 March 2011, 33949/05 *Potomska i Potomski v. Polska*, LEX 784737.

71 T. Gardocka, *Cmentarze jako dobra kultury*, in: *Prawna ochrona dóbr kultury*, (eds.) T. Gardocka, J. Sobczak, Toruń 2009, pp. 144–145.

The lack of procedure enabling private entities to institute the expropriation proceedings with respect to an immovable monument was considered a breach of principles due to a failure to maintain balance between the parties and allow private entities to renounce the ownership of a monument.[72] Under the Immovable Property Management Act[73] and the APGM, the situation of the owner as regards expropriation is unbalanced. Under Article 50(3) of the APGM only when an immovable monument entered into the register is threatened with destruction or damage can it be taken over by the State Treasury. In this respect, the Act, giving the right to institute proceedings to a heritage protection agency, creates an unfavourable situation for the owner by treating him or her solely as the addressee of a duty once a competent agency has taken advantage of a norm of competence. It seems, however, that the study of heritage protection and the effective management of heritage should thoroughly investigate ownership not only as to the powers of the owner, but also as to its permanence and the possibility of deciding about its transfer to another entity. The findings of the ECHR have contributed towards the rise of a new argument since then used by owners in proceedings involving monuments. The 'argument from balance', so to speak, has been used to judge the actions of heritage protection agencies. On many an occasion, this argument is wrongly used, not to say unreasonably, by the owners of monuments without taking heed of its real meaning in the heritage protection law.

Meanwhile, by the judgment of 4 November 2014 in the case of *Potomska & Potomski v. Poland*, involving a redress of damage, the applicants were afforded a compensation of EUR 14 000 (EUR 10,000 in respect of pecuniary damage, EUR 4,000 in respect of non-pecuniary damage) and a sum of EUR 800 in respect of costs of proceedings before the Court. The conclusion of the proceedings and case of the historic cemetery shows how ownership is viewed in international law and how norms in international and national law relate to each other.

The judgment has not aroused any discussion about the model of heritage protection. Adopted in the Act, the model of an entity consciously exercising control over a monument concerns specific ideal situations. When the findings

72 An interesting *de lege lata* proposal suggests to assume, before the statute is amended, that a petition for expropriation filed by the owner of a monument with a voivodeship inspector obligates the latter to petition the local *starosta* to expropriate the immovable monument. M. Górski, *Commentary to the ECHR judgment of 29March 2011*, 33949/05, LEX/el. 2011.

73 Ustawa z dnia 21 sierpnia 1997 r. o gospodarce nieruchomościami [Immovable Property Management Act of 21 August 1997], consolidated text Dz. U. 2010, No. 102, item 651 as amended.

of fact are as complex as in the case of *Potomska & Potomski v. Poland*, it is hardly possible to transpose an individual situation onto an entire law. Nevertheless, relieving from the 'burden' of bearing the costs of monument upkeep is one thing and preventing the use of a property – in this case historic cemeteries – is quite another. In this situation, the State must not be left the role as the sole guardian of cultural heritage. Arguments in favour of this opinion include a lack of response of the legislator to the judgment and controversial amendments to the APGM.[74]

A mention has already been made of the absence of any mechanism which would enable an owner to freely alienate a historic immovable object by the person under whose control it remains on account of limitations imposed on its economic or living use. In the case of cemeteries and their limited or non-existent usability for persons exercising control over them, the matter is doubly complex. Perhaps, a need will arise to make some modifications, while keeping its major assumptions, to the conception of a person consciously exercising control over monuments.

Many disputes between an investor and administrative agencies arise from decisions on the range and manner of property development. These agencies are responsible for project execution, its approval and making sure that cultural heritage protection concerns are not ignored.[75] Sorting out interests in heritage protection, one can speak of the community of interests of heritage protection on national and international planes, and possible variance in the assessment and selection of the most favourable solution for heritage.[76] Differences may appear even if a common interest and heritage are preserved, but are differently interpreted. A situation may arise, however, where heritage attracting interest and care of the international community is underappreciated by the community of the region. While in such a situation a consideration should be given to the commonality of heritage, its history, the conception of 'making heritage one's own',[77] however, the discussion of interest planes and areas where they can be reconciled

74 For instance, a proposal to make entries of movable and immovable monuments equal as regards the decision on the entry into the register of monuments on the inspector's own initiative.

75 V. Vadi, *Cultural heritage in international investment law and arbitration*, Cambridge 2014, pp. 107–123.

76 Ibid. pp. 107–108; V. Vadi, *Culture, Development and International Law: The Linkage between Investment Rules and the Protection of Cultural Heritage*, in: *Cultural Heritage, Cultural Rights...*, pp. 415–416.

77 J. Purchla, *Naród – Dziedzictwo – Pamięć*, "Zagadnienia Sądownictwa Konstytucyjnego" 2012, No. 2, p. 64.

must end the moment heritage is deliberately devastated during military operations.[78]

The concept of heritage important for the international community is also encountered when Article 12 of the Convention concerning the Protection of the World Cultural and Natural Heritage 1972 is interpreted.[79] Under it, signatory states should afford protection to other heritage components not included in a list, provided they have an outstanding universal value. The principles laid down in Articles 4 and 5 of the Convention, should be applied by State Parties to cultural property not included in a list but meeting the criteria specified in Articles 1 and 2 of the Convention.[80] The public interest embodied in the protection of monuments is many a time marginalised on the regional level in favour of the economic interest following from the need to carry out development projects and create new jobs, and caused by progressing urbanization of cities. Hence, the search for a balance in the area of owner's powers may be inextricably linked to the rise of indemnity claims based on limitations imposed on ownership,[81] suffered expropriation and amount of compensation.[82]

The other question circles around the mobility of objects. In some situations the principle of free movement of goods is restricted on account of the object. This can be seen in domestic and EU legislation. Under Article 51(4) of the APGM, the following categories of monuments permanent export abroad is prohibited: entered in the register, forming part of public collections belonging to the State Treasury, units of local government and other organisational units counted among the sector of public finance, included in museum inventories and the National Library Collection. To export permanently other objects specified using

---

78 Then, international law norms concerning the protection of cultural property in case of armed conflicts become applicable.

79 Convention concerning the Protection of the World Cultural and Natural Heritage adopted on 16 November 1972 by the General Conference of the United Nations Educational, Scientific and Cultural Organization meeting in Paris at its seventeenth session, http://portal.unesco.org/en/ev.php-URL_ID=13055&URL_DO=DO_TOPIC&URL_SECTION=201.html (accessed: 18.01.2016).

80 K. Piotrowska-Nosek, *Konwencja w sprawie ochrony światowego dziedzictwa kulturalnego i naturalnego*, in: W. Kowalski. K. Piotrowska-Nosek, H. Schreiber, K. Zalasińska, *Konwencje UNESCO w dziedzinie kultury. Komentarz*, (ed.) K. Zalasińska, Warszawa 2014, pp. 280–281.

81 For Polish forms of the protection of immovable monuments see M. Drela, *Formy ochrony zabytków a wyrównanie szkody doznanej przez właściciela nieruchomości*, in: *Prawna ochrona zabytków*, (eds.) T. Gardocka, J. Sobczak, Toruń 2010, pp. 167–178.

82 V. Vadi, *Cultural heritage…*, p. 119.

money value and age criteria, a permit is required (Article 51 of the APGM,). The current legislation represents the evolution of export law from a prohibition on export, when export was an exception, towards its declared liberalization, accompanied, however, by the increasingly stronger marking of object categories to which interdicts and restrictions will apply.

Free movement is thus restricted, which builds ties between the country and an object stronger than those between an object and its owner. Of course, on many occasions, a permanent export permit is not related to the movement of the owner himself, but rather his intention to bring the object to the foreign market with the aim of obtaining a higher price for its sale. Studies of export procedures have found that a buyout is possible not only in respect of objects undergoing export procedures but also those which may not be exported.[83] In this situation, an owner leaving the country may not take an object with him or her, because its export is *ex lege* not possible. In this context a prohibition imposed on export of objects – movable monuments entered into the relevant register – in 2010 put owners in an entirely new situation. For filing a petition to have an entry made, they began a procedure for including an object in the register of monuments.[84] The change introduced by the amendment did not represent a liberalization of the export law,[85] but instead created an artificial and inexportable set of movable monuments. The question of the elements of this set and their value for the national heritage is not absolutely clear, because on the foundation of the register of monuments, a completely new legal mechanism has been built with an altogether different purpose. The legislative measures taken to adjust national law to EU policy have been wrongly superimposed on the oldest form of heritage protection whose primary function is the protection of monuments and not the control of export streams.

Among ownership-related issues connected to the export procedure, the following deserve mention: lowered confidence in the legislator, information asymmetry concerning objects entered into the register and the contravention of the principle of free movement – one of the freedoms of the European Union. This

---

83 A. Jakubowski, O. Jakubowski, *Pierwokup przy wywozie dóbr kultury za granicę – analiza kierunkowych zmian w prawie polskim*, in: *Kultura w praktyce. Zagadnienia prawne*, Vol. 3: *Muzea a rynek sztuki. Aspekt prawny*, (eds.) A. Jagielska-Burduk, W. Szafrański, Poznań 2014, p. 229.

84 Ibid. p. 219.

85 K. Zalasińska, *Wpływ zmiany przepisów dotyczących wywozu zabytków za granicę na rynek sztuki w Polsce*, in: *Rynek sztuki. Aspekty prawne*, (eds.) W. Kowalski, K. Zalasińska, Warszawa 2011, p. 171.

freedom suffers a major restriction for extra-economic reasons listed in the Treaty on the Functioning of the European Union, Article 36 (TFEU). They include prohibitions or restrictions on imports, exports or goods in transit justified on the grounds of protection of national treasures possessing artistic, historic or archaeological value. Such prohibitions or restrictions shall not, however, constitute a means of arbitrary discrimination or a disguised restriction on trade within the European Union. Increasingly greater importance is attached to national supportive legislation, covering objects not subjected to any special legal regime (for instance, blanket statutes concerned with the state ownership of some objects and their exclusion from private-law transactions). Furthermore, another aspect of legislation is coming to the fore, which directly affects private property. Export bans or restrictions as such will affect the privately-owned objects that are important for a given state, because of incorporated values.[86] The introduction of such legislation may result in the development of a mechanism enabling alienation of an object; but then again, the absence of such a provision puts the owner of an object entered into the register of monuments in a less favourable situation upon their decision to leave.

The role of the State as the entity assigned the task of safeguarding heritage also through legislation restricting the free movement of cultural property follows from the supreme law of the land. Under Article 5 of the Constitution, the Republic of Poland is to safeguard the national heritage. The degree of the involvement of the public authorities in the protection of private or public heritage was examined by the Constitutional Tribunal Court.[87] In the context of

---

86 S. Vigneron, *Protecting cultural objects: Enforcing the Illicit Export of Foreign Cultural Goods*, in: *Art, Cultural Heritage and the Market Ethical and Legal Issues*, (eds.) V. Vadi, H. Schneider, Berlin – Heidelberg 2014, p. 118.

87 Verdict by the Constitutional Tribunal Court dated 8 October 2007 K 20/07, OTK-A 2007/9/102, Dz.U.2007/192/1394. Faced with the absence of a legal definition of heritage, the Tribunal, for the purpose of judicial review of the provision concerning the conduct of archaeological investigations by the investor, used the definition formulated by Prof. Jan Piotr Pruszyński, who defined heritage as 'the collection of movable and immovable objects together with related spiritual values, and historical phenomena, customs and traditions found worthy of legal protection for the good of society and its development, and transfer to successive generations, owing to comprehensible and acceptable historical, patriotic, religious, scientific and artistic values important for the identity and continuity of political, social and cultural development, proving truths and commemorating historical events, cultivating the sense of beauty and civilization community' (J. Pruszyński, *Dziedzictwo kultury Polski. Jego straty i ochrona prawna*, Vol. 1, Kraków 2001, p. 50).

the participation of private entities in the management of cultural heritage, one fragment of the opinion delivered by the Constitutional Tribunal Court is worth quoting:

> in principle, the Constitution does not exclude the possibility of imposing public-law burdens on ownership above and in excess of profits borne by property. However, admissibility of such duties (burdens) is not unlimited for they may not interfere with the essence of ownership nor be a concealed (indirect) form of expropriation. Neither can they consist in shifting the duties incumbent on the public authorities onto the owner.[88]

While the conduct of archaeological investigations is a necessary element of heritage protection, the role of the State in safeguarding heritage brings up the question of sharing the cost of such protection.

This cooperation of the State and its citizens, the latter acting either as individuals or persons involved in the work of the third sector, i.e. NGO's, is, as it were, the aim and foundation of the State in themselves. The conception of the common good used in Article 1 of the Constitution, has an important bearing on the national heritage which 'should be protected by the State as well as, pursuant to Article 82 of the Constitution, by the citizens'.[89] Expressing a similar view as regards the sharing of duties, another author of a commentary maintained that 'the protection of heritage is not only a public, but also a universal task, incumbent by law on private entities as well'.[90] It can hardly be overlooked that the institutionalised protection of cultural heritage therefore is directed towards objects of a special value. Their value makes authorities extend extra protection to them, using one of the available protective measures – whereas the management of heritage components by private entities may embrace not only objects of a special value but also those beyond the compass of the interest of heritage protection agencies. In this respect, private entities have far more leeway, for they can discretionarily manage their assets. The limits of their discretion, nonetheless coinciding with care, are reached when the object in question is covered by one form of protection.

The ownership of cultural heritage or monuments, although left to national legislation (TFEU, Article 345) to be defined, strongly interacts with the cultural

88 Verdict by the Constitutional Tribunal Court dated 8 October 2007 K 20/07, OTK-A 2007/9/102, Dz.U.2007/192/1394.

89 K. Zalasińska, *Glosa do wyroku…*, pp. 3 et seq.

90 M. Drela, *Glosa do wyroku TK z dnia 8 października 2007 r. K 20/07*, "Państwo i Prawo" 2008, Issue 11, pp. 138–142.

policy pursued in the area of heritage and relevant EU legislation. It can be even claimed that through the changes of the EU legislation, the Polish legal system has new restrictions imposed on cultural heritage owners. For instance, the principle of the free movement of goods has begotten a legislative amendment which lists objects – national cultural property objects – that cannot be exported permanently. Changes in legislation are not a result of conception studies or fundamental research, but are strongly politically motivated. Moreover, newly adopted protection measures draw on the EU legislation or refer to it, for instance, to objects that may be subject to restitution at the same time indicating items worth including in the Heritage Treasure List (Article14a(2) of the APGM) in the wording submitted to the President for signature and sent to the Constitutional Tribunal Court for review).

The moulding of ownership of monuments depends on the model of heritage protection adopted in the APMG by the Polish legislator. With no visible direction or stable line of development being followed by the heritage protection law, there is hardly any strategy of the legislator that could be discussed, a strategy that would take into account both heritage protection needs and the limited capacity of the institution of ownership. The expanding of heritage protection forms makes a thing – monument – an object of community rights rather than an object of owner's rights. In this regard, it does not matter who the owner is – if it is a private or public entity. Public entities – units of local government – also as owners of monuments, should care first about heritage protection, which is one of the task they have been assigned by law. On many an occasion, this task yields to development interests seen in local spatial development decisions unfavourable to historic immovable objects located within a given district. Therefore, the finding that owners' interests and those of future generations entitled to heritage differ concerns equally all the owners of cultural heritage.

The direction in which the restrictions of ownership of monuments move in Poland is inconsistent with the conception of common European heritage. Viewing on the one hand cultural heritage as belonging to the European Union, the legislator unreasonably creates, on the other hand, sets of national cultural heritage objects within it. New restrictions have been imposed on the owners of movable cultural heritage without proper reflection on the purpose of export regulations. In turn, the ECHR judgment is a clear signal for the Polish legislator that the ownership of immovable monuments and the scope of owner's discretion in exercising control over them will be assessed on each occasion in the context of fundamental rights, making sure that restrictions are proportional and do not pose an excessive burden for an individual. It appears that the ownership of monuments and cultural property items that may become monuments is at a crossroads. To leave it safely and dynamically, the legislator must quicken its pace.

The knot based on the ownership of cultural heritage, despite being anchored in the principal real right, appears incongruous with ideal ownership, because of the nature of cultural property and the manner they can be used as determined by legal norms. The study of restrictions of powers enjoyed by the person exercising control over a monument and the fact that they apply not only to the owner make the regime of using the object escape ownership and gain a broader impact. The transferability and permanence of the right to certain goods should be enjoyed by an entity embodying the continuity of societies. It is the belief of the present authors that future generations should constitute this entity. Provided that they are made sufficiently definite and that secure transfer of ownership is ensured, or ownership is rejected altogether as unsuitable for cultural heritage, future generations will be a credible entity in legal relationships extant in a regime of using things selected by the legislator. Summing up, perhaps the chance for the evolution of property law as regards cultural heritage lies in the conception of the Eternal Rhombus of the Law, which is a consequence of the conception of successor interest protection and presents the relationship between an object and the successive persons exercising control over it. In the exercise of ownership with regard to cultural heritage components, a key role is, therefore, played by responsible and conscious decisions on the part of the owner both when merely transferring possession and performing momentous dispositive acts as well.

The choice of management instruments depends on the status of ownership. Different reasons will guide public and private entities. With the expansion of the protection system, the role of owners – private sector entities – therefore is strengthened. The building of this awareness in private collectors has a strong public dimension in the long run. With the lapse of time, collected works, at least some of them, become monuments and the collectors become increasingly aware of the public role of their collections. Thus, time is equally important for cultural heritage and the building of awareness in the private sector. While choosing an instrument, an institution exercising control over a collection – a public entity, say, a museum – even if it admits the possibility that the collection it possesses belongs to a private entity, will search for quasi-public solutions. In the case of ownership problems involving large collections, up till now decisions have been reached by negotiations to establish a foundation. Whereas in cases where fewer assets were involved, the parties chose civil-law agreements. The choice of a legal mechanism was often connected with the need to complete a specific administrative procedure, for instance a decision to have objects struck out from the inventory of museum pieces. With each mechanism, objects continued to be available to the public and owing to the collaboration between the institution and owners in caring for objects, the risk of their destruction or loss were brought down to a minimum.

The graphic model below shows decision options available to a private owner of cultural property which is at present or will be in future considered a monument. The model gives also the costs to be borne at the moment of making the decision and afterwards, necessary organisational involvement and actual say in management. The costs at the moment of making the decision are understood as the costs of effecting the relevant change and the costs borne after the decision is made, meaning the costs borne after the chosen mechanism is implemented. On the diagram, mechanisms unavailable in Poland are specially marked: *fidei-commissum* which does not exist and a trust which is foreign.

In the case of public collections, there are no doubts that they serve future generations. With private collections, the decision slowly takes shape while available mechanisms are conducive to the building of owner's awareness. The aim pursued by the person exercising control over heritage objects is to participate in the promotion and protection of heritage. Their decision depends on many factors. First, such a person faces the choice of the legal status of objects; namely, are they to remain their property or are they to be separated from their estate and form private or public collections. If the person concerned wills to continue the private character of the amassed heritage, they will look for solutions ensuring its safety or, when there is no danger, ones that will help promote it. If the decision-maker wishes to promote their objects, they may choose between more or less, costly solutions and among the costly ones between those calling for their active organisational participation or others that do not but ensure control over collections anyway. A given decision is influenced by the need to undertake organisational efforts, likelihood of such further needs and possible economic benefits. The possible benefits will be identified with doing business and collecting profits from works.[91]

91 The diagram does not include loaning collections for a fee as this mechanism is relatively rarely used in Poland and only in respect of works of a great value.

The least demanding mechanisms, as far as making a decision is concerned, are civil-law agreements. Apart from signing an agreement and actual handing over the object, the owner is not expected to take any other action, regardless of their purpose – promotion or providing security. A deed of gift (donation) is in a sense the mechanism of last choice, as it changes the status of objects from private to public. It can be claimed that a deed of gift is a mechanism representing a mature choice, resting on many years of awareness building in the collector whose ties to the object are severed. In the case of agreements, their success does not depend on the size of a collection. The choice of other mechanisms will also depend on the kind of collection held by the decision-maker.

Because of the legal-economic setting they find themselves in, entities possessed of cultural property seem to prefer some mechanisms to others. Depending on what is economically affordable and organisationally feasible, and whether the owner agrees to part with the property, the decision-maker makes their choice. As a rule, every private entity wishes for the collection to survive and searches for a settlement conducive to this end. In the long run, such collections take on a public character or nuance (e.g. private foundations).[92]

The conduct of public and private depositaries and heritage guardians is similar despite differences in legal systems. It is worth noting that some systems are friendlier than others to the decisions of transferring heritage components to the public sector, including tax regulations. If one were to venture a general rule, then it could be claimed that countries with more developed art markets create legal mechanisms conducive to taking on public character or nuance by cultural heritage objects. The mechanisms involve both the fiscal policy and the appreciation of private collectors as one of the prime movers of cultural development. Ultimately, an object originally possessing the so-called double identity: private (as far as the owning entity is concerned) and public (as far as its value is concerned[93]), takes on a full public character, thus losing its duality.

---

92 Cf. E. Moustaira, *Art, Collections, Private and Public: A Comparative Legal Study*, Cham – Heidelberg – New York – Dordrecht – London 2015, p. 7.

93 Ibid.

Decision diagram of a private decision-maker (AJB)

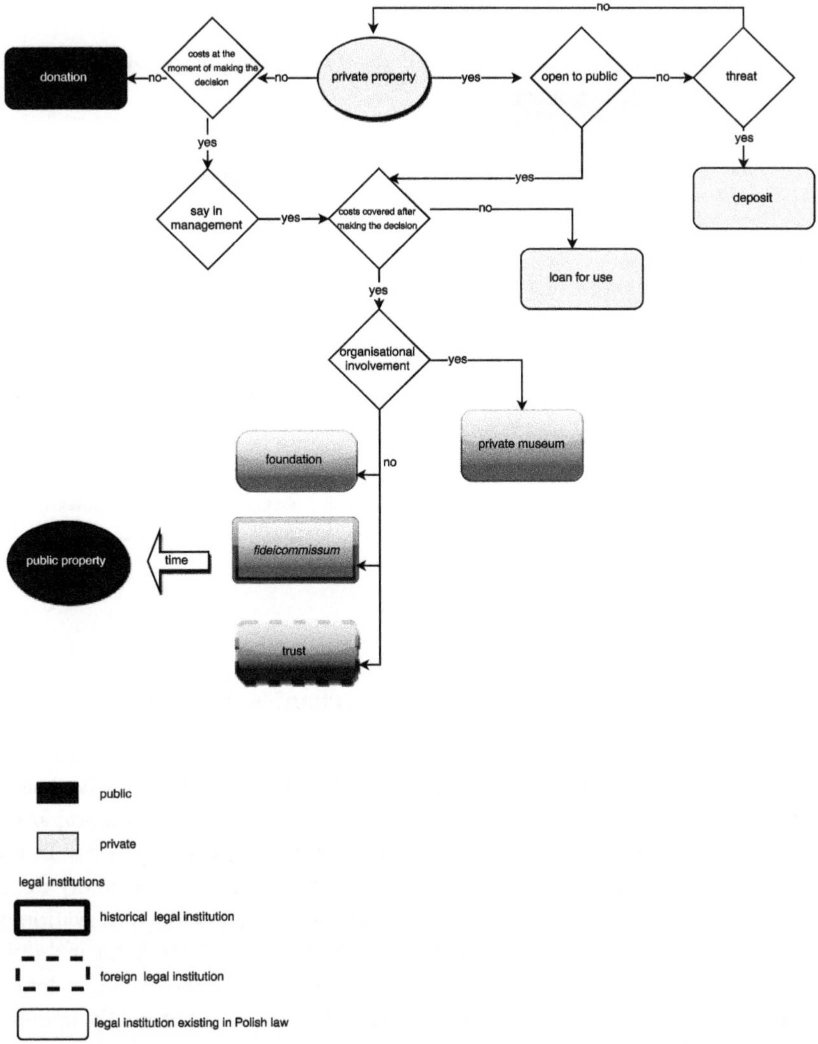

The decision ladder shows various legal mechanisms and the necessary organisational and financial involvement of the entity (Fig. a). The owner of cultural heritage objects, choosing a management mechanism, is guided by their wish to keep the objects together. If, however, only costs borne at the making of the decision and afterwards are taken into account, then a gift is less demanding on the decision-maker than making the cultural heritage property into a separate estate and setting up independent entities (Fig. b).

Degree of financial and organisational involvement of the decision-maker (AJB)

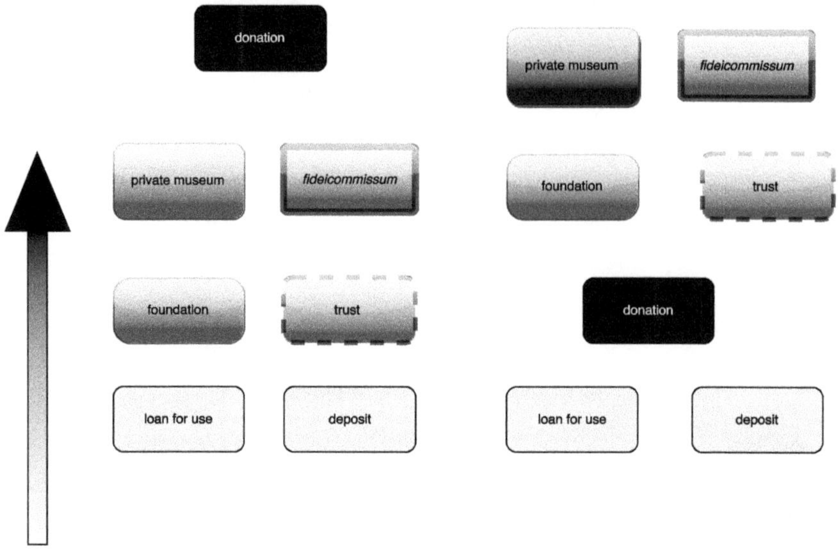

II.1.2 Heritage protection forms as a mechanism of cultural heritage management

In heritage protection, a special role is assigned to law. When successive enactments are adopted, the analyses of particular provisions are always accompanied by emotions on the part of those participating in the legislative process. In the application of the heritage protection law, emotions may, alas, on many occasions harm and hinder the achievement of its purpose, that is the preservation of heritage; heritage protection, as well as the appropriation of funds for it should proceed progressively. The development of a protection system and the definition of protection objects should be an ongoing process, continually updated and elaborated. This entails constant control and monitoring of the effectiveness of legal mechanisms. Furthermore, the process of updating should include collection exploration and control while elaboration should incorporate research results.

In order to assess statutory heritage protection forms as a mechanism of cultural heritage management, a thought should be given first to the function and place of protection forms in the Polish heritage protection law. Heritage protection forms were introduced to the APGM for the purpose of distinguishing legal regimes directed at monuments according to their kind (movable or immovable) and value for cultural heritage. Since different forms of monument protection have been identified, the Act defines heritage protection forms as 'special rules according to which individual monuments may be protected, depending on particular circumstances'.[94] The literature on the subject has distinguished two meanings of a heritage protection form: one restricting the meaning of heritage protection forms to the narrow meaning adopted in the Act (catalogue of forms set out in Article 7 of the APGM) and the other broadly encompassing also other protective measures beyond the administrative-legal plane. Among the latter, factual acts undertaken at monuments were included.[95] In the literature grounded in the APGM, a still different meaning of a heritage protection form has been adopted; it was taken to mean a form of administrative action, i.e. issuing a decision on an entry in the register of monuments. In this case, a distinction was made between the legal forms of protecting heritage and the legal means of its protection, for instance, administrative decisions requiring their addressees (entities exercising control over a monument) to embark on a specific conduct with respect to a monument.[96] In the majority of publications, their authors understand a heritage protection form as a legal institution.[97] Below, statutory heritage protection forms, as a legal mechanism of cultural heritage management, shall be analysed.

In 2003, during proceedings in the Polish lower chamber of parliament (the Sejm)'s Culture and Media Committee, its members discussed the actual

94 R. Golat, *Ustawa o ochronie zabytków i opiece nad zabytkami. Komentarz*, Kraków 2004, p. 28. In the APCP, the concept of a protection form was not employed at all and provisions on institutions corresponding to the present protection forms and detailed provisions elaborating on them were set out in different places. For instance, Chapter IV was devoted to the register of monuments, while means of protection were set out already in Chapter II entitled 'Object of Protection'.

95 K. Zeidler, *Prawo ochrony dziedzictwa kultury*, Warszawa 2007, p. 139.

96 P. Dobosz, *Formy i sposoby ochrony zabytków*, in: *Prawo ochrony zabytków*, (ed.) K. Zeidler, Warszawa – Gdańsk 2014, pp. 232–233.

97 Ibid. p. 233. W. Kowalski, K. Zalasińska, *Prawo ochrony dziedzictwa kulturowego w Polsce – próba oceny i wnioski*, in: *System ochrony zabytków w Polsce – analiza, diagnoza, propozycje*, (ed.) B. Szmygin, Lublin – Warszawa 2011, p. 20.

significance of the introduction of heritage protection forms in Article 7 of the APMG.[98] At the meeting, a relation between Article 4 of the AGM, which describes the means of heritage protection and defines what protection is, and Article 7 of the APGM, which defines heritage protection forms, was explained as well. An expert of the Committee, Jan Błeszyński, in a reply to a question about the significance of an entry in the register of monuments, explained that upon extending a protection form to a monument 'a number of consequences ensue which give rise to a special regime'. These consequences embrace the permissible conduct of an entity exercising control over a monument, conduct requiring a permit from a competent agency, subsidies for works at monuments and tax aspects related to the management of an immovable monument. The mention of a 'special regime' is important for this discussion, for it refers to all forms of heritage protection and indirectly interprets how a heritage protection form, as a legal institution, is to be understood.

Heritage protection forms function as intended by the legislator as separate legal institutions, with a predominance of administrative law norms, making the ownership of monuments more specific. The legal norms making up heritage protection forms are applied pursuant to: (1) the sources of the law (a regulation [monument of history], in the jurisdiction of agencies which have enacted it, (2) local bylaws [cultural park, heritage protection stipulations in a local spatial development plan]) and (3) administrative actions (administrative decisions [entry in the register of monuments] or heritage protection stipulations in the case of the fourth form [decision on public construction project location, outline planning permission, road project permission, decision on railway project location or public airport project permission]).

The APGM does not provide for the contractual defining of a monument status as a form of heritage protection. One must not fail to mention, however, that in the course of work on the APGM, the need to introduce elements typical of civil-law relationships was stressed many times, because they help maintain the equal status of the parties. This is important in relations between entities exercising control over monuments and heritage protection agencies,[99] at least at the first stage of contacts when no administrative acts (e.g. decisions) need to be issued. A special relationship between a heritage protection form and the

98 The meeting of the Committee on 21 January 2003 to hear the report of the *ad hoc* sub-committee on the Cabinet bill on monuments (Sejm paper No. 624) and Deputies' bill on national heritage protection (Sejm paper No. 537), *Biuletyn Komisji Sejmowych* No. 1425/IV, Culture and Media Committee, No. 68.

99 A. Jagielska-Burduk, *Zabytek ruchomy*, Warszawa 2011, pp. 172–173.

other norms from the legal system is best presented on the example of heritage protection stipulations in a local spatial development plan, which is based on a bylaw and other provisions of the heritage protection law. In the opinion of an administrative court 'the protection stipulated in a spatial development plan may not replace or modify existing statutory provisions and, in addition, must be grounded in the provisions authorizing the commune legislative body to stipulate it'.[100] This means that protection stipulations must be consistent with the APGM legal norms and norms of competence directed at the legislative bodies of local government units. In this approach, heritage protection forms, with respect to an object as an element of ownership, have limits set by the legislator.

Heritage protection forms are legal institutions defined as 'permanent (relatively permanent) forms of legal regulation of typical social relationships.[101] In the cultural heritage protection law, the permanence of legal regulations is undeniably one of its basic features, because of, among others, the object of regulations – monuments – and the assumptions about the longevity of protection institutions made by the legislator when enacting new regulations. The social relationship, to which heritage protection forms refer, considered as complexes of legal norms distinguished from others and being a functional whole,[102] is ownership of a specific type of things – monuments as defined by the APMG. Zygmunt Ziembiński's preferable definition of a legal institution reads as follows:

> A clearly designed legal institution is a complex of norms concerning a set of actions in a specific domain of affairs, in which the relationship holding between these norms raises no doubts and in which functional ties making up the institution are uncontested, with all these norms having other justification than only thetical as, for instance, axiological in the form of an ordered system of judgments and preferences.[103]

A clearly designed legal institution is an ideal model, therefore, interactions between the norms and their discernible hierarchy help remove any doubts as to component norms. An ideal legal institution is made up of legal norms belonging to a single domain. In the case of heritage protection forms, these would be legal

---

100 Verdict by the Voivodeship Administrative Court in Wrocław dated 15 February 2012, file No. II SA/Wr 723/11, LEX No. 1139028.

101 See T. Stawecki, P. Winczorek, *Wstęp do prawoznawstwa*, Warszawa 2003, p. 104; K. Zeidler, *O dobre prawo dla zabytków – rozważania na gruncie ustawy z 2003 roku o ochronie zabytków i opiece nad zabytkami*, "Gdańskie Studia Prawnicze" 2010, Vol. XXIV, p. 587.

102 W. Gromski, entry: *Instytucja prawna*, in: *Wprowadzenie do nauk prawnych. Leksykon tematyczny*, (ed.) A. Bator, Warszawa 2012, p. 209.

103 Z. Ziembiński, *Podstawowe problemy prawoznawstwa*, Warszawa 1980, p. 34.

norms belonging to various branches of law (civil law, administrative law), which is an indirect consequence of the interdisciplinary nature of heritage protection. Recognizing, however, as a fact, the emergence of cultural heritage protection law as a separate branch of the law, one has to conclude that the legal norms making up heritage protection forms will belong to this new branch of the law of the dynamically growing legal system.[104] The last finding has a serious consequence for cultural heritage protection, namely it presupposes the application of legal principles adopted in a given branch of law, which is of paramount importance in the practical application of law.[105]

In the APMG, the legislator has used the term heritage protection *forms* with good reason in a new legal sense different from the intuitive one. The concept of form should be taken to mean the means of protection provided for in independent legal institutions set up by the legislator for the purpose of attaining specific objectives[106] – in this case, protection adjusted to the kind of monument and its properties. The functioning of legal institutions entails the grouping of legal norms, which in turn brings order to the internal system of the law. It can hardly go unnoticed that certain legal norms will be repeated or will dominate several institutions. It follows that the institutions defined in Article 7 of the APGM, can be distinguished and considered a common institution type.[107] In the studied legal institutions, legal norms tend to reoccur.[108] The identical objective of the legal institutions and the properties they have in common have made the legislator, compiling their closed catalogue, call them heritage protection forms.

To analyse the legal institutions named in Article 7 of the APGM, it is desirable to trace how the concept of heritage protection form is used in judicial decisions. It can be concluded that adjudicating benches variously understand heritage protection forms when they interpret the law. A broad understanding of heritage protection forms, close to seeing them as forms of administrative action, was presented in the judgment by the Voivodeship Administrative Court in Warsaw dated 18 March 2010[109] in which the court held that 'an entry in the register of monuments is a special, more exacting form of heritage protection

104 K. Zeidler, *Prawo ochrony dziedzictwa kultury jako nowa gałąź prawa*, in: *Prawo ochrony zabytków…*, p. 33.

105 Ibid. p. 32.

106 T. Stawecki, P. Winczorek, op. cit., p. 104.

107 Z. Ziembiński, op. cit., p. 35.

108 For example, the duty to obtain a permit.

109 Verdict by the Voivodeship Administrative Court in Warsaw dated 18 March 2010, file No. I SA/Wa 1978/09, LEX No. 606524.

(in comparison to that defined in Article 4 and for instance in Articles 27, 29, 30, 36(1)(2, 5) of the Act on Protection and Guardianship of Monuments 2003)'. Additionally, the court in its opinion graded protection forms and held that an entry in the register of monuments 'far more strongly limits and interferes with the ownership enjoyed by the owner of a historic immovable'.[110] Hence, it was assumed that inspector of monuments recommendations, defined in Article 27a, may also constitute a heritage protection form, provided they are issued in writing by a voivodeship inspector of monuments on the motion of the owner or the possessor. They determine how the monument is to be used, what protective devices are to be put in place and how conservation work is to be carried out. They also specify admissible alterations to a monument. Finally, under Article 29 of the APGM, heritage protection agencies are empowered to inspect *in situ* monuments or ones having the features of a monument by appointment with their owners or possessors. Assuming this line of reasoning, heritage protection forms set out in Article 7 of the APGM, can be considered as qualified forms together with already existing relationships within this catalogue.

Thus, it appears that it was wrong to equalise heritage protection forms and their relevant means, composed of legal instruments listed as protection forms, ranking below the register of monuments. The judgment by the Voivodeship Administrative Court in Wrocław dated 15 February 2012 lists together heritage protection forms and heritage protection means, finding that 'heritage protection stipulations in a local spatial development plan are one of the forms and means of heritage protection'.[111] It was assumed that heritage protection stipulations in a local spatial development plan were both a heritage protection form and the modus of protection provided. Relying on the above view, one can draw a distinction in the concept network between heritage protection forms, as a special means of protection making up separate legal institutions, and protection measures taken to mean all protective actions, taking advantage of legal instruments defined in the APMG. In turn, the judgment by the Voivodeship Administrative Court in Warsaw dated 30 January 2013,[112] in the context of making a finding whether an object was a monument as defined in the APMG, found that 'a heritage protection agency must ascertain whether a given object has characteristics listed in the statutory definition [...] and if so, whether its historic characteristics

110 Ibid.

111 Verdict by the Voivodeship Administrative Court in Wrocław dated 15 February 2012, file No. II SA/Wr 723/11, LEX No. 1139028.

112 Verdict by the Voivodeship Administrative Court in Warsaw dated 30 January 2013, file No. VII SA/Wa 2211/12, LEX No. 1298787.

merit extension of the legal form of conservator protection by entering it in the register of monuments'. In this case, the adopted meaning of a heritage protection form is identical with that used by the legislator and assumed to be the principal one in this work. What is more, the judgment strongly emphasised the process of adjusting the heritage protection form to a monument and its characteristics. This process is vital as one can choose between a regular or a qualified form, or indeed decide to choose neither.

In Article 7 of the APGM, the legislator has distinguished four heritage protection forms. Among the forms found in previous legislation, an entry in the register of monuments and recognition as a monument of history have been considered worthy of retention. In addition, because of 'new challenges related to the necessity of protecting historic space shaped by human activity and in particular a cultural landscape,'[113] two new forms have been added, namely, creation of a cultural park and protection stipulations in a local spatial development plan. The fourth protection form was modified by the Act of 18 March 2010 to amend the Act on the Protection and Guardianship of Monuments and several other Acts[114] by expanding protection stipulations beyond a local spatial development plan.

The provisions on heritage protection forms divide them by subject, distinguishing together forms applicable to movable and immovable monuments, as well as those dedicated solely to immovable ones, because of their specific character. The heritage protection forms applicable to immovable monuments may be graded by separating regular forms from qualified ones (entry of an immovable monument into the register, recognition as a monument of history).[115] Importantly, the order of enumerating the relevant heritage protection forms does not reflect the level of protection *per se*. Neither is there a clear division into forms applicable to movable and immovable monuments. The relationships holding between individual forms rather, are seen in provisions concerning each form, permitting to build a hierarchy of heritage protection forms. The order, however, it must be emphasised, is not haphazard. The legislator has enumerated the forms in their historical order, beginning with the first two, known already

113 A. Soldani, D. Jankowski, *Zabytki. Ochrona i opieka. Praktyczny komentarz do nowej ustawy. Tekst ustawy z dnia 23 lipca 2003 r.*, Zielona Góra 2004, p. 19.

114 Ustawa z dnia 18 marca 2010 r. o zmianie ustawy o ochronie zabytków i opiece nad zabytkami i zmianie niektórych innych ustaw [Act of 18 March 2010 amending the APGM and some other Acts], Dz. U. 2010, No. 75, item 474.

115 K. Zalasińska, *Prawna ochrona zabytków nieruchomych w Polsce*, Warszawa 2010, p. 212.

when the Act on the Protection of Cultural Heritage (APCH) was in force.[116] However, in the literature on the subject an opinion can be encountered that the functioning of qualified heritage protection forms is not properly emphasised in respect of the major principles of practical heritage management.[117]

Furthermore, the legislator allows for heritage protection forms to function in parallel within the register of monuments. This takes the form of an entry of an immovable monument next to an entire layout or complex of immovable monuments. Under Article 9(3) of the APGM, the entry into the register of a historic urban or rural layout, or a historic building complex does not preclude the issuing of a decision to enter into the register component immovable monuments, making up these layouts or building complexes. In judicial decisions and opinions voiced by the authors of authoritative juristic publications, there is a set division between an entry of a layout or a complex of immovable monuments and an entry of an individual immovable monument in the sense that 'an entry into the register of monuments of an urban layout mentioned in the APGM, Article 6(1)(1b), does not automatically entail the extension of protection to the individual objects of the layout'.[118]

Upon the extension of a heritage protection form to an object, it acquires a new legal status, which can be called a new regime of using a thing. The position that 'only in respect of objects covered by one of these forms, it is admissible to use the instruments of conservator supervision (instruments of an imperious character)',[119] should, however, be slightly moderated. Under the APMG, a voivodeship inspector of monuments enforces heritage protection and guardianship provisions. The enforcement may embrace immovable monuments, too, which are not entered in the register. In such situations, authorised conservation

116 However, there is barely any justification, in view of the arrangement adopted so far, for placing an entry in the List of Heritage Treasures immediately after the register of monuments in item 1a in the Act amending the Act on Protection and Guardianship of Monuments. Then, in the event the new form enters the legal system, the enumeration of forms given in the Article 7 would be closer to a division by subject.

117 The possibility of taking into account the fact that a monument has been recognized as a monument of history in the allotment of funds is mentioned *inter alia* in K. Zeidler, *Pomniki historii*, "Spotkania z Zabytkami" 2006, No. 8, p. 36.

118 K. Zalasińska, *Ochrona zabytków. Orzecznictwo z komentarzem*, Warszawa 2010, p. 83. Verdicts delivered when the APMG and the APCP were in force: Verdict by the Supreme Administrative Court in Warsaw dated 27 January 2011, II OSK 31/10, LEX No. 953062, Verdict by the Supreme Court dated 10 June 2005, II CK 729/04.

119 P. Antoniak, M. Cherka, in: *Ustawa o ochronie zabytków i opiece nad zabytkami. Komentarz*, (ed.) M. Cherka, Warszawa 2010, p. 40.

personnel may enter any premises upon reasonable suspicion of destruction of or damage to a monument (Article 38(3)(1) of the APGM). The instruments of conservator supervision are designed to be used by heritage protection agencies also for other purposes such as exploration of historic resources. For this purpose, the owner or possessor of a monument or other object having characteristics of a monument (either movable or immovable) is required to give access to it in accordance with Articles 29 and 30 of the APGM.

The Act features a closed catalogue of heritage protection forms. For that matter, in the course of work on the APGM, a proposal was tabled to expand heritage protection forms by a fifth form, namely, records of monuments. Finally, the Committee did not recommend the proposal to the Sejm. The reasons given for the Committee's position read that records kept by the General Inspector of Monuments were not a form of protection but merely documented monuments and informed about the size of historic resources in a commune, province and the country itself. An opinion by a Ministry official seems important; it maintained that 'the records provide no heritage protection' and 'they do not cause any protection to be extended to the objects covered by them'.[120] The recognition of records as a heritage protection form might remove doubts concerning the restriction of ownership enjoyed by entities exercising control over monuments[121] and allay fears expressed by practitioners.[122]

In some works, monument records and the protection of objects inscribed in the UNESCO World Heritage List are called innominate heritage protection forms.[123] In support of this practice it is claimed that the legislator, besides the

---

120 The meeting of the Committee on 21 May 2003 to consider amendments and motions proposed in the second reading to the Deputies' national heritage protection bill and the Cabinet monument bill (Sejm papers nos. 537, 624 and 1527).

121 In the matter, the Human Rights Defender intervened. Letter of 14 November 2012, RPO-706860-IV/12/JP, http://www.sprawy-generalne.brpo.gov.pl/pdf/2012/06/706860/1682077.pdf (accessed: 29.06.2015).

122 I. Mikiciuk, *Gminna ewidencja zabytków w świetle zmian wprowadzonych ustawą o zmianie ustawy o ochronie zabytków i opiece nad zabytkami oraz zmianie niektórych innych ustaw*, "Kurier Konserwatorski" 2010, No. 9, pp. 5ff. The question of the constitutionality of the commune monument records and their consequences for the powers of an owner will be settled when the Constitutional Tribunal Court adjudicates on a constitutional complaint filed by a private entity, case No. SK 3/15. The unconstitutionality of the records was suspected already in 2010 by K. Zeidler, *O dobre prawo…*, p. 593. See also A. Krzyżanowska, *Resort nie przyznaje się do wad w ewidencji zabytków*, "Gazeta Prawna", 3 July 2015.

123 P. Dobosz, *Formy i sposoby ochrony…*, p. 232.

forms named in the Act, has enacted provisions giving rise to legal forms similar in function (innominate forms), but has not decided to distinguish them. It is hardly believable, given such a strong determination of the legislator shown in the drafting of the catalogue in Article 7 of the APGM, that it intended to treat functionally similar legal institutions as heritage protection forms. It appears, however, that if monument records were to be given the status of a heritage protection form, it would be a less onerous form than an entry in the register of monuments. Additionally, to the extent it covers monuments entered in the register, it would be a parallel form and in respect of monuments named in Article 22(5)(2 and 3) of the AMGM, a subordinate form to an entry in the register of monuments, which in this case is a qualified form.

In turn, the inscription of an object in the UNESCO World Heritage List connected with its recognition as a monument of history is an extra-statutory regulation, following from international obligations assumed by Poland. The recognition of the inscription in the World Heritage List would, therefore, be yet another, qualified protection form of the third degree (first-degree protection form – entry in the register of monuments, second-degree protection form – recognition as a monument of history, third-degree protection form – inscription in the World Heritage List), not involving any clear change in the legal status of a monument. Set out in the Convention, Article 4, the duties of signatory states comprising identification, protection, conservation, presentation and transmission to future generations are of a general and systemic character. The duties are performed therefore pursuant to national law regulations, ascribed to specific heritage protection forms, as far as the entirety of cultural heritage is concerned, and in the case of the inscription in the World Heritage List – by a recognition as a monument of history. The duty to cooperate is actualised only if a state party is incapable to perform its duties on its own. In this sense, an inscription in the World Heritage List is not one of the protection forms mentioned in Article 7 of the APGM, defined above as legal institutions having a specific purpose and regulating social relationships.[124]

In the discussion about the catalogue of innominate heritage protection forms, a proposal was put forward to consider an agreement for letting land in perpetual usufruct as such a form.[125] In the case of immovable monuments,

---

124 See claims K. Piotrowska, *Aspekty prawne zarządzania dziedzictwem na przykładzie pomników historii i miejsc światowego dziedzictwa*, in: *Prawo ochrony zabytków...*, pp. 267–269.

125 T. Sienkiewicz, *Umowa o oddanie gruntu w użytkowanie wieczyste jako nienazwana forma ochrony zabytków*, in: *Kultura w praktyce. Zagadnienia prawne*, Vol. 3: *Muzea a*

perpetual usufruct arises not only by a purposeful agreement but also requires a prior permission from an inspector of monuments.[126] Under Article 13(4) of the Act on Real Estate Management Act (AREM), letting in perpetual usufruct of real estate be entered in the register of monuments,[127] owned by the State Treasury or a unit of local government, as well as contributing such real estate as non-pecuniary assets into companies or partnerships, requires permission from a voivodeship inspector of monuments. A permission is also necessary for other forms of disposing of a property, including contracts of sale, exchange or donation.[128] The agreement of perpetual usufruct was called a contractual heritage protection mechanism, with special attention being drawn to the potential of the stipulations that can be made in the agreement.[129] The manner of use stipulated in the agreement binds also the successors and assigns of the usufructuary,[130] which is a guarantee safeguarding the monument concerned. Under Article 29 of the AREM, in the agreement, a usufructuary may be imposed additional duties such as the renovation or rebuilding of objects.[131] In the scope defined by Civil Code provisions, a usufructuary may be also obligated to keep monuments in good condition or given deadlines and terms for rebuilding them in case of their destruction (Article 239 of the Civil Code).[132]

A perpetual usufructuary's duties may also follow from a statute,[133] in this case the APGM. In Article 63 of the AREM there are additional instruments providing for financial penalties for a usufructuary in the event of failure to

---

rynek sztuki. Aspekty prawne, (ed.) A. Jagielska-Burduk, W. Szafrański, Poznań 2014, pp. 245 et seq.

126 The permission mentioned in Article 13(4) of the IMA, is granted by a Voivodeship Inspector of Monuments in the form of a decision.

127 On the scope of application of the legal norm exclusively to monuments entered in the register of monuments see E. Bończak-Kucharczyk, *Ustawa o gospodarce nieruchomościami. Komentarz*, Warszawa 2014, p. 157.

128 G. Bieniek, G. Matusik, in: *Ustawa o gospodarce nieruchomościami. Komentarz*, (ed.) S. Kalus, Warszawa 2012, pp. 172–173, E. Bończak-Kucharczyk, op. cit., pp. 156–157.

129 T. Sienkiewicz, op. cit., p. 256.

130 A. Cisek, K. Górska, in: *Kodeks cywilny. Komentarz*, (eds.) E. Gniewek, P. Machnikowski, Warszawa 2014, p. 470.

131 E. Bończak-Kucharczyk, op. cit., p. 236.

132 A. Tułodziecki, in: J. Jaworski, A. Prusaczyk, A. Tułodziecki, M. Wolanin, *Ustawa o gospodarce nieruchomościami. Komentarz*, Warszawa 2013, p. 186.

133 Z. Truszkiewicz, *Użytkowanie wieczyste. Zagadnienia konstrukcyjne*, Kraków 2006, p. 181.

meet deadlines set for developing a land immovable. In such a situation, a competent authority may set an additional deadline and if duties are not performed by the first and additional deadlines, additional annual fees may be imposed on a usufructuary, above and beyond the perpetual usufruct fees. Moreover, with regard to the safety of cultural heritage, the owner may terminate the agreement when the perpetual usufructuary uses the immovable in question in a manner inconsistent with that agreed by the parties.[134] This power follows from Article 240 of the Polish Civil Code, to which Article 33(3) of the AREM referred. However, the termination of a perpetual usufruct agreement is not obligatory. Having regard to its narrow application – only to the immovables (real estate) owned by the State Treasury or units of local government – perpetual usufruct ought to be considered a very interesting mechanism of managing cultural heritage offering broad possibilities, but, due to its character of a limited real right, arising out of an agreement establishing it or letting an immovable in perpetual usufruct, incapable of recognition as a heritage protection form.

The major argument in favour of maintaining a closed catalogue of heritage protection forms is the purpose for which they have been established as an internal, domestic regulation – setting up specific protection regimes for immovable and movable monuments. The principal purpose, which is heritage protection, cannot be achieved with monument records and perpetual usufruct. In these cases, heritage protection is only secondary to the principal purpose which in one case is the accumulation of information and in the other, determination through the establishment of a limited real right as to how an immovable owned by the State Treasury or units of local government is to be used by other entities. Moreover, partially overlapping in terms of subject matter, monument records and the relevant register should not create overlapping protection regimes, seen in extending to an object a new protection form within national law. It must not be ignored that upon recording an object in commune monument records, its management undergoes many changes provided for in the APGM. They are not as broad as those provided for by the legislator in the case of heritage protection forms, but are a significant side element of the process of heritage exploration in the context of project execution.

134 T. Sienkiewicz, op. cit., p. 255.

HERITAGE PROTECTION FORM MOVABLE		MONUMENTS (number)	
		MOVABLE	IMMOVABLE
1	Register of monuments	246960[135]	70190
2	Monument of history	--------------	71
3	Cultural park	--------------	26
4	Protection stipulations in a local spatial development plan, in a decision on public construction project location, outline planning permission, road project permission, decision on railway project location or public airport project permission	--------------	Number is unknown
5	*List of Heritage Treasures*[136]	Over a dozen declared	-----------------
6	Commune monument records	-----------------	No nationwide data available

Source: author's description (A. J.- B.)

Indirectly, the function of individual heritage protection forms, differences in scope with respect to movable and immovable monuments, while taking into account the overall size of the heritage in question, as well as the introduction of two levels of protection, are shown by the number of objects covered.

In conclusion, when heritage protection forms are compared, a clear majority of forms designed to be used with immovable monuments is noticeable, including regular, qualified and parallel forms. In contrast, movable monuments can be embraced by a single protection form, namely an entry in the register of monuments. It appears that in the case of the fourth form, the impossibility of keeping its continuous record makes its usability for carrying out a coordinated cultural heritage protection policy insufficient. There is no doubt, however, that the fourth form of protection must not be inconsistent with documents of a nationwide rank, including the National Spatial Planning Policy and Province Development Strategy. Even with distributing the activities of entities competent to establish heritage protection forms between heritage protection agencies and local government units, the legislator consciously diversifies protection forms

135 Number of decisions 14889.

136 A heritage protection form not in force at the time of publication. The Act was sent to the Constitutional Tribunal Court for review.

into those closer and more distant to a region or possible, or impossible to be centrally planned or verified.

Register of monuments

Historically the oldest form of monument protection, entry in the Register of Monuments,[137] has undergone numerous changes as it has evolved over time. This was connected with the terminology adopted, extending on a cultural property and a monument and, consequently, a definition of a monument as an object which through entry in the Register has attained the status and protection of a monument. A register of monuments was originally the only form of recording historic resources in practice. The current Act on the Protection and Guardianship of Monuments (APGM) provides for a different manner in which movable and immovable monuments are entered in the Register on the basis of a decision of a voivodeship inspector of monuments. Pursuant to Article 9 clause 1 of the Act, today, an immovable monument may be entered in the Register of Movable and Immovable Monuments either by a decision of a voivodeship inspector of monuments issued *ex officio,* following a request by the owner of the immovable monument, or by the perpetual owner of the land upon which the immovable monument stands. A movable monument may, in principle, be entered in the Register by a decision of a voivodeship inspector of monuments issued following a request by the owner of the monument (Article 10 of the APGM). The decision to enter a movable monument in the Register may be issued *ex officio* in the event of a justified concern that a monument of exceptional historic, artistic or scientific value may be destroyed, damaged or illegally exported abroad. The removal of a monument from the Register of Monuments is governed by the provisions of Article 13 of the APGM. One of the premises justifying the removal of a monument from the Register is damage to a monument to an extent resulting in the loss of its historic, artistic or scientific value, or a situation where the historic, artistic or scientific value has not been confirmed by a subsequent scientific examination. The decision to remove is made by the Minister of Culture and National Heritage.

The entry of a monument in the Register of Monuments entails a number of duties for its holder.[138] They not only pertain to the manner of handling a

---

137 Compare remarks on the form of this protection P. Dobosz, *Formy i sposoby ochrony…*, pp. 233–234.

138 Compare Verdict of the Voivodeship Administrative Court in Warsaw of 23 April 2009, file I SA/Wa 48/09, LEX No. 550267, and in particular the reasoning concerning

monument but also to planning work in relation to it, as referred to in the construction law. This restriction is noteworthy especially in the light of the recent attempt (in 2015) to eliminate the distinction between movable and immovable monuments and their different treatment. The report on the functioning of the Polish system of national heritage protection after 1989 pointed out a "two track" method of issuing decisions on the entry of a monument in the Register of Movable and Immovable Monuments, which led to a situation where a decision issued "exclusively in the higher interest of conservation as seen by the issuing office" was in fact "frequently an example of an ineffective official form of protection by the conservator".[139] It was also reported that the principle of the equality of subjects before the law was violated because this mechanism of entering monuments into the Register did not apply to immovable monuments and their owners. However, when the constitutionality of the provisions was examined, the differing or differentiated procedures were the focus of attention, while the legal impact on the owner of a decision to approve the entry of a movable monument passed unnoticed.[140]

The rationale behind the proposed amendments made in 2015 seeking to eliminate this "two-track" path, was that "the scope for the effective protection of movable monuments is very limited because protection cannot be commenced any earlier than when a monument has already been exposed to different risks. This situation is not right. A failure to intervene in time may result in the irreparable loss of priceless objects".[141] Such a brief statement of the reasons for a proposal for radical change was however insufficient. What the proposed amendment actually intended to secure was a decision supporting the entry of a monument in the register independently of its holder's will. However, the specific character of a movable object means that its entry in the Register would substantially limit its mobility as such an object would forthwith become subject to the

---

those entitled to inherit that: "a monument ceases to be only and exclusively the private property of its owner"

139 A. Böhm, P. Dobosz, P. Jaskanis, J. Purchla, B. Szmygin, *Raport na temat funkcjonowania systemu ochrony dziedzictwa kulturowego w Polsce po roku 1989*, (ed.) J. Purchla, Kraków 2008, p. 42.

140 Ibid. pp. 68–69.

141 Private member's bill to amend the Act on the Protection and Guardianship of Monuments and the Law on Museums, Seym of the VIIth term print No. 3112, http://orka.sejm.gov.pl/Druki7ka.nsf/0/747FA7FAF793D658C1257DE200390A5A/%24File/3112.pdf (accessed:15.06.2015).

prohibition on permanent export that is inherent in the provisions of Article 51 of the APGM.[142]

The model of ownership of a movable monument entered in the Register of Monuments as described in the APGM is the ideal model. However, as has frequently been pointed out, the execution of the ownership right is difficult to supervise and it may even be claimed that the protection of ownership provided for in the Act is rather illusory. When the benefits to the owner of a monument entered in the Register are compared with the obligations which the draft law imposed on the owner, it is clear that "from the point of view of the constitutionality of the proposed provisions, a balance of the rights and duties should be sought, having regard to the principle of proportionality".[143] What is more, to ensure the satisfactory fulfilment of the obligations imposed on owners of monuments, some supervision would be needed, and this would require establishing regular contact with owners or their successors. This would not be easy to achieve in practice. Real protection of monuments may be easier to achieve when society grows more aware of the need for such protection and this consciousness spreads to all levels, regional, national and international.

Luckily, the draft amendment proposing the *ex officio* entry of movable monuments in the Register was rejected by the Senate which found that the proposed amendments, and the obligations connected with entry in the Register which arose from them, were incompatible with the objective to be achieved. This objective was to be reflected in the extension of supervision over certain objects in the absence of any reason to justify the implementation of protection mechanisms. It was also claimed that entering movable objects in the Register *ex officio* would have negative consequences on the antiquarian market, with a number of transactions moving to what might be termed a 'grey' area. The biggest concern was a substantial limitation of cross-border movement of art objects and damage to the transparency of transaction that has been laboriously built up in recent

142 As Wojciech Szafrański noted, even before the proposed amendment became the subject of a parliamentary debate, there were attempts to have 'added to it unnoticed' a provision allowing the entry of an immovable object in the Register of monuments by an *ex officio* decision, thus substantially limiting their owners' rights without any real benefits for them. This was to be done when debating the List of National Treasures. See W. Szafrański, *"Dama" na liście skarbów*, "Rzeczpospolita", 8 January 2014, http://prawo.rp.pl/artykul/1077063.html (accessed: 15.06.2015).

143 K. Zalasińska, *Ochrona ruchomego dziedzictwa kulturowego w Polsce – wybrane zagadnienia*, "Opolskie Studia Administracyjno-Prawne" 2011, Vol. 8, p. 43.

years by the Association of Polish Antiquarians.[144] In discussions on the amendments to the existing regulation, fostering art collecting has been presented as one of the indirect, but extremely important ways of protecting monuments.

The APGM provides for two different ways of regulating movable and immovable monuments entered in the Register of Monuments. In the case of movable monuments, the investment process and its regulation are of key importance. Any work to be done in relation to monuments is subject to regulatory provisions in the binding Act and in secondary legislation. The latter frequently takes the form of decrees or regulations of the Minister of Culture and National Heritage, which, for various reasons, are frequently difficult to execute in practice. Yet it seems justified that movable monuments are treated differently and this difference ought to be continued owing to their different characteristics. The fact of entering a movable monument in the Register of Monuments means that such a monument is prohibited by law from being taken across the border. Such a ban on exports, however, distorts one of the basic forms of protection. Added to that, the list of protective measures now also included a duty to build up a resource of movable monuments that are objects of heritage ascribed to a certain territory.

List of National Treasures

Another amendment concerned movable objects which it was proposed should be put on a list in order of priority, similar to that existing for immovable monuments. A proposal for amendments to the Act on the Protection and Guardianship of Monuments and the Law on Museums was made in 2013.[145] The idea behind the proposed amendments was to ensure a stronger financial contribution by the State for the protection of the most valuable movable monuments. These monuments were to be entered on the List of National Treasures by, accompanied by a recommendation of the Minister of Culture and National Heritage.[146] There was much controversy about the proposed amendments, practically at each stage of the legislative process,[147] which ultimately caused the President of the

---

144 www.antykwariusze.pl.

145 Private member's bill to amend the Act on the Protection and Guardianship of Monuments…

146 Compare the way in which museum personnel communicated regarding the transfer of "Lady with the Ermine" to a museum abroad, or refused to issue a permit the transfer abroad of Memling's "Last Judgement".

147 Compare: W. Szafrański, "*Dama*"…; Ł. Gazur, *Dama z łasiczką i ministrem*, "Dziennik Polski", 21 January 2014, http://www.dziennikpolski24.pl/artykul/3304068,dama-z-lasiczka-i-ministrem,id,t.html?cookie=1 (accessed 15.06.2015).

Republic of Poland Bronisław Komorowski to use his right to refer the act to the Constitutional Tribunal Court before giving it final approval.[148]

If the proposed amendment to create a List of National Treasures is finally approved, it will be necessary to draw up a definition of objects destined for entry.[149] The decision on which items ought to be on the List of National Treasures may be based on the provision of a draft wording of Article 14a of the APGM that reads that a movable monument "of particular value to cultural heritage shall be entered on the List of National Treasures if it falls in one of the categories referred to in Article 64 clause 1 of the APGM". The terms that were frequently used in the debate when referring to this new category of monument included "distinction", "prestige", and "exclusivity". Recognising the financial consequences of creating a List of National Treasures, it was decided that it would contain a limited number of objects. These objects must meet the criteria specified in the legal definition of a monument referred to in Article 2 of the APGM. They provide that the maintenance of a given monument is in the public interest and that the monument itself is of particular significance to the cultural heritage. Thus, the administrative procedure related to the entry of an object on the List of National Treasures, requires that first it must be determined whether the object in question is indeed a monument, even if it had been considered as such before, and whether it fulfils the criteria of being of particular significance for cultural heritage.

The first question that must be asked is about the framing of this provision. Is there anything that may be of particular significance for the cultural heritage as a dynamic asset whose definition has evolved over the years? Another question concerns the understanding of "cultural heritage' that has not been specified. Thus a doubt arises whether we are dealing in this case with a shift of category assuming that something may have a value for heritage when treated as tangible and intangible assets, but not for others, in this case the recipients or

---

148 Motion put to the Constitutional Tribunal Court by Poland's President requesting examination of the compliance with the Constitution of the Act amending the act on the protection and guardianship of museums of 31 July 2015, http://www.prezydent.pl/download/gfx/prezydent/pl/defaultaktualnosci/2073/16/1/20150731_wniosek_do_tk_ws_ustawy_o_ochronie_zabytkow.pdf (accessed 15.06.2015).

149 Also see P. Dobosz, *Koncepcja Listy Skarbów Dziedzictwa w systemie prawa ochrony zabytków w Polsce, in: Kultura w praktyce. Zagadnienia prawne*, Vol. 2: *Wokół problematyki prawnej zabytków i rynku sztuki*, (ed.) A. Jagielska-Burduk, W. Szafrański, Poznań 2013, pp. 199–224; P. Dobosz, *Ewoluujące prawne formy ochrony zabytków w Polsce, in: Prawo ochrony zabytków…*, pp. 235–243.

beneficiaries. The situation is slightly clearer in relation to historic monuments which should be "of particular significance for culture" and qualify for the 'exceptional' purpose of the legislation. The term "of particular significance for cultural heritage" is new and its meaning and scope require definition, while reference to terms already defined for the sake of the legislation applicable to historic monuments would certainly be easier.

The reference to Article 64 clause 1 of the APGM also seems wrong, since this article refers to categories of objects eligible for restitution. It raises doubts particularly because as has been reported on the work on a new EC directive, "the new directive breaks with the existing link between the definition of a national cultural property and a catalogue contained in the Annex to the current directive, in consequence of which the quota thresholds have been abolished".[150] As can be seen, the references made in the draft of the new Polish legislation are to Polish provisions applicable under Polish law, but they may have to be amended in the future to comply with EU legislation. Under Article 11 of the APGM, an object entered on the List of National Treasures will not appear in the Register of Monuments, a museum inventory, or any national library resources. Thus it has been decided that new objects added to the List of National Treasures will not be entered in these registers or lists. It has also been decided that although objects which already are in the register of museums will not be removed from these inventories upon entry on the List of National Heritage, unless otherwise provided for elsewhere, new entries on the List of National Treasures will not be reflected in the Register of Monuments. Thus an entry on the List of National Treasures will not lead to removal from the museum pieces inventory, unless there are provisions to the contrary. In the second case, there will emerge a need to make an additional list of objects entered in the List of National Treasures, but which are not part of any resources of museum inventories or registers of deposits.[151]

The Act obliged the Ministry of Culture and National Heritage to subsidise the making of an inventory of objects of national heritage, which, in the view of the representatives of the ministry, was meant to "ensure the axiology and

150 P. Stec, *Dyrektywa 93/7/EWG z perspektywy dwóch dekad funkcjonowania*, "Santander Art and Culture Law Review" 2015, No. 1, p. 112.

151 A similar problem arises with collections of which a museum is the legal possessor although not the owner. See A. Jagielska-Burduk, K. Mularski, *Problematyka reprywatyzacji zabytków ruchomych. Uwagi na marginesie wyroku Sądu Najwyższego z dnia 16 lutego 2012 r. (III CSK 208/11), in: Kolekcje i zbiory muzealne: problematyka prawna*, (eds.) P. Stec, P. P. Maniurka, Opole 2016, pp. 201–216.

the values",[152] to make sure that the List of National Treasures is not unlimited. However, it is not an easy task to judge whether a given object fulfils the criteria of a national treasure if this judgment depends entirely on the financial resources available to the decision maker. This model would then resemble the model of judging the efficiency of a grant subsidy used for financing academic research, restricted to the availability of the resources granted. In the case of historic monuments, there are constant additions to their resources, which means that the fixed sum allocated in the ministerial budget for works related to the recording and classifying of monuments would need to be regularly reviewed. Among objects mentioned as potential "national treasures" were items belonging to private owners (natural and legal persons), the Church and the State. To give a few examples, the list included *Szczerbiec* – the coronation sword of Polish kings, Leonardo da Vinci's painting "Lady with an Ermine", and Altarpiece by Veit Stoss in St. Mary's Basilica in Kraków.[153] Following the adoption of the APGM, the list was complemented and subsequently endorsed by the Monument Protection Council appointed at the Ministry of Culture and National Heritage, and now it includes the Gniezno Doors in Gniezno Cathedral, the Sigismund Bell in Wawel Cathedral, "The Final Judgment" by Hans Memling, Jan Matejko's painting The Battle of Grunwald, Rembrandt's Scholar at a Desk, Girl in a Picture Frame and Landscape with the Good Samaritan, The Black Madonna of Częstochowa, and the Dąbrówka Chalice from Trzemeszno.[154] What is missing from this preliminary list are the Jagiellonian tapestries from Wawel Castle, despite an earlier promise by the General Inspector of Monuments, Piotr Żuchowski. The most plausible reason for this absence is the fact that their poor state means that they are in need of costly repair. This, in turn, would consume a large proportion of the total financial resources allocated. Once an object is entered on the List of National Treasures, the State automatically becomes responsible for its maintenance and all related conservation costs of any work that needs to be done in relation to it. Therefore, the first monuments entered on the List were those not

152 As stated by P. Żuchowski, a Special Commission for recognition proposal of bill to amend the Act on the Protection and Guardianship of Monuments and the Law on Museums, print No. 3112 of 17 March 2015, http://www.sejm.gov.pl/sejm7.nsf/transmisje_arch.xsp?unid=B23E24E2F20CE19DC1257E03003F16DB (accessed: 15.06.2015).

153 A special subcommittee for recognition a private member's bill to amend the Act on the Protection and Guardianship of Monuments…

154 J. Bończa-Szabłowski, *Lista Skarbów*, interview with P. Żuchowski, "Rzeczpospolita", 21 August 2015, p. 12.

requiring immediate repair.[155] This also shows that it is not always the value or exceptional significance of objects which is the determining factor in the decision to enter them on the List, but rather the immediate goals and available funds. Nobody from the Ministry will openly admit that the above is true but this is the reality. The fate of the tapestries is particularly remarkable because King Sigmund Augustus left a Will in 1571 in which he disposed that if his sisters died leaving no heirs, the ownership of the tapestries was to be given to the Republic of the Two Nations, the Crown and the Grand Duchy of Lithuania. As Stanisław Waltoś has pointed out, this was one of the first instances "of the nationalisation / of cultural goods in Europe, whereby a royal collection changed owners and became the property of the nation".[156]

From the point of view of cultural heritage management, the new status of objects possessing a "particular significance for cultural heritage" whose objects constitute at the same time part of a museum inventory, the national library resources, or national archives resources is worth a word here. According to the view presented by the Ministry, the List of National Treasures is primarily meant to support and promote non-public, i.e. privately owned items of heritage. However, a legal act adopted to that end will become part of domestic legislation and the benefits deriving from it will allow public museums as well to rely on it and become beneficiaries of subsidies originally not intended for them. The recommendations on which objects should be entered on the List of National Treasures has been moved from the *ex officio* approach applicable in respect of the Register of Museums, to the ministerial level to become one of the competences of the Ministry of Culture and National Heritage. And yet, since the minister of culture and national heritage has been appointed to be the organ of the first instance, the discussion on the qualifications expected of voivodeship inspectors of monuments, when no such requirements are expected from the General Inspector of Monuments who is to act in the name and on behalf of the Minister in matters relating to succession, will certainly return. It has also been noted that the regulations, when eventually adopted, will increase in significance after the introduction of new forms of monument protection. However, whether it is a good idea to let

155 This policy of the Ministry of Culture and National Heritage has been commented on by W. Szafrański – P. Szymaniak, *Dzieło sztuki będzie można znacjonalizować*, "Gazeta Prawna", 15 June 2015, http://prawo.gazetaprawna.pl/artykuly/877250,dzielo-sztuki-bedzie-mozna-znacjonalizowac.html (accessed: 7.08.2015).

156 S. Waltoś, *Prawna ochrona dóbr kultury w Europie (Tezy)*, in: *Spotkania w Willi Strucego 1998–2001. Wykłady o dziedzictwie kultury*, (ed.) K. J. Kwiecińska, Warszawa 2001, p. 235.

ministerial decisions govern these new forms of monument protection and introduce a radical systemic change without a prior comprehensive legislative process is a big question.

Protection extended to movable monuments differs in its forms and principles from the protection of immovable monuments. For example, an immovable object, to be regarded as a monument of history, must first be entered in the Register of Monuments or be part of a cultural park. And yet, entering an immovable object on the List of National Treasures is possible regardless of its being entered in the Register of Monuments. The procedure for entering a movable object in the Register requires a motion requesting its entry, but may also in certain situation be made *ex officio*, while in the case of entries on the List of National Treasures, they are made *ex officio* as well as being initiated by a motion. As can be seen, an attempt was made (by the legislator) to depart from the earlier proposal made in respect of immovable monuments in which a transparent levelling of the protection was recommended. The List of National Treasures has thus become a separate form of protection, different from the basic protection extended to objects entered in the Register of Monuments. What is more, when an object qualifies for entry on the List, an *ex officio* decision to that end may be made even in the absence of the owner's consent. Such a differentiation of protection applicable to movable and immovable monuments in the adopted legislation was not expected and came as a surprise. If efforts were to focus on promoting monuments only, which for movable monuments is nothing more than value added, then the creation of a List of National Treasures based on Monuments of History could be considered as an option. This would mean that the basic form of protection would be maintained. Although this solution is being criticised as well, it is nevertheless less prone to be deemed to be infringing the rights of holders of these objects.

Monument of History (Pomnik Historii)

A Monument of History (*Pomnik Historii*) is the highest form of protection of immovable monuments but it lacks detailed regulation. This legal form of cultural heritage protection is not used to the full. An analysis of the existing provisions regulating protection of monuments classified as Monuments of History suggests that the function of monument of history protection is not merely a 'formal springboard' for different actions procedures focused on heritage protection. This form of protection may also play an important role internationally in the management of items of cultural heritage of universal value. The promotional as well as the economic aspect of creating a region's 'trade mark' or a cultural site is becoming of increasing importance today when the approach to national heritage is changing. This is also the result of the increasing professionalism of bodies responsible for heritage management as well as the recent discussions on new solutions, including proposals for the inclusion of local communities in the process.

A Monument of History has always been a form of monument protection dependent on international law regulations. In the original version of the Act on the Protection of Cultural Property, Article 6 clause 2 provided that, pursuant to the Convention on cultural property protection, a monument of culture was subject to registration in the International Register of Cultural Property Under Special Protection applicable in the event of armed conflict. However, when this provision was applicable, not even one monument of history was registered in Poland. The first one registered was at the time when an amended provision of the above Article came into force.[157] Under the amended provision, monuments of culture must be presented to the World Heritage Committee if application is made for inclusion on the World Heritage List and, arising from this, subsequent protection pursuant to the Convention concerning World Cultural and National Heritage. The APGM has retained the connection of monument protection with entry on the World Heritage List although this entry is no longer obligatory. There is a clear trend towards the loosening of a strict connection between internal (national) and international monument protection. It even seems that tying the internal protection of a monument with making internal protection dependent on obligatory entry in the international register (currently the List of World Heritage), did not work and resulted in no protection at all, or very limited protection (at the national level). This, of course, does not mean that in the case of the List of World Heritage, the international models are inappropriate. On the contrary, but there their application still has a different scope and a different objective. However, an analysis of the existing regulations shows that if a new regulation aimed at protecting movable or immovable monuments is to be considered in the future, it should be made separate from the national regulations, or at least structured in such a way that internal and international forms of protection and their regulations are independent of one another. During the time that the Act on the Protection of Cultural Property was in force, no ordinance referred to in Article 6 clause 3 of the APCP was issued that would provide

157 Ustawa z dnia 19 lipca 1990 r. o zmianie ustawy o ochronie dóbr kultury i o muzeach [Act of 19 July 1990 amending the Act on the protection of cultural property and on museums], Dz. U. 1990, No. 56, item 322.

certain norms according to which Monuments of History should be protected and how this protection be organised. This absence of a prescribed norm had most probably influenced the regulation contained in the APGM which provided that a similar delegation of the issuance power of a relevant secondary act (norm) to a minister competent for culture and national heritage is absent, and the procedure itself has been determined in a document that is not binding.

Under Article 15 clause 1 of the APGM, upon a motion by the minister competent for culture and national heritage, the President of the Republic of Poland may confer the status of a Monument of History on an immovable monument entered in the Register of Monuments or to a cultural park of particular importance for culture, specifying its borders. The ministerial motion must be preceded by an opinion of the Monument Protection Council. Recognition of an immovable monument as a monument of history requires a regulation issued by the President. The ordinance contains the official name of the monument of history, the form of protection applicable to the monument and the values that are of particular importance for culture. The procedure allows for the withdrawal of the recognition of a monument as a Monument of History. It should be noted that contrary to the decision on the entry of a monument in the register (issued by a voivodeship inspector of monuments) the removal of a monument from the register requires a decision of a minister competent for culture and heritage protection, an higher organ in the hierarchy.

The role of third parties in the protection of Monuments of History is not specified in the Act. This is probably because the protection of a Monument of History has been given a prestigious function, based on the fundamental legal framework of monument protection (entry in the Register of Monuments or being a cultural park). In this context the owner of a monument may still be excluded from the proceeding because a change in the status of a monument does not entail any change in the owner's rights. The document *Kryteria procedury uznawania obiektu za Pomnik Historii* (Criteria for the procedure of recognition of an object as a Monument of History) adopted by the Monument Protection Council on 6 October 2005[158] specifies the type of procedure laid down in the process of recognising a monument as a Monument of History. According to the procedure, an application requesting extension of the higher protection of a monument must be filed with the General Inspector of Monuments *via* a

158 Criteria of the procedure of recognising object as a Monument of History adopted by the Monument Protection Council of 6 October 2005, www.nid.pl/pl/Dla_wlascicieli_i_zarzadcow/opieka-nadzabytkami/dobre-praktyk/Kryteria_procedury_uznawania_obiektu_za_pomnik_historii.pdf (accessed: 1.06.2015).

voivodeship inspector of monuments and with an opinion of the latter. The entity filing such an application may frequently be the owner of a monument, or, in the case of a complex of monuments, the managing body of a given self-government territorial unit, capable of preparing the necessary documents. An endorsed local spatial development plan is often a prerequisite although it is not an absolutely binding condition and its absence cannot be grounds for a refusal to commence the proceeding. Pursuant to the Criteria, once the application is filed with an opinion on the proposal, it is then forwarded *via* the Department for Monument Protection to the National Centre for Research and Documentation of Monuments (now the National Heritage Board of Poland where the attached documents are reviewed and an opinion justifying conferral to a monument of the status of a Monument of History is drawn up. This opinion is subsequently presented by a competent minister to the Monument Protection Council. A positive opinion issued by the Council results in the documentation returning to the National Heritage Board of Poland. The Board prepares a draft of a regulation which includes the rationale for the decision with an illustration attached. Once endorsed by the Department of Monument Protection, it is forwarded to the relevant minister for final approval. The minister applies to the President of the Republic of Poland for the monument to be awarded the status of a Monument of History. The President's consent is announced in the Official Gazette (*Dziennik Ustaw*). These criteria have been considered satisfactory in the literature.[159] It was also stated that "recognising a monument as a Monument of History is a special form of distinction.[160] Objects to be recognised as monuments of history must fulfil the criteria specified in the document and in the case of monuments of architecture they may, in certain situations, be grouped into complexes of monuments. The statement that "such essential elements as the criteria and procedure in which a monument is recognised as a monument of history should be specified in an ordinance issued by a minister competent for culture and national heritage"[161] should be promoted. Unfortunately this recommendation has not yet met with any reaction on the part of the legislator.

No other regulations of Monuments of History have been envisaged in the APGM. What it also means is that the owners of items that are part of the cultural heritage do not acquire any new rights, nor have been given more duties.[162] Thus the same rights and duties acquired by holders of objects of cultural heritage

159 K. Zalasińska, *Prawna ochrona…*, pp. 267–269.
160 Criteria of the procedure of recognising object as a Monument of History…, p. 1.
161 K. Zalasińska, *Prawna ochrona…*, p. 267.
162 A. Böhm, P. Dobosz, P. Jaskanis, J. Purchla, B. Szmygin, op. cit., p. 69.

at the time when these objects were entered in the Register of Monuments or were considered a cultural park, continue to apply upon the recognition of such objects as monuments of history. Regarding the promotion of cultural heritage and when applying for grants or other financial subsidies, the status of a monument of history may be a supporting although not a determining factor. It is very probable that owners of monuments of history which take the form of a multi-object complex will be excluded from taking part in the application procedure regarding recognition of a monument as a Monument of History. Therefore establishing relationships based on collaboration with owners for the sake of the promotion of monuments in the future is recommended. All other measures and actions undertaken in relation to multi-object monuments should have the form of a dialogue conducted by co-participants in the monument protection project. The absence of legal solutions that would oblige local self-governing authorities to develop local spatial development plans and collaborate with holders of monuments in the area of monument protection is certainly a great weakness.[163] Under the provisions of the Act on the Protection of Cultural Property), the President of the Republic of Poland may confer the status of a monument of history on an immovable object of particular significance for culture. Under the Act on the Protection and Guardianship of Monuments, the range of monuments on which may be conferred the status of a monument of history has been widened owing to the fact that the requirement that they link the culture with the nation has been deleted.[164] This change in the wording, however, has had no influence on the choice, or a different choice, of monuments being recognised as monuments of history. Each decision constituting the basis for recognising a monument as a monument of history, refers to the value of a monument for the region and for the country, very infrequently referring to any universal value. Some of the expressions used in the decisions issued in the last decade, include "particular significance for the culture and history of Poland"[165] e.g. Trzebnica – the former Cistercian nuns' Abbey complex, or, with a special role in the development and the building of Polish identity upon regaining independence – Gdynia, the

163 Ibid. pp. 69–70.

164 R. Golat, op. cit., p. 38.

165 Rozporządzenie Prezydenta Rzeczypospolitej Polskiej z dnia 4 lipca 2014 r. w sprawie uznania za pomnik historii "Trzebnica – zespół dawnego opactwa cysterek" [Regulation by the President of the Republic of Poland of 4 July 2014 on the conferral of the status of a Monument of History" to "Trzebnica – the former Cistercian nuns Abbey complex"], Dz. U. 2014, No. 957.

historic layout of the city centre[166]. References to worldwide or European values, such as those referring to Łódź as a multi-cultural industrial town landscape and "the biggest in Poland and one of the largest 19th century centres of the textile industry in Europe"[167] are less frequent.

The form of monument protection is the first step in the procedure of entering a monument in the List of World Treasures. However, today this entry is optional. Under the former Act (ACPP) recognition of an object as a monument of history was equivalent to the preparation of an application to the World Heritage Committee. It is possible that such recognition and the related requirement of producing necessary documentation, did, in some way, hinder the possibility of recognising other monuments as of historic value, because it required submission of a number of documents necessary to accompany an application for an entry on the List of World Treasures.[168] Freeing protection of monuments from the obligation for a monument to be entered on the List of World Treasures, was meant to draw a line between the national protection of immovable monuments of particular significance and measures undertaken to identify objects of universal value that would be common at an international level and were possible to implement. In the case of an application for entry on the List of World Treasures, a plan describing the subsequent management of the object must be submitted.[169] The recognition of a monument as a monument of history, meaning that it is attached special importance because of its particular significance for culture, does not entail any change in the legal regime applicable to and binding

166 Rozporządzenie Prezydenta Rzeczypospolitej Polskiej z dnia 23 lutego 2015 r. w sprawie uznania za pomnik historii "Gdynia – historyczny układ urbanistyczny śródmieścia" [Regulation by the President of the Republic of Poland of 4 July 2014 on the conferral of the status of a monument of history" to "Gdynia, a historic layout of the city centre"], Dz. U. 2015, No. 356.

167 Rozporządzenie Prezydenta Rzeczypospolitej Polskiej z dnia 16 lutego 2015 r. w sprawie uznania za pomnik historii "Łódź – wielokulturowy krajobraz miasta przemysłowego" [Regulation by the President of the Republic of Poland of 4 July 2014 on the conferral of the status of a monument of history" to "Łódź – a multi-cultural landscape of an industrial town"], Dz. U. 2015, No. 315.

168 T. Zielniewicz, statement found in: "Biuletyn Forum Debaty Publicznej. Pomniki historii – źródło dziedzictwa kultury. Twórczość, dziedzictwo kulturowe i przyrodnicze bogactwem Polski" 2012, No. 10, p. 32.

169 About the constituent elements of the management plan read in: *The management plan for the World Cultural Heritage*, http://www.unesco.pl/kultura/dziedzictwo-kulturowe/swiatowe-dziedzictwo/procedurawpisu/plan-zarzadzania/ (accessed: 10.08.2015).

this object. In the current wording, a monument of history is a prestigious form of monument protection, strengthened in eyes of the market by the fact that the President of the Republic of Poland has been involved in the process that has eventually led to the recognition of the monument as a monument of history.

Cultural park

A cultural park is a form of monument protection whose implementation is contingent upon the will of the commune (*gmina*), which is a local self-government unit. This provision satisfies the requirement of Article 7 clause 1 point 9 of the APGM which provides that monument protection is the responsibility of local authorities. In the discussion the role of the commune in monument protection was widely discussed, including the financial aspect of the obligation. Pursuant to Article 16 clause 1, a commune council may establish a cultural park in order to protect a cultural landscape and preserve areas of outstanding landscape with immovable monuments characteristic of local construction and settlement tradition.[170] Article 6 of the APGM refers to a cultural landscape as an immovable property, defined as a space historically shaped by human activity, comprising products of civilisation and elements of nature. In the context of this definition a doubt arose whether "the concept of a cultural landscape does actually comply with the legal definition of an immovable monument" owing to the fact that such a landscape is "mere proof of Man's interaction with nature".[171]

A resolution to establish a cultural park must be preceded by an opinion of a voivodeship inspector of monuments. The latter requires a specific type of formal decision. The resolution establishing a cultural park must include: the name of the cultural park, its boundaries, form of its protection as well as any potential prohibitions and limitations that may arise when a cultural park is established. The *wójt* (or head of a commune, mayor of a town) is obliged to draw up a cultural park management plan in consultation with the voivodeship inspector of monuments. The plan requires endorsement by the commune council. A cultural park may be established by several communes or associations as a joint undertaking. If this is the case, all interested parties must adopt relevant resolutions. Unlike in the case of a monument of history, in that of a cultural park, a local

---

170 About the recommendation to include in the Act a provision that a voivode be the entity responsible for the establishment of a cultural park see A. Soldani, D. Jankowski, op. cit., pp. 31–32.

171 K. Zalasińska, *Prawna ochrona…*, p. 267.

spatial development plan is essential.[172] Under Article 10 clause 3 of the APGM, the obligation to commence work on a local spatial development plan arises within three months of, in this case, the adoption of a resolution to establish a cultural park. The decision whether an immovable monument is to be made into a cultural park is to be made in stages. Apart from the requirements specified in Article 16 clause 1 of the APGM, another necessary condition is recognition that the "maintenance of the values (of the potential areas of the park – authors' note) will only be made possible by establishing a cultural park, i.e. that for the satisfactory completion of the task the provisions of the currently applicable local spatial development plan, or the existing entry of the monument in the Register of Monuments, will not suffice".[173]

In order to ensure that the whole procedure for implementing this form of monument protection does not infringe existing legal regulations an overall assessment of the potential cultural park must be made, taking into account the protection already in place and the proposed new form, having regard to the principle of proportionality. Certain prohibitions and limitations may also be imposed with regard to the property to be protected, and they arise from the provisions of Article 17 of the APGM, and include: carrying out building works as well as industrial, breeding, commercial and service provision activity; modifying the type of use of immovable monuments; placing boards, inscriptions, advertisements and other signs not connected with the protection of the cultural park except for road signs and signs connected with the protection of public order and safety, subject to Article 12 clause 1, storing or warehousing waste. Should the prohibitions and limitations in the use of the property made into a cultural park cause inconvenience, a compensation scheme for those affected has been envisaged, with reference to the Act of 27 April 2001 – the Law on Environment Protection. The resolution adopted by the commune council should only refer to prohibitions and limitations referred to in the APGM. Anything other than these statutory prohibitions and limitations applicable to the use of the property covered by a protected cultural park may constitute legal grounds for declaring the adopted resolution invalid[174]. The decisions contained in the commune council resolution influence the rights of the owners situated within the cultural park. On 6 October 2005 the Monument Protection Council adopted

172 Within three months of the decision to establish a cultural park an obligation arises to prepare a spatial development plan.

173 P. Antoniak, M. Cherka, op. cit., p. 101.

174 Verdict of the Supreme Administrative Court of 7 December 2007, file II OSK 1487/07, LEX No. 424539.

a document entitled: "The Principles for establishing a Cultural Park, its management, and the preparation of a plan for its protection. The guidelines for commune self-government units, authors of protection plans, and voivodeship and self-government unit inspectors of monuments".[175]

The initiative for the process of establishing a cultural park has been left with a number of entities such as local communities, territorial self-government, or an initiative by an official. These entities are required to prepare a description of the place and the objects situated within the boundaries of the area where a potential cultural park is to be established. A study of the advantages deriving from the establishment of a cultural park and the social cost of its activities has shown that the declaration of a social will, or intent, to create a cultural park may be identified on the basis of primary sources. The management of the park may be delegated to a separate organisation specially appointed by the commune council. Such a specifically appointed organisation may function in a manner which includes collaboration with the local community. Its representatives may participate in the carrying out of tasks performed in different ways: advisory (in advisory groups), volunteer work performed for the sake of a cultural park, or as a collaborating entity (entrepreneurs from the tourism sector may form a cluster around a given cultural park). Entities operating in the third sector may also take part in the management of a cultural park as consultants, or may take up a role as the park's operator.

It seems that despite the intense information campaign carried out by local self-governments and state administration, the need for cultural parks and the awareness of the values offered by a cultural landscape is still unrecognised or is insufficiently present in the public mind. The participatory model of cultural heritage management requires the participation of local communities, which is of key importance to the outcome of the proceedings. An objection raised by the community involved is not infrequently a reason for abandoning the idea of a cultural park altogether. Hence the need to raise awareness of the value of cultural heritage and cultural landscape within society and increase sensitivity to the values of cultural landscape heritage. This seems to be almost as important

175 Principles underlying the establishment of a cultural park, its management and the preparation of its protection plan. Guidelines for commune self-governing units, authors of protection plans and voivodeship and commune inspectors of monuments, http://www.nid.pl/pl/Informacje_ogolne/Zabytki_w_Polsce/Parki_kulturowe/Zasady%20tworzenia%20Parku%20Kulturowego,%20zarz%C4%85dzania%20nim%20oraz%20sporz%C4%85dzania%20planu%20jego%20ochro ny.pdf In these documents the legal aspects permeate the managerial issues (accessed: 15.06.2015).

as the transparency of the legal grounds upon which decisions to create cultural parks may be based.

Monument protection stipulations

Another form of monument protection are directives contained in local spatial development plans and stipulations referred to in decisions determining a public construction project location, road project permission, or decisions on a railway project location, or the location of a new public airport. The amendments to the APGM of 2010[176] extended the protection of monuments and its Article 7 point 4 refers to six different measures that may be taken in respect of immovable monument protection, of which the last five may be undertaken in the event of the location not being subject to, or covered by, an urban spatial development plan. This form of monument protection has been widened as an answer to the problem of the absence of local spatial development plans in Poland. These plans are subject to endorsement by the voivodeship inspector of monuments. The limited extent of local spatial development plans has prompted the legislator to move the protection stipulations to an even lower level, indirectly connected with the investment process. Under Article 18 clause 1 of the APGM, the protection and guardianship of monuments is already taken into account when plans for the spatial development of the country are being drawn up or up-dated. Considerations related to monument protection are also included in the form of stipulations in strategies for the development of regions (voivodeships) and their spatial development plans, spatial development plans of inland sea waters, territorial waters and the exclusive economic zone, studies and analysis of the spatial development of *poviats* and the development strategies for communes (*gminas*), studies of the conditions and stipulations pertaining to spatial management of communes and local spatial development plans, or decisions specifying public construction project location, outline planning permission, road project permission, decisions specifying the location of a railway, or decisions on public airport project permission. Only the last six types of decisions are structured in a way which makes them forms of monument protection.

Depending on the needs, the results of a feasibility study and stipulations of local spatial development plans, zones of conservation protection are determined, where the prohibitions, limitations and orders specified in local plans and

---

176 Ustawa z dnia 18 marca 2010 r. o zmianie ustawy o ochronie zabytków i opiece nad zabytkami i zmianie niektórych innych ustaw [Act of 18 March 2010 amending the APGM and some other Acts], Dz. U. 2010, No. 75, item 474.

intended to protect monuments are applicable. In the event of real estate situated within the territory subject to the predetermined limitations and prohibitions depreciating in value owing to the binding regulations of the local spatial development plan, compensation is available under the provisions of Article 36 of the Act on Spatial Planning and Development.[177] The fact that this fourth form of monument protection (stipulations) can be found at several levels indicates the poor progress of urban and spatial planning throughout the whole country. At the same time, however, it shows a will on the part of the legislator, to make up for this shortcoming and to mitigate its effects. Unfortunately, the result is that this creditable purpose is being realised with too diversified a range of tools and with the participation of too many subjects. Article 19 clause 1 of the APGM provides that the local area development plan should in particular consider the protection of: immovable monuments entered in the Register and their surroundings; other immovable monuments that are in the commune inventory of monuments. The use of the term 'in particular' leads to a situation in which the above provision may be extended also to monuments not entered on any list, register or inventory.[178] Thus, as can be seen, looking for a 'substitute form' of protection does not seem right in this case. A decision on planning (construction and development) permits issued by an administrative body without consultation with a monument protection body is not linked to any compensation system referred to in the Act on Spatial Planning and Development and applicable to limited ownership rights. It may be therefore be stated that the legal position of an owner of a monument under special protection within the fourth form of protection is not equal when it comes to the compensation issues whereas it should be based on the same principles. This inequality is present at the stage of the collaboration of an administrative body with a monument protection body, as well as in the compensation scheme designed for the holders of monuments. Despite having a common purpose – monument protection – the same purpose may be realised with or without the possibility of compensation in relation to the same real estate. The reason for this is not, however, the scope or burden of the need to implement protection, or the value of a given monument but the type of measures undertaken to realise this protection.

---

177 Ustawa z dnia 27 marca 2003 r. o planowaniu i zagospodarowaniu przestrzennym [Act of 27 March 2003 on spatial planning and development], uniform text, Dz. U. 2015, No. 199.

178 See P. Antoniak, M. Cherka, op. cit., p. 115.

Conclusions

Article 4 of the APGM provides that "containing a framework regulation"[179] specifies that the activity of organs of public administration related to monument protection consists in, among other things, ensuring adequate legal, organisational and financial conditions to facilitate the preservation of monuments, as well as their proper use and maintenance. The provision identified three pillars of protection: laws, organisational issues, and financial issues. All three are responsible for the success of the protection system. These pillars are of importance from the point of view of the implementation of monument protection and related forms of monument protection, as well as the manner of exercising ownership law. However, the legislators's declaration is not always fulfilled to the same degree, neither when it comes to the protection activities undertaken in relation to movable and immovable monuments, nor with regard to the effectiveness of the forms of protection directed at protecting the immovable resources of cultural heritage. The forms of protection referred to in Article 7 of the APGM constitute the legal grounds for the protection upon which it is possible to apply, *vis a vis* holders of monuments, the instruments referred to in the APGM. The under-used forms of protection are cultural parks and monuments of history, of which the latter are not, by mistake, subject to the obligation of being accompanied by a local spatial development plan.

The form of monument protection ought to be a legal institution which defines the status of a monument. The form of protection should relate to the holder of the monument as well as the compensation scheme. It should at the same time take into account the principle of proportionality of limitations with regard to the protected value. Each form should be clearly based upon legal norms and a clearly identified subject responsible for the implementation of the protection and relying on a predictable financing system. The absence of such an approach results in the protection system losing credibility on the grounds of a violation of norms of constitutional weight. It seems that nothing needs to be more creditworthy than the State's activities with regard to cultural heritage protection conducted with the aim of passing on to future generations the heritage of humankind. The building up of confidence through the actions of the legislator in the area of culture heritage pays dividends because the private sector joins in the efforts to ensure the proper protection of heritage, engaging in the process economically. Confidence building in heritage protection should

179 Verdict of the Voivodeship Administrative Court in Warsaw of 24 August 2005, I SA/Wa 1260/04, LEX No. 191976.

not only consist in the development of new forms of monument protection, but in a constant revision of existing forms, as well as the conscious abandonment of certain solutions. First and foremost, though, the aim should be the maintenance of a protection model which stands the test of constitutionality. There are two basic factors that have an impact on the structure of the contemporary system of monument protection: one is the consequence of the permitted private and public ownership of cultural heritage, the other results from what is known as the loss effect in resources that has occurred in the course of recent centuries. These two are the dominant factors influencing the intervention level that the legislator exercises in particular matters. One must be aware of the fact that a decision to resign from the protection of cultural heritage is not easy to make even if legal and economic conditions, instead of being supportive, constitute obstacles of implementing effective protection in practice. The issue of proportionality has reoccurred regularly with regard to the restrictions on ownership rights and the actual exercise of their application under Article 31 clause 3 of the Constitution, and when it comes to the economics, with regard to their effectiveness.

The business approach has so far been neglected in the literature because of a conviction that monuments must be protected "at all costs". The issues of costs were discussed selectively in the course of discussions on the procedures for creating a cultural park and identifying the commune as a decision maker and at the same time the entity that bears the cost of a cultural park once it is established and its subsequent maintenance. The commune must also assign in its budget funds to finance works to be done in relation to the monuments entered on the List of National Treasures and their level must be treated as a limiting criterion, restricting the number of objects upon which protection cover may be extended. It would seem that a simulation of the cost-effectiveness of individual forms of monument protection would help to understand the economic potential of each. The real size of funds available to spend on cultural heritage in Poland will always be lower than the desired amount. Skilful use of a part of the heritage for commercial purposes will supplement the budget assigned for culture. It must be first assumed, though, that monuments differ in their commercial potential, although that potential is not the measure of their value.

Under Polish monument protection law different levels of monument protection are being developed in order to differentiate elements of heritage of greater and lesser value. New categories enforce or provoke legislative activity with regard to ownership and the culture market, i.e. the derivatives of monument protection. International categories are incorporated in the domestic system and new forms of protection are developed based on these categories. And yet, the amendments that have been introduced since 2003 have not helped to unify or liberalise the principles of monument protection. The regulations are short of a uniform stance of the legislator regarding the protection of movable and immovable monuments. While in the case of immovable monuments the investment process is supported by the legislator, the protection level of movable monuments increasingly intervenes in ownership rights.

At the EU level, the new approach that advocates leaving to the State the freedom to define precisely which are the State's national treasures, may result in too excessive creativity of national legislators who may wish to increase existing resources.[180] While national legislators are given freedom to decide, the building up of common, EU cultural property resources should be more structured. For public opinion in Poland, the problem of clear-cut definitions of what constitutes national cultural property occurs only in the context of media coverage in cases of exports or attempts to export cultural property. Before the principles of exporting cultural property changed, there was much discussion regarding leaving the archival resources of Zbigniew Herbert in Poland. The Ministry of Culture and National Heritage proposed an individual treatment of this particular case and offered a Solution pursuant to which in 2005 the Institute of Documentation and Studies on Polish Literature at the Adam Mickiewicz Museum of Literature was established.[181] Eventually, Herbert's heirs granted the archive to the National Library. In 2013 there was an animated debate concerning export regulations in connection with the painting Castaway (*Rozbitek*) by Henry Siemiradzki from Ryszard Krauze's collection sold for GBP 1,000,082.5 at auction at Sotheby's.[182] In this case it would be difficult to separate personal reasons from the fundamental question of national heritage protection. A similar price for such work of art would not have been possible in Poland. Additionally, establishing a brand and value is important for Polish cultural heritage in general, when all, not only recent Polish works of art are introduced to foreign markets.

In the system of museum protection, there are special events as well as individual focused activities. One cannot avoid the impression that the activities

180 Compare the French solution P. Stec, *Dyrektywa* 93/7/EWG…, p. 113.

181 [rom], *Archiwum Herberta zostaje w Warszawie*, "Gazeta Wyborcza", 29 December 2004, http://wiadomosci.gazeta.pl/wiadomosci/1,114873,2469418.html (accessed: 1.08. 2015) [Mm], *Co z archiwum Herberta*?, "Gazeta Wyborcza" 3 November 2004, http://wyborcza.pl/1,75475,2373893.html (accessed: 1.08.2015).

182 I. Kadłuczka, *"Rozbitek" Siemiradzkiego sprzedany. "To wielka strata dla Polski"*, "Gazeta Wyborcza", 28 November 2013, http://wyborcza.biz/biznes/1,100896,15035897,_Rozbitek__Siemiradzkiego_sprzedany___To_wielka_strata.html (accessed: 1.08.2015).

undertaken are designed to match existing resources, regardless of their constant growth and the possibility of enriching Polish collections with foreign works of art. It must be noted, though, that a model of monument protection based on responses to media reports will never be really effective. The work on new legal solutions is being carried out alongside research into the subject. The final provisions can anyway only be shaped by the political decision makers taking part in the legislative process. Although the development of the doctrine is based on the (ever)-changing system of the law on monument protection, the reverse is not true. It seems that the legislator does not pay enough attention to the experts' opinions.

II.1.3 *Res extra commercium*

The protection of cultural heritage only rarely is an effect of a well-thought out and properly introduced system. Over the stages of both its design and 'disassembly' in an amending process, not only ad hoc political decisions following from current events, cast their shadow.[183] *Res extra commercium* is a category, although known to and applied in the Polish legal system for the protection of heritage, which, however, is still used inconsistently. It has never been the subject of comprehensive discussion at the stage of legislative decision-making, despite the fact that practically every year elements appear which touch upon the category of *res extra commercium* in the course of discussions or suggestions of legislative amendments, which can be seen recently in connection with:

a) work on the ratification of the 1995 UNIDROIT Convention on Stolen or Illegally Exported Cultural Objects;[184]
b) work on the ratification of the 2001 UNESCO Convention on the Protection of the Underwater Cultural Heritage;

---

183 Such a situation occurs practically in every country. In Poland, an example may be the rather 'too spontaneous' actions taken with regards Zbigniew Herbert's inheritance, the export of Henryk Siemiradzki's painting "Castaway", or an attempt to introduce the List of National Treasures made in connection with Leonardo da Vinci's "Lady with an Ermine".

184 Conference at the Ministry of Foreign Affairs held on 17 December 2014 on the occasion of the ratification in the near future of the UNIDROIT Convention in Poland. Presentations by: A. Nowak-Far, W. Kowalski, A. Jagielska-Burduk, P. Stec and W. Szafrański published in "Santander Art and Culture Law Review" 2015, No. 1.

c) work on the implementation of Directive 2014/60/EU into the national legal system and thus leaving to Member States the decision on defining national cultural treasures;[185]
d) completed work on the Act of 20 February 2015 on Unclaimed Property and the establishment of the National Register of Lost Cultural Property;
e) work on a new form of cultural property protection, namely an entry in the List of National Treasures, provided for in the amendment to the Act on the Protection and Guardianship of Monuments 2015;[186]
f) work on the National Programme of Heritage Protection and Care, the principles of which were adopted by the Cabinet in 2014 and which provides for the ratification of the UNESCO Convention on the Protection of the Underwater Cultural Heritage and "drafting a legal diagnosis of the protection of movable cultural property;"[187]
g) the ongoing discussion on archaeological heritage;[188]
h) the resumption of discussion about the de-accession of museum pieces (for instance at the 1st Congress of Museologists held in Łódź in 2015, a resolution was adopted, calling for making the rules for de-accession of museum pieces clearer and more precise; it met with criticism and protests from historians);[189]
i) ongoing discussion among jurists engaged in heritage protection on the directions in which the system should change and measures which are used in

185 Currently work is being carried out at the Ministry of Culture and National Heritage on a bill on national cultural treasures.

186 The Act that was on 31 July 2015 referred to the Constitutional Tribunal Court by President of the Republic of Poland to review its compliance with the Constitution, http://www.prezydent.pl/download/gfx/prezydent/pl/defaultaktualnosci/2073/16/1/20150731_wniosek_do_tk_ws_ustawy_o_ochronie_zabytkow.pdf (accessed: 15.06.2015).

187 See The National Programme of the Protection and Guardianship of Monuments 2014–2017 (appendix to resolution No. 125/2014 RM of 24 VI 2014), pp. 52–56, http:/bip.mkidn.gov.pl/media/download_gallery/20140818Krajowy_Program_Ochrony_Zabytkow_i_Opieki_nad_Zaby.pdf (accessed: 15.06.2015).

188 See M. Trzciński, *Definicja zabytku archeologicznego – problemy i kontrowersje wokół stosowania prawa,* in: *Prawo ochrony zabytków,* (ed.) K. Zeidler, Warszawa – Gdańsk 2014, pp. 115–122.

189 See Resolution No. 4 adopted at the "First Congress of Polish Museologists", http://kongresmuzealnikow.pl/projekty-uchwal/ (accessed: 14.06.2015).

other European countries (France, Italy, Switzerland) which make a wider use of the category of *res extra commercium* than Poland does.[190]

The category of *res extra commercium*, known from the ancient handbooks of Roman Law (Gaius, Justinian), derived from *res extra patrimonium*, i.e. things outside of an estate, and as such were excluded from private-law transactions. Among them, a distinction was made between things belonging to divine law (*res divini iuris*) and those belonging to human law (*res humaniiuris*). These two categories broke up into subcategories. And so, *Res diviniiuris* comprised:

a) *res sacrae* or sacred things such as temples, altars, sacrificial vessels. The Romans considered as sacred only those objects which had been sacrificed with the consent of Roman people given in a statute or resolution of the Senate;[191]
b) *res religiosae* or places where the dead had been buried such as cemeteries and tombs;
c) *res sanctae* or inviolable things – entrusted to the care of gods – such as town walls and gates or camp ramparts. Their violation carried *poenam capitis* (death sentence).

What was subject to divine law could not be part of anybody's estate. Things subject to human law, in turn, could be either public or private and only the former were excluded from legal transactions. *Res humaniiuris* comprised:

---

190 This discussion concerned the possibility of acquiring an artwork from a non-owner (non-entitled vendor) (remarks on Articles 169 and 174 Polish Civil Code triggered by the fact that for over 25 years the Polish legal system lacked provisions that would effectively protect the owner from whom an object was stolen. Compare W. Kowalski, *Nabycie własności dzieła sztuki od nieuprawnionego*, Kraków 2004, pp. 262–264; or his *Prawna ochrona zabytków w świetle aktualnych problemów zachowania dziedzictwa kulturowego Polski*, in: *Prawna ochrona dziedzictwa kulturowego. Wokół problematyki prawnej zabytków i dzieł sztuki*, Vol. 3, (eds.) W. Szafrański, K. Zalasińska, Poznań 2009, pp. 79–87; or his *Trust and res extra commercium in search of legal instruments to strengthen the protection of cultural heritage*, in: *Ius est ars boni et aequi: festschrift für Stanisława Kalus, red.* M. Hadbas, A. Wudarski, Frankfurt 2010, pp. 227–242.

191 To make a thing sacred, vows were necessary (*votum*), subsequently endorsed by a resolution – *dedicatio* (of the people, the senate, and later the caesar) and finally, consecrated by priests (*consecratio*). See F. Zoll, *Pandecta czyli nauka rzymskiego prawa prywatnego*, Vol. I: *Część ogólna*, Kraków 1914, pp. 294–295; Gai, *Institutiones*, text and translation W. Rozwadowski, Poznań 2003, p. 41.

a) *res omnium communes* or things common to all which, therefore, could not be owned by anybody, i.e. air, flowing (running) water, sea, seashores,[192]
b) *res publicae* or things belonging to the Roman State or to individual communes (*res universitatis*) and designated for public use by all its members.[193]

They included public roads, streets, bridges, public squares, ports, theatres, monuments, and stadiums.[194]

Would Ulipan, Gaius or Paulus be surprised by an attempt to extend the category of *res extra commercium* to cultural property? And under which class of these mentioned above would it be subsumed or would it be divided among different ones? The questions are difficult in that no analogy can be used in this respect. For contrary to what can be expected, such objects would not find their way only to the category in which the ancients placed monuments, i.e. among *res publicae* as the category of *res humaniiiuris* was closed only in the period of Justinian. Thus, it developed for a rather long time although – like today – the direction of its development was clear: making the category broader and more precise rather than narrowing it. What else matters is a difference in the mindset of people then and today, not so much in respect of the protection of heritage itself but the construction of categories of important exemptions. In ancient Rome, the areas of *ius* and *fas* merged considerably, making for a quick development of the category of *res diviniiuris*. From the point of view of modern jurisprudential constructions, cultural property as *res extra commercium* would be placed among both *res diviniiuris* and *res humaniiuris*; in the former, in particular in the subcategory of *res sacrae*, as it is from this category that the protection of heritage has developed.

The history of cultural property protection has its beginnings in the construction of protection (a separate legal regime) for objects worshipped in given times. In antiquity and the Middle Ages, they were worshipped for their divine or supernatural values (relics of saints) and in modern times because of their

192 This concept was proposed in the 3rd century A.D. by Aelius Marcianus. This category, extending on things with no economic value, was totally alien to lawyers of the early classical period.

193 W. Dajczak, T. Giaro, F. Longchamps de Bérier, *Prawo rzymskie. U podstaw prawa prywatnego*, Warszawa 2009, p. 352.

194 However, in the pre-Justinian period, some movables which belonged to the Roman nation could be traded in. This category was 'closed' later on, in the actual Justinian period. See *Instytucje Justyniana*, translated by C. Kunderewicz, Warszawa 1986, pp. 58–59.

ancient provenance.[195] As today, exclusion from private-law transactions was not caused by some unique physical properties but followed from the purpose a given thing was supposed to serve.[196] In the other category, i.e. *res humaniiuris*, cultural property would be assigned to both classes because today importance is attached to the necessity of combining natural heritage with a human one and treating them jointly, hence considering a part of them as belonging to *res omnium communes*.[197] Of equal importance is the 'designation' of the heritage belonging to the State (local government) for public use (*res publicae*) with an additional aim: to preserve it for future generations. This supports even more the construction of the *res extra commercium* category.

One question that arises in this respect is the direction of penetration by the *res extra commercium* regime in respect of heritage. Has it first found its way to the international legal stage from a national perspective or indeed vice versa? In contemporary times, countries have chosen various models of heritage protection, depending on the share of the *res extra commercium* regime. Thus, there are countries which do not use this construct at all, others that use only vestiges of it – in respect of some narrow categories of cultural property. Finally, there are still others in which the category of objects excluded from private-law transactions is very broadly defined indeed (covering all objects belonging to the public domain) and, additionally, has a long tradition dating back over one hundred or almost two hundred years. It was these latter countries, among them France, Belgium and Italy, that actually albeit indirectly set the tone for international discourse in this domain, taking advantage of their own national experience.

---

195 Also see K. Pomian, *Dlaczego chronimy zabytki*, in: *Spotkania w Willi Struvego 2001–2003. Wykłady o dziedzictwie kultury*, (eds.) D. Królak-Merska, K. J. Kwiecińska, Warszawa 2004, pp. 243–254.

196 Compare M. Drela, *Własność zabytków*, Warszawa 2006, p. 184.

197 Today, the Roman category *res omnium communes* is used for the conception of the common cosmos or the nature. Compare: F. Tronchetti, *The Exploitation of Natural Resources of the Moon and Other Celestial Bodies. A Proposal for a Legal Regime*, Leiden 2009, pp. 10–14. The contemporary researchers are looking for the anchor point to introduce the Roman category *res extra commercium* in respect of cultural property. However they point out at the same time to two other categories *res communis omnium* and *res communis humanitatis*. These categories serve to build concepts of the common human heritage which since the beginning of the 60s of the 20th century have been developing as a justification of the direction of changes in international public law – see K. Baslar, *The Concept of the Common Heritage of Mankind in International Law*, Martinus Nijhoff, The Netherlands1998, pp. 40–43.

For example, objects belonging to the public domain, meeting specific criteria, as for instance in France where they must be owned by a collective public entity and be designated for public use or public service (or adapted to activities in the interest of the general public) are excluded from private-law transactions and thus always subject to restitution. Such legal constructs of the public domain were reinforced with specific statutes with time, constructing a special status of cultural property entered into an appropriate register. In France for example, the purpose of reinforcing the provisions of the Napoleonic Code was served by a statute on *monuments historiques* enacted in 1913, imposing considerable restrictions on trade.[198] A similar statute was also adopted in Italy in 1909.[199] In this chapter, however, an example from Belgian law serves best to illustrate this very point. In Belgium, the early construction of public domain in law was modelled on French measures from the time of the French Revolution. However, even after Belgium had become independent in 1830 and adopted a new constitution, a distinction between the public and private domains was in effect a consequence of authoritative juristic publications and judicial decisions.[200] Already in the 19th century, Belgian judicial decisions confirmed that works of art on display in museum and church collections belonged to the public domain. In 1872, the Court of Cassation analysed the criterion of public service for recognizing this inclusion, finding that parish churches, and riches held therein, were burdened with permanent tasks of providing public services.[201] In 1886, the Court of Cassation upheld this position, maintaining that parish churches were part of the "municipal public domain" and thus any accessories belonging to these churches were inalienable. As grounds for the decision were given permanent 'tasks' of such church accessories (church furnishings) in the service of glorification/holiness, which made for their inclusion in the public domain.[202] The importance of this decision lay in the fact that the Versailles Treaty of 1919, ending the First World War, provided for the restitution of cultural property. Under Article 247,

---

198 See, for instance M. Anton, *Zivilrecht – Guter Glaube im internationalen Kunsthandel*, Berlin 2010, pp. 246–252, and about the significance of this Act for other solutions, see L. K. Morisset, *Des régimes d'authenticité. Essai sur la mémoire patrimoniale*, Rennes 2009, p. 41 et seq.

199 Compare A. Jagielska-Burduk, *Zabytek ruchomy*, Warszawa 2011, pp. 27–28.

200 For more see C. Romainville, *Le statut des collections publiques muséales en droit domanial, in: L'inaliénabilité des collections de musée en question. Actes du colloque tenu au Musée royal de Mariemont le 28 avril 2009*, Morlanwelz 2010.

201 Cour de Cassation, 10 VI 1872, in: *Pasicrisie Belge*, 1872, I, p. 352.

202 Cour de Cassation, 11 XI 1886, in: *Pasicrisie Belge*, 1886, p. 401.

Germany undertook to deliver up to Belgium, through the agency of the Reparation Commission, the wings of the triptych *Mystical Lamb* by the Van Eyck brothers, which at that time were in a Berlin museum (and earlier in a church in Ghent) and the wings of the triptych *Last Supper* by Bouts kept in a Berlin museum and the Pinakothek in Munich (and earlier in a church in Louvain).[203] These works were to be returned to their respective places to preserve the integrity of the church interiors for which they had been painted in spite of the fact that the Germans bought them from merchants in 1821 and 1834. This demand rested on an assertion that these works of art belonged to the public domain and were treasures representing common values. In this case, even the lapse of time did not bar their return.

That such reasoning was actually used can be deduced also from the practical enforcement of Article 247. The Germans argued that ultimately a forced sale of these works of art was meant rather than their gratuitous delivery. The Reparation Commission found, however, that the delivery had to be made free of charge, relying on the grounds cited above. There are thus certain connections between the reasoning applied to Article 247 of the Versailles Treaty (and its enforcement) and the national authoritative juristic publications, and Belgian judicial decisions, which have been internationally adopted. Since the construct of public domain in law had been known to the Belgian system already earlier, it was important not so much as to extend the grounds relied on by the Belgians to Article 247, but to convince the Reparation Commission that the public domain ought not to be identified with state property, but with public property. Consequently, the fragments of the triptychs by both Bouts and the Van Eyck brothers, owned by the two churches in Belgium, were part of furnishings in the service of holiness, because they had been painted specially for this purpose. For this reason they were seen to be elements of the public domain and as such were not subject to private-law transactions; ergo, they could not be effectively purchased by the Germans.

The Belgian case cited above is an example how international law gradually grew cognizant of the need to restrict the freedom of transactions in cultural property and construct the category of *res extra commercium* for a certain kind of such property. Initially, the cognizance of exclusion from transactions applied only to single objects (less frequently to single categories of property) and was reflected in bilateral and multilateral agreements.[204] They did not comprise though

203 See S. Nahlik, *Grabież dzieł sztuki. Rodowód zbrodni międzynarodowej*, Wrocław – Kraków 1958, pp. 241–242.

204 See A. Weidner, *Kulturgüter als res extra commercium im internationalen Sachenrecht*, Berlin – New York 2001, pp. 224–231.

any norms that would outright provide for *res extra commercium* but rather referred to the national systems that made use of such exclusions from private-law transactions.[205] This comes as no surprise, having regard to the only budding system of heritage protection on the international arena. A breakthrough in this respect could be expected from the UNESCO Convention on the Means of Prohibiting and Preventing the Illicit Import, Export and Transfer of Ownership of Cultural Property, 1970.[206] Prior recommendations and the work leading up to the Convention show that the market and interests of individual countries continued to prevail over a system of cooperation in supranational protection at that time.[207] This tendency was not without effect on the text of the 1970 Convention when studied from the point of view of the possibility of excluding, on an international level, certain categories of property from private-law transactions. One could opine that this was hardly a breakthrough in cultural property protection from the perspective of *res extra commercium*. On the one hand, it was an effect of the very nature of this act, for the Convention cannot be directly applied, providing only for few binding duties and giving much leeway to signatory countries so as to implement its objectives.

What is more, it has been ratified only by a few countries – the most popular destinations of stolen or illegally exported cultural property. On the other hand, the Convention itself has shied away from introducing outright a *res extra commercium* regime, adopting a 'softer' wording of its Article 13. An international recognition of the status of *res extra commercium* could have been attained if the norm of Article 13(d) of the Convention had not been drafted to contain the phase "consistent with the laws of each State" and were directly applied or if States had been obligated to legally recognise cultural property as excluded from private-law transactions by amending their legislation.

Unfortunately, certain shortcomings of the Convention from the perspective of *res extra commercium*, resulting from its excessive 'softness', only in practice

---

205 Ibid. pp. 231–233.

206 It was preceded by two UNESCO recommendations: one regarding the international principles applicable to archaeological excavations of 1956 and the measures aimed at the prohibition and prevention of illegal export, import and transfer of the ownership title of 1964 – H. Nieć, *Ojczyzna dzieła sztuki. Międzynarodowa ochrona integralności narodowej spuścizny kulturalnej*, Warszawa – Kraków 1980, pp. 72–80; W. Kowalski, K. Piotrowska-Nosek, H. Schreiber, K. Zalasińska, *Konwencje UNESCO w dziedzinie kultury. Komentarz*, (ed.) K. Zalasińska, Warszawa 2014, pp. 174–176.

207 See C. Forrest, *International Law and the Protection of Cultural Heritage*, London – New York 2010, pp. 166–195.

exposed its weaknesses.[208] It is a pity that an important opportunity was missed but even in the present state of affairs, the States Parties to the UNESCO Convention cannot ignore an announcement by another signatory State, including a given piece of cultural property among *res extra commercium.*[209] The significance of the 1970 Convention from the perspective of *res extra commercium* rests only, or as much as, on soft measures: for the first time in an international agreement (not merely a regional one), a provision was made for common convictions and values concerning the protection of cultural property and the combat of illicit trade in art. It has become a standard even for those countries that have not ratified the Convention and a point of reference – a kind of guidelines for the courts of law which referred to the UNESCO Convention – even where it did not apply to specific facts of a case. The Conventions of the 70s and 80s, even of the 90s of the 20th century do not contain any strengthening or any shift of emphasis of *res extra commercium,* that would go much further than the UNESCO Convention of 1970.[210] A certain new quality between *res extra commercium* and international law is discernible only in the case of the 1995 UNIDROIT Convention, which was a watershed in that it unequivocally imposed a duty to restore stolen cultural property and control export thereof, making it a principle

208 More on the strengths and weaknesses of the UNESCO Convention of 1970 see in: L. V. Prott, *Strengths and Weaknesses of the 1970 Convention: An Evaluation 40 years after its adoption*, 2nd edition, 2012, pp. 1–12, http://www.unesco.org/new/fileadmin/MULTIMEDIA/HQ/CLT/pdf/Prott_2_en.pdf (accessed: 15.06.2015).

209 A. Weidner, op. cit., pp. 244–245.

210 For instance, the Convention of 1976 on the archaeological, historical and artistic protection of the heritage of the American people (so called San Salvador conference), left the legal regulation of the ownership of cultural property and its transfer within the borders of countries belonging to the jurisdiction of the domestic law, and thus constituted a principle that each country may undertake "all measures which it deems effective in order to prevent and stop the illegal export, import, or removal of cultural properties as well as to return such properties to the mother state". In a similar manner the European convention on offences related to cultural property of 1985, pursuant to Article 3 of that Convention stated that each State was entitled to pronounce that it also considers to be an offence acts defined in Appendix III point 2 which includes: alienation of cultural goods that are otherwise inalienable pursuant to the internal part of the Convention. And so, although passed, the Convention was not ratified although it continues to constitute another example of the sanctioning of the principle of a recognition of the national *res extra commercium* in the international order.

of the law on the protection of cultural heritage in its international aspect.[211] Narrowing the scope of the Convention to international relations only should not take away from its overall highly-positive assessment, bearing also in mind the history of its drafting and the real threat of it being ultimately disapproved. At the preliminary stage, discussion focused on the consequences of excluding cultural property from private-law transactions within individual national legal systems, which can be seen in two studies by Gerte Reichelt and a draft convention authored by Roland Loewe.[212] Particularly strong opinions are formed in Reichelt's second study where all cultural property is divided into items excluded from any transactions and others which can be traded in.[213] Consequently, every country was to decide on its own which cultural property items were to enjoy the status of *res extra commercium*. Since not every legal system was familiar with this conception, the proposal did not aim at the international recognition of national law, but rather attempted to make every country define the items of cultural property it considered particularly important and that would be treated next by the signatory countries as *res extra commercium*. These items, in their country of origin, would not have to enjoy the status of goods exempted from trading. This was a rather bold construction and had it been introduced, would have certainly brought about later a recognition of the category of *res extra commercium* (known to international law) by those national legal systems to which it was alien. Later, Reichelt's conception – exclusion of certain items of cultural property from private-law transactions under international agreements – was again dropped without any broader discussion. An analysis of the work of the commission preparing a preliminary study shows that initially primary attention was given to the special status of public cultural property and – importantly – much emphasis was laid on the special nature of the principles of inalienability and imprescriptibility (exemption from the statute of limitations).[214] Later, these were more often mentioned with a ban on export and in the context of

---

211 W. Kowalski, *Droga do Konwencji* UNIDROIT *z 1995 roku oraz jej podstawowe rozwiązania*, "Santander Art and Culture Law Review" 2015, No. 1, p. 78.

212 See W. Kowalski, *Nabycie własności…*, p. 77; Raports and and internal preliminary document: G. Reichelt, *The Protection of Cultural Property*, UNIDROIT, 1986, Study LXX – Doc. 1; *The International Protection of Cultural Property*, UNIDROIT, 1988, Study LXX – Doc. 4; R. Loewe, *Preliminary Draft Convention on the Restitution of Cultural Property*, UNIDROIT, 1988, Study LXX – Doc. 3.

213 See G. Reichelt, *The International Protection…*, p. 38 (Conclusion point 2).

214 See R. Monaco, *Outlines for a Private Law Convention on the International Protection of Cultural Property*, UNIDROIT, 1988, Study LXX – Doc. 2, pp. 3–4.

the general problem of the recognition of foreign statutes on the protection of cultural property.[215] Their universal recognition, however, was found to be impossible due to differences in protection norms between countries; later, the issue was settled by imposing limitations in the UNIDROIT Convention, Article 5. The convincing of Convention drafters to introduce an absolute duty to return all stolen cultural property, falling under the scope of the Convention, resulted in the natural expiration of discussion on *res extra commercium*. As a consequence, the clear need to grant special protection, taking advantage of the *res extra commercium* regime, to a specific item of cultural property disappeared.[216] A desire to avoid making distinctions between various categories of cultural property might have also been an argument in favour of dropping this regime.

The finally adopted text of the 1995 UNIDROIT Convention did not provide for a direct recognition of the status of an item of cultural property as one of *res extra commercium*. Instead, the Convention provided for only indirect recognition of a cultural property item as a thing excluded from private-law transactions.[217]

Such an indirect construction can be also found in *acquis communautaire*. The fundamental EU principle of free movement of goods has an exception in Article 36 of the Treaty on the Functioning of the European Union (TFEU) (former Article 30 of the Treaty on the Establishing the European Community), giving to Member States the possibility to depart from prohibitions defined in Articles 34–35 and the following for the purpose of *inter alia* "the protection of national treasures possessing artistic, historic or archaeological value". It does not, however, specify what cultural property may be subject to an export ban without breaching the principle of free movement of goods.[218] Practically every Member State treats this principle differently: from a very broad scope (Germany), through intermediate (Italy, Spain, and Poland), to very narrow (initially

215 See *The International Protection of Cultural Property. Observations L. Prott*, UNIDROIT, 1988, Study LXX – Doc. 7, p. 2.

216 Doubts regarding the limitation clause which had to appear due to the lack of a classical exemption from trading, was solved by the authors by determination of special principles of the prescription of time with regards cultural property worthy of special protection.

217 For more see A. Weidner, op. cit., pp. 263–267.

218 For more see W. Paczuski, *Handel dziełami sztuki w Unii Europejskiej*, Kraków 2005, pp. 139–195.

France – although today it has moved to the group of countries which apply the principle broadly).[219]

The margin of freedom in this respect may not make protective regulations a disguised restriction on trade between Member States. Neither Council Regulation 3911/92 (EEC) on the export of cultural goods[220] nor Council Directive 93/7 (EEC) on the return of cultural objects unlawfully removed from the territory of a Member State constitute a breakthrough in the direct recognition of certain categories of cultural property as *res extra commercium* in EU law. However, it is worth mentioning a few elements that might show reasons behind this EU approach. EU law leaves the decisions as to which objects are to be protected as national cultural heritage to the competence of Member States and does not provide any rules or standards in this respect. Council Directive 93/7 (EEC) did create separate categories in an annex but the cultural property items which were protected by national law and belonged to the public collection or were listed in the inventories of church institutions, enjoyed a special status even without being listed in the annex. A criterion for qualifying a collection as 'public' was its state ownership or ownership by a regional or local authority or institution which in accordance with the law of a given Member State is considered a public institution, for instance because it is financed with public funds.

In many legal systems, museum, archive and library collections, constituting public property, are treated as inalienable and exempt from a statute of limitations by reason of their status as part of public domain or by reason of a special classification. The property of church institutions, too, is partially classified as *res extra commercium*. The Directive took account of this special treatment accorded to public and church cultural property. Cultural property considered *res extra commercium* was partially protected in an explicit manner by a ban on its export. If, in spite of the ban, such property was exported, law on the protection of national cultural property was violated and, therefore, such cultural property was treated under the Directives as unlawfully removed from the territory of a Member State.[221]The situation of an indirect recognition of the status of *res extra*

219 The moved view of France is noticeable in the implementation of EU Directive 2014/60, OJ L 159, 28.05.2014.

220 Amended by the Ordinance of the Council (EC) No. 116/2009 of 18 December 2008 on the export of cultural property, OJ L 39, 10.02.2009.

221 The EU regulations in the area of cultural heritage management have led to the separation of a special category of property that is subject to the return procedure known as *res extra commercium europapaeum*. This concept is only seemingly convergent with the concept of *res extra commercium*. In reality, it covers cultural properties which

commercium practically did not change with the introduction of new Directive 2014/60/EU.[222] The departure therefore from the annex and giving freedom to Member States in determining the categories of national cultural property on their own cannot be taken to be a harbinger of the quick construction of a single but direct category of *res extra commercium* within the EU legal system, without paying any regard to national legal systems.

In the area of international law (Conventions), the process was quicker in this respect mainly because of the optionality of accession to the convention (ratification) which provides for a supranational exclusion of certain cultural property items from private-law transactions. This is the case in the UNESCO Convention on the Protection of the Underwater Cultural Heritage, adopted on 2nd November 2001. It was the first instance in international law of so direct and uniform an establishment of the category of *res extra commercium*; in this case with respect to underwater cultural heritage meaning "all traces of human existence having a cultural, historic or archaeological character which have been partially or totally under water, periodically or continuously, for at least 100 years".[223] Under Article 2, paragraph 7, of the Convention, underwater cultural heritage may not be commercially exploited and, next to the principle of preserving underwater cultural heritage *in situ*, this is the priority of the Convention, which is seen not only in its formulation in the "Objectives and general principles" but also in its specification in the Annex – "Rules concerning activities directed at underwater cultural heritage".[224] Under Rule 2: "The commercial exploitation of underwater cultural heritage for trade or speculation or its irretrievable dispersal is fundamentally

---

pursuant to the domestic law are treated as *res extra commercium* and that have maintain the same status also upon their return, or recovery, and also to all other cultural properties fitting with the concept of cultural goods as specified in the Directive, "*Res extra commercium europaeum*" does not just mean that objects are excluded from legal circulation, except when they are excluded from free trading within the EU territory. Thus in this case one cannot claim that the rhetoric of a formulum was more successful than the successful rhetoric of the *stricte* legal one.

222 For the assessment of Directive 93/7 and premises of adopting a new one (2014/60) see P. Stec, *Dyrektywa 93/7 EWG z perspektywy dwóch dekad funkcjonowania*, "Santander Art and Culture Law Review" 2015, No. 1, pp. 103–118.

223 Indirectly, its adoption was triggered off by bilateral or multilateral agreements concluded by states interested in the protection of certain named shipwrecks, which sought a way to exclude a possibility of trading in such objects.

224 For more see V. Cogliati-Bantz, C. Forrest, *Consistent: The Convention on the Protection of the Underwater Cultural Heritage and the United Nations Convention on the Law of the Sea*, "Cambridge Journal of International and Comparative Law" 2013,

incompatible with the protection and proper management of underwater cultural heritage. Underwater cultural heritage shall not be traded, sold, bought or bartered as commercial goods."[225]Currently, the Convention has been ratified by 51 countries.[226] The exclusion of such heritage from private-law transactions (without settling the problem of the ownership of wrecks) shows the practical realization of the 1997 UNESCO Declaration on the Responsibilities of the Present Generations Towards Future Generations.[227]

The growing popularity of the category of *res extra commercium*, introduced either directly or indirectly in international law, has triggered a rebound effect in both countries that have applied this regime earlier to certain categories of cultural property and others for which it is an entirely novel measure. An example is offered by Switzerland where in 2003 a federal statute was enacted, one devoted to the international transfer of cultural property (known as KGTG),[228] largely begotten by the 1970 UNESCO Convention, and regulating the import, export

---

No. 2, pp. 536–561; B. Gadecki, *Ochrona podwodnego dziedzictwa kultury – aspekty prawnokarne i kryminologiczne*, Warszawa 2014, pp. 25–34.

225 Without doubt, the new category *res extra commercium* had an effect on the dissemination of the concept of a *planetary trust*, based on the undertaken obligation towards future generations that the heritage acquired from the past generations will be passed on to the next ones. In this scope the form of trust (not classical ownership) owing to its specific character, fits the underwater heritage even better than other generally defined cultural properties.

226 Among the countries missing, apart from Poland, are some states (that are important for the practical functioning of the principles contained in the Convention and actual exclusion of trading in such objects) such as: USA, UK, Australia, Japan, Brasil or China. See http://www.unesco.org/eri/la/convention.asp?KO=13520&language=E&order=alpha (accessed: 1.09.2015).

227 Declaration UNESCO on the Responsibilities of the Present Generations Towards Future Generations, adopted on 12 November 1997, http://portal.unesco.org/en/ev.php-URL_ID=13178&URL_DO=DO_TOPIC&URL_SECTION=201.html (accessed: 10.06.2015).

228 It must be emphasised that Under Article 724 archaeological objects belong to the canton in the territory of which they have been found. They are not subject to acquisition in good faith, through acquisitive prescription, or under the statute of limitations. Without the consent of canton authorities they may not be sold and are treated under Swiss law as *res extra commercium* – For more see M. Weber, *New Swiss Law on Cultural Property*, "International Journal of Cultural Property" 2006, No. 13, pp. 105–106.

and transit of cultural property.[229] Under the statute, cultural property objects, owned by the Swiss Confederation and entered into the Federal Register, are *res extra commercium*, thereby their export is prohibited, they cannot be acquired in good faith nor through acquisitive prescription, and actions for their restitution are not barred by the statute of limitations.[230] Individual cantons, too, may introduce the regime of *res extra commercium* in respect of cultural property owned by them, which must be shown in a special register as well. The Swiss legislator has laid down lax criteria for counting a cultural property object among those excluded from private-law transactions, being guided primarily by the construction of 'ownership' and only as its consequence by that of 'value'. The Swiss law is a typical example of introducing the category of exclusion from private-law transactions by referring to minimum standards of protection set by international conventions and indirectly recognizing exclusion from transactions in international law. This process, however, has not taken place in all countries – even where demanded by national authorities.[231]

Attempting to draw a diagram of the 'permeation' of the *res extra commercium* regime (Fig. 1), one has to show first that such regulations existed in relation to public domain constructions (or single categories of property covered by the regime of exclusion from private-law transactions) within national legal systems. Next, such regulations made their individual way to the international forum – initially only indirectly as is seen from the Belgian case from the time of the Versailles Treaty.[232] In this way, from among various national legal systems, the *res extra commercium* regime permeated into the international legal system (to which it was originally alien with respect to cultural heritage). Only rarely, however, did it pass as an autonomous element, but rather as a point of reference and respect for national legal systems in this[233]. At the next stage, the principle

229 *Bundesgesetz über den internationalen Kulturgütertransfer* (KGTG or CPTA) of 20 June 2003 (in force as of 1 June 2005).

230 See Article 3 KGTG.

231 For example such as Israel Antiquites Authority which demanded implementation of a prohibition to trade and a category of *res extra commercium* for the antiquities in Israel. This regime has not been as yet introduced with regards archaeological objects. See T. Einhorn, *Israel*, in: *Handbook on the Law of Cultural Heritage and International Trade*, (ed.) J. A. R. Nafziger, R. K. Paterson, London 2014, pp. 228–232.

232 Exercising pressure on Germans (in whose legal system such a category was non-existent) to indirectly follow this principle in respect of triptychs shows how *res extra commercium* permeates from the national regime to the international.

233 Therefore in the graph in is represented by the dotted line.

of recognizing the national *res extra commercium* regime was sanctioned in the international legal system (as is the case with the 1970 UNESCO Convention or the 1995 UNIDROIT Convention). Likewise, European Union Law only indirectly recognised the characteristic of cultural property as *res extra commercium*. Only with time, was a specific category of property recognised as *res extra commercium* by international law, while in the national legal systems that had used this regime earlier (including those in which public domain existed), judicial decisions and authoritative juristic publications solved meanwhile many practical problems related to the functioning of such a category (in French, Belgian and Italian legal systems).

Fig. 1. The popularization of the res extra commercium *regime*[234].

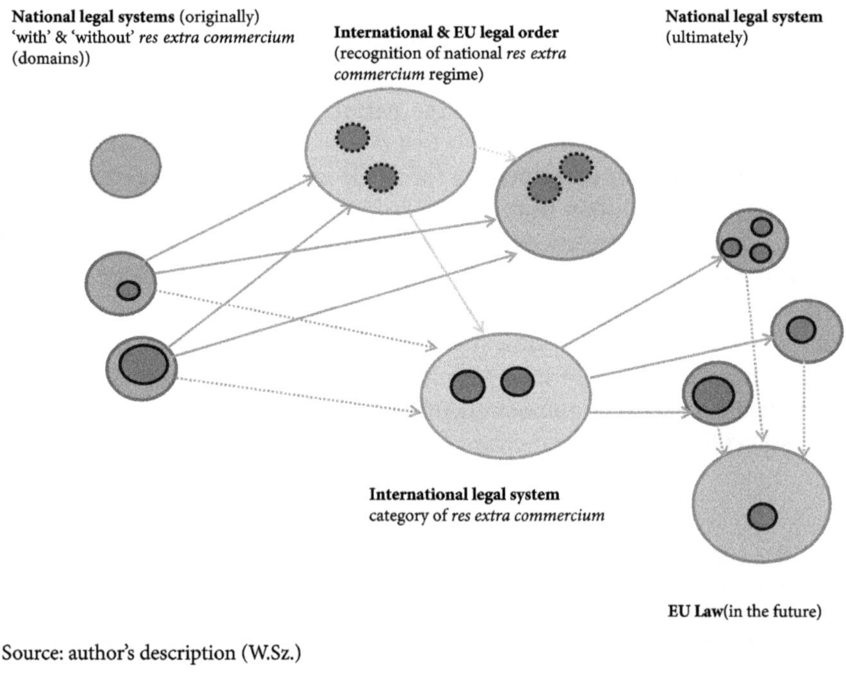

Source: author's description (W.Sz.)

234 The blue circles denote national regimes, the green ones international and the orange the EU's regime. The small red circle denotes *the res extra commercium* category, the bigger one – the public domain. Circles with a dotted line represent recognition of the national category of *res extra commercium*. Arrows drawn with a dotted line denote indirect influence and with a solid line – direct influence.

The spread of the exclusion from private-law transactions in international law brings about/will bring about the introduction of the *res extra commercium* regime, at least in respect of some kinds of cultural property (underwater archaeological heritage), to these national legal orders in which this regime has not functioned at all. A possible extension to other categories of cultural property is often an effect of an internal choice made by a country. Ultimately, every national legal system will have such a category; only what is not known is how broad and how defined it will be (relying on value or ownership or described in a mixed manner). With the spread of the *res extra commercium* category across national legal systems, it will permeate into EU law, which currently is 'shy' of such a solution due to a great dissimilarity in this respect between the respective legal systems of EU Member States. Hence, it leaves the decision about the manner of protection (using the *res extra commercium* regime or not) to Member States.

The category of *res extra commercium* in respect of cultural heritage objects appeared in Poland relatively late – as it did only in Act on the Protection of Cultural Property and Museums[235] in respect of archaeological objects and in Act on the National Archival Resource and State Archives[236] in respect of the non-state archival collection. Earlier, one could mention only certain restrictions imposed on an owner. These included a ban on sale within a certain time, a duty to notify or obtain permission for sale from a competent state authority, or a registration of sale or purchase of an historic object (work of art).

The first such restrictions were found already in the 1918 Decree of the Regency Council on Guardianship of Monuments of Art and Culture.[237] Its Article 20 stipulated that movable objects which were the property of "the country or cities, administrative or religious communes, parishes and social institutions" could not be "sold" or "exchanged" without prior permission from a competent

235 Ustawa z dnia 15 lutego 1962 r. o ochronie dóbr kultury [Act of 15 February 1962 on the Protection of Cultural Property and Museums], Dz. U. 1962, No. 10, item 46 as amended.

236 Ustawa z dnia 14 lipca 1983 r. o narodowym zasobie archiwalnym i archiwach [Act of 14 July 1983 on the National Archival Resource and State Archives], Dz. U. 2011, No. 123, item 698 as later amended.

237 Dekret Rady Regencyjnej o opiece nad zabytkami sztuki i kultury z dnia 31 października 1918 r. [Decree of 31 October 1918 of the Regency Council on the Guardianship of Monuments of Art and Culture], Dz. U. 1918, No. 16, item 36. Regarding the significance of this Decree see P. Dobosz, *Ponadczasowe wartości Dekretu Rady Regencyjnej z dnia 31 października 1918 r. o opiece nad zabytkami sztuki i kultury*, in: *Prawna ochrona dziedzictwa...*, pp. 21–52.

conservation authority. The same restrictions applied to excavations and finds owned by the entities mentioned above. A failure to obtain permission from a conservation authority resulted in the invalidity of the "sale, exchange, pledge or donation" of movable historic objects or excavations and finds. The 1928 Regulation by the President of the Republic on the Care for Monuments,[238] as part of preliminary protection (when it was not certain whether a given object had properties typical of an historic object), made it possible for a conservation authority to put "a ban on alienation either for a valuable consideration or gratuitously of such an object". [239] In addition, it was incumbent on private owners of historic objects to notify in advance the authorities of any transaction involving such objects. This duty followed from the pre-emptive right to buy such objects enjoyed by the State Treasury and meant in consequence that historic objects owned by private persons "could be alienated only with the prior notification of a conservation authority".[240] A greater burden was placed on legal persons (religious unions, associations, municipal unions) owning movable historic objects. In this case, alienation required the approval of the Minister of Religious Denominations and Public Enlightenment. Historic objects in the form of "excavations and finds" did not automatically become the property of the State Treasury but could be expropriated for its benefit and for the benefit of local government unions or legal persons engaged in the care for historic objects. Thus, the 1928 Regulation did not introduce the category of *res extra commercium* in respect of archaeological artefacts.

The status of *res extra commercium* was not introduced, either, by the Decree of 1st March 1946 on the Registration and Export Prohibition of Works of Fine Art and Objects of Artistic, Historical and Cultural Value.[241] Its purpose was to create a legal vehicle for taking over objects of high class by the State and

238 See Article 12 of the Regulation by the President of the Republic of Poland of 6 March 1928 on the Care for Monuments (Rozporządzenie Prezydenta Rzeczypospolitej Polskiej z dnia 6 marca 1928 r. o opiece nad zabytkami, Dz. U. RP No. 29, item 265 as later amended), repealed in 1962.

239 This ban could remain in force for a maximum of 3 months during which time a decision regarding the value of the object needed to be made. Also see A. Jagielska-Burduk, op. cit., p. 109.

240 See Article 19 of the Regulation of 1928.

241 Dekret z dnia 1 marca 1946 r. o rejestracji i zakazie wywozu dzieł sztuki plastycznej oraz przedmiotów o wartości artystycznej, historycznej lub kulturalnej [Decree of 1st March 1946 on the Registration and Export Prohibition of Works of Fine Art and Objects of Artistic, Historical and Cultural Value], Dz. U. 1946, No. 14, item 99.

subjecting to state control all privately-owned works of art. The requirement of registration applied to all entities: state, local-government, corporate, and religious which "possessed or held" any works of art. An exemption was made only for museums of various types, including private ones, which had their own inventories. Obligatory registration extended also to accepting an object for sale on a commission basis, alienating, acquiring or finding a work of art or an object, possessing characteristics stipulated in the decree. The decree provided for a penalty of up to three years of imprisonment or a fine for evading registration or providing false information or withholding information. The court could also decree the forfeiture of an object subject to registration owned by the offender. The decree was an oddity – in practice it did not result in a single "private registration" but for those in power at that time it was a convenient instrument to take over works of art, as for instance the collections of Andrzej Potocki.[242]

The Act of 14th July 1983 on the National Archival Resource and State Archives has unequivocally introduced, practically as the only enactment now in the area of heritage protection in Poland, the status of *res extra commercium* in respect of a certain category of objects.[243] It contains anti-alienation provisions, varying, however, in scope, depending on the kind of archival collection. Materials included in the National Archival Resource "may not be alienated" while those comprised in inventoried non-state archival collections (produced and owned by political parties, political, cooperative and social organisations, churches and religious unions and other non-state organisational units) may not be subject to any transactions. This varied protection of archival collections – stronger in the case of inventoried non-state collections – is certainly unfavourable for the former and hard to explain, because it follows that the most important archival materials on Poland's past are protected less.[244] An explanation for this difference in archive material protection, maintained for such a long time, should be sought in a failure to understand the category of *res extra commercium*. As was the case with the discussion continuing once in Poland about extending the category of

---

242 For more see W. Szafrański, *Dekret o rejestracji i zakazie wywozu dzieł sztuki z 1946 r. – czy praktyka rozmijała się z celami regulacji prawnej?*, "Studia Iuridica Toruniensia" 2012, Vol. 10, pp. 225–238.

243 The earlier decree of 19 March 1951 did not contain any detailed regulations, but a general provision pursuant to which: "without a consent of competent authorities the archival collection was not to be shredded or destroyed".

244 There have been many occasions for amending the legislation and equalising the two categories by giving the status of *res extra commercium* to the archival material constituting part of the state archival collection, the last one of 2015.

res extra commercium to museum pieces, also in the case of archive materials, forming part of the National Archival Resource, there was a fear of the effects of granting them such a status. This was considered to be too far-reaching a measure which ultimately could significantly restrict an adopted collection policy.[245] The standing legislation would have to be purged of the admissibility of the sale of museum pieces and archive materials.

In the case of archive materials, it has been decided not to introduce the regime of *res extra commercium* also because otherwise it would not be possible to move items between institutions (and not sell as this is banned). Under the 1983 Act, archive materials forming part of the State National Archival Resource may not be alienated; neither can they be, except in cases defined in the Act, transferred to organisational units other than those specified in the Act. Specifying clearly the limits of transfer and the institutions to which archive materials belonging to the State Archival Collections may be transferred, does not preclude the conferring of the *res extra commercium* status on these archive materials in the future.

From the point of view of this status, it is important if the ownership of such materials will be retained by the State Treasury. It is worth observing in this context that archive materials (like museum pieces) are not owned by archives (or museums) but by the entity which has created them. Thus, ownership would need to remain vested in the State Treasury with any transfer of archive materials. Then, from the point of view of civil law, the *res extra commercium* status would not be at all restricted with any exceptions. Alternatively, the status can be introduced with respect to archive materials forming part of the National Archival Resource and an exception made for transferring such materials. Such constructions are known to other legal systems and only part of authoritative juristic publications raise the issue of violating the uniformity of exclusion from

245 See statement by P. Żuchowski, Secretary of the State at the Ministry of Culture and National Heritage who, responding to a question posed by a deputy in the parliament in 2013 regarding the status of a public collection said that "introduction of the institution of *res extra commercium* with regards public collections would limit the independence of cultural institutions in the area of their policies of building up museum collections. What must be mentioned is that collections which institutions hold are enriched, among other things, also by exchanges of exhibits with other institutions or private collectors […] And an undesirable effect of an introduction of a total ban on the alienation of the museum property would be a loss of this possibility of accessions" http://www.sejm.gov.pl/sejm7.nsf/InterpelacjaTresc.xsp?key=34230811 (accessed: 15.06.2015).

private-law transactions. The line between the restriction of transactions and exclusion from them is very thin indeed, especially when we deal with a "mixture' of private and public law (and administrative decisions as well) or the situation as with archive materials where only moving them is allowed and at that – only under specific conditions.[246] In Poland, neither Acton the Protection of Cultural Property and Museums,[247] nor the Act on the Protection and Guardianship of Monuments, currently in force,[248] status outright in respect of specific categories of objects. Only archaeological objects, in the Act on the Protection of Cultural Property and Museums called excavations and finds, and in the Act on the Protection and Guardianship of Monuments (APGM) archaeological artefacts were made *ex lege* the property of the State Treasury. One kind of proof of the exclusion of movable archaeological artefacts from transactions was performed by Monika Drela.[249] Under the APGM, a voivodeship inspector of monuments may by administrative decision hand over a recently found archaeological artefact to a museum or another organisational unit for safekeeping and, at the request of the director of the museum, the voivodeship inspector of monuments may transfer the ownership of the artefact to the museum. Hence, no transfer of ownership under civil law takes place and a voivodeship inspector of monuments must not transfer the ownership of such a movable archaeological artefact to any other entities. Since the statute provides for issuing an administrative decision, an agency like a voivodeship inspector of monuments may not decide on its own to perform an act in any other form. At the same time, museums do not own museum pieces: they are actually the property of the entity that has created them, in this case, the State.

246 The creation of a state archival collection and analogous to it national library resources provided for in the Act of 1997 on libraries, failed to effect in an introduction of any special protection of library resources, even the most valuable ones, that would be based on *res extra commercium*. The lack of "internal" categories or groups of categories with no protection cover restricting transactions is rather strange since the two categories, archival collections and library resources are related. What is more, it may be that in some cases a doubt arose as to the classification of certain resources, and consequently the availability of the limited circulation regime in relation to these collections.

247 Dz. U. 1962, No. 10, item 48 as amended.

248 Ustawa z dnia 23 lipca 2003 r. o ochronie zabytków i opiece nad zabytkami [Act on the Protection and Guardianship of Monuments, currently in force], Dz. U. 2003, No. 162, item 1568 as amended.

249 See M. Drela, op. cit., Warszawa 2006, pp. 185–189.

Thus, such an archaeological artefact will remain the property of the State Treasury. For this reason, movable archaeological artefacts are objects excluded from private-law transactions and as such are not subject to acquisitive prescription or acquisition in good faith (pursuant to the Polish Civil Code, Article 169).[250]

Did these questions look similar under the rule of the old Act on the Protection of Cultural Property and Museums with respect to excavations and finds? Pursuant to its Article 24, a voivodeship inspector of monuments handed over movable finds and excavations, once their historical value was established, to an appropriate museum or a research institution. The Act did not specify whether he or she handed over such objects for the purposes of safekeeping or ownership (as is the case under the rule of the APGM).

Regardless of the fact whether the handing over was only factual, whether it took place in the form of ownership transfer by decision, and not a civil law act, movable finds or excavations remained the property of the State. Movable finds and excavations were handed over to "appropriate museums", in this case state museums, which, under Article 48 of the Act, were owned by the State at that time. It is hard to pinpoint though what the legislator had in mind, providing for a possibility of handing over a movable find or an excavation to an appropriate research institution. Nevertheless, they were generally treated as state entities at that time and since a voivodeship inspector of monuments in practice handed over movable finds and excavations to few select institutions, it was the State that continued to hold title to such objects. Movable finds and excavations were therefore indirectly treated as *res extra commercium* and thus excluded from private-law transactions. It seems that despite the fact of a model of rational legislator being used even today, one can hardly speak of the conscious building of *res extra commercium* with respect to archaeological artefacts. Otherwise, the legislator would have decided outright to exclude archaeological artefacts from private-law transactions.

A slightly different case is encountered in the Act on Museums,[251] which initially replaced in this regard Act on the Protection of Cultural Property and Museums. The category of museum pieces set up in it – objects entered in an inventory and owned by the museum – has not attained the status of *res extra commercium*. For originally, it was admissible to exchange and alienate museum

---

250 Ibid.

251 Ustawa z dnia 21 listopada 1996 r. o muzeach [Act of 21 November 1996 on Museums], Dz. U. 1997, No. 5, item 24 as amended.

pieces. The latter had to follow a procedure defined in the Act and was possible only with the approval of the Minister for Culture. Act on Museums, Article 23, concerning the possibility of alienating a museum piece has been amended and currently provides for the Minister's approval of an exchange, sale or donation of museum pieces only in justified cases and at the request of the director of a museum. The request must be preceded by the museum's council opinion. Any funds raised by selling museum pieces may be allocated only for the enlargement of museum collections.

The question arises therefore as to the status of museum pieces. In authoritative juristic publications, the opinion can be rarely encountered that until the Minister gives approval, museum pieces are excluded from transactions. Nonetheless, museum pieces cannot be held to be full-fledged, classical *res extra commercium* then; meanwhile, there are no other separate regulations, as is the case with archive materials belonging to a specific collection, restricting their alienation. Hence, museum pieces do not enjoy the status of *res extra commercium* in Poland now and the ongoing debate about the de-accession of museum collections is also a debate about *res extra commercium*. The demands made in authoritative juristic publications concerning de-accession vary.[252] However, the details of an appropriate de-accession policy of a museum are not as much important as the ideas of political decision-makers in this respect.

Today, in Poland, one can speak of a certain turning of the tables for as a rule de-accession liberalization is opposed by those responsible for heritage protection, including museologists. It is they who are inclined to take in principle positions close to *res extra commercium* in respect of museum pieces. Whereas, de-accession is supported by entities connected to the art market who favour its liberalization. In Poland, however, the division is not as sharp as elsewhere. The community of museologists (at least its members present at the 1st Congress of Museologists in 2015) wishes for a more precise definition of de-accession, hence, it does not make the *res extra commercium* regime its aim. Similarly, the Ministry of Culture and National Heritage has argued against introducing such a regime in respect of museum pieces by claiming that it will strongly restrict the free hand of cultural institutions in formulating museum collection policies. A debate about this issue is beginning to grow, sparked off by a basically forced

---

252 A comprehensive approach to the advantages and disadvantages of a de-accession policy in Poland *vis a vis* other countries has been presented in N. Fyderek, W. Szafrański, *Sprzedaż muzealiów – niewykorzystana szansa czy brak konieczności,* in: *Kultura w praktyce. Zagadnienia prawne,* Vol. 3: *Muzea a rynek sztuki. Aspekty prawne,* (eds.) A. Jagielska-Burduk, W. Szafrański, Poznań 2014, pp. 11–51.

introduction of the *res extra commercium* regime in respect of the cultural heritage, related to the ratification of the 2001 UNESCO Convention for the Protection of the Underwater Cultural Heritage.

When the Convention is ratified, a major change will be introduced into Polish law, as hitherto it will have been lawful to transact in artefacts extracted from the sea.[253] Thus, there will not be any space for the sidestepping the Polish legislator intends to use when implementing Directive 2014/60/EU. The new Directive 2014/60/EU replacing Directive 93/7(EEC) no longer contains a definition-connecting factor between a national cultural property object and the catalogue that was stipulated in the Annex to the previous Directive 93/7(EEC). Consequently, individual countries may determine for themselves what a national cultural property object is.[254] It will depend on their decision therefore if they give a broad or narrow treatment to the catalogue of national cultural property objects. Implementing the directive to their respective legal systems, they will be able to confer the status of *res extra commercium* on such objects. The Polish legislator is unwilling to take this step now, hence the sidestepping mentioned earlier, but the implementation of the directive and development of a catalogue of national cultural property objects would be a good pretext for establishing the category of objects excluded from civil-law transactions. Nevertheless, this does not mean that Poland will not want to draw the limits of national cultural property rather broadly and will face the decision of drawing the limits of national cultural property sooner or later.[255]

Since the regulation concerning export has not been amended yet, there may not be sufficient correlation between the catalogue of national cultural property objects compiled pursuant to the Directive 2014/60/EU and the objects that may be taken out of the country. Since Poland has not ratified the 1995 UNIDROIT Convention yet and the directive is its suitable complement, making any claim for restitution more effective, there is a need for cooperation or at least correlation between these provisions as far as the definition of national cultural property is concerned.

---

253 See W. Kowalski, *Konwencja UNESCO o ochronie podwodnego dziedzictwa kulturowego z 2001 r.*, "Cenne, Bezcenne, Utracone" 2014, No. 3–4, pp. 66–68.

254 P. Stec, op. cit., p. 112.

255 The first experiences of the implementation of the directive in French law point to such a tendency (showing, for instance, in the introduction of underdefined notions such as e.g. "and other cultural properties"). This indicates a rather loose approach of the French legislator to the principle of the exception of the rule, and in practice this means that exports of cultural property will be considerably restricted substantially and substantial supervision of transactions implemented.

A discussion concerning *res extra commercium* in respect of specific categories of cultural property ensued when work on the Act on Unclaimed Property Act adopted in 2015 began.[256] It amended the APGM by establishing a National Register of Lost Cultural Property kept by the minister for cultural affairs. The purpose of the register was to exempt objects listed in it from the provisions on acquisitive prescription and purchase under voidable title. The Polish legislator could introduce the *res extra commercium* regime, but it chose another path in an attempt to avoid a total exclusion of a number of State-owned cultural property objects from private-law transactions and provide at least fragmentary protection for private owners against the unfavourable effects of the Civil Code, Articles 174 and 169. In this case, objects owned by these entities must be entered into either the inventory of a private museum or into a register of historic objects. The special treatment accorded to private objects entered into a register of monuments results also from the need to compensate their owners for administrative burdens imposed on them by the APMG. A prerequisite for making an entry is the loss of the actual control over a thing in question by the owner as the consequence of one of prohibited acts specified in the provisions on theft, burglary, robbery, or larceny by extortion. An entry is made pursuant to an administrative decision issued by the minister for cultural affairs at the request of competent authorities (*inter alia* Police, public prosecutor's office, voivodeship inspector of monuments) or the owner of the object in question.

An entry in the National Register of Lost Cultural Property entails specific legal consequences, namely it makes the owner immune against the loss of ownership of the movable object concerned through purchase under voidable title and acquisitive prescription. In practice, the question arises if an entry in the National Register of Lost Cultural Property makes the thing entered a *res extra commercium*. The juristic construction suggests that one can speak here of a temporary quasi exclusion from private-law transactions, because in the period between an entry into and the striking out of the Register, the object in question is not subject to the provisions of the Polish Civil Code, Articles 169(1 & 2) and 174.

Not in every case will an entry in the National Register of Lost Cultural Property provide as effective protection to the owner as the conferment of the *res extra commercium* status, because an object concerned is temporarily excluded from private-law transactions only from the moment of its entering into the National Register

256 Ustawa z dnia 20 lutego 2015 r. o rzeczach znalezionych [Unclaimed Property Act], Dz. U. 2015, item 397.

of Lost Cultural Property.[257] The *res extra commercium* construction would protect public collections against insider theft, which often comes to light only after many years. The Polish legislator by establishing the National Register of Lost Cultural Property afforded, however, a chance of protection to privately-owned objects, too, provided that they are entered into a register of monuments or an inventory of a private museum. The *res extra commercium* status could not be extended to such objects as this would considerably restrict ownership. The creation of an inducement for private owners to file petitions for an entry in a register of monuments by constructing protection against purchase under voidable title, involving a National Register of Lost Cultural Property, is a step in the right direction.

An analysis how the *res extra commercium* regime functions in the system of heritage protection provokes the legitimate thought whether the introduction of the National Register of Lost Cultural Property will bring about a resignation from expanding the category of *res extra commercium* in the national legal system and from constructing the conception of public domain and extending the status of the exclusion from private-law transactions to it. The fact that legal measures unfavourable to the owners of works of art or cultural property, due to the possibility of acquisitive prescription or effective purchase under voidable title, have been in force for many years has often made the conception of *res extra commercium* resurface in discussions. The compilation of a Register will not cause a complete resignation from a decision to exclude specific categories of state-owned cultural property from private-law transactions, but will only postpone it to a later date. This is so because of the "permeation" of the *res extra commercium* regime from international law prompted not only by the looming necessity to extend this status to certain categories of cultural property (as in the case of underwater heritage) but also owing to the practical revelation how effective the recognition of the changeable status of objects entered in the National Register of Lost Cultural Property by other national legal systems will be. It is possible that a truly strong protection in this respect is ensured by extending the *res extra commercium* regime to state-owned objects, regardless of the many

257 The past practice regarding the functioning in Poland of the "National Register of Stolen or Illegally Exported Objects" (recognising the differences between these registers and procedures) shows how frequently the passage of time between the theft and the effective reporting thereof was long enough to allow for a successful acquisition of the stolen object from an unentitled seller – Compare P. Ogrodzki, *Rola baz danych w zwalczaniu przestępczości przeciwko dziedzictwu narodowemu*, in: *Prawna ochrona dziedzictwa…*, pp. 195–197 and 202–203.

disadvantages this construction has (including the prohibition on alienating museum pieces even with the minister's approval).[258]

The question arises how far the introduction of the *res extra commercium* regime in the future, if at all, should concern only state-owned objects/categories of objects and how far it should concern privately-owned ones, including historic objects owned by churches and religious unions. Any answer to this question boils down to the decision whether the criterion of exceptional value as well, and not only that of ownership, should matter to any significant degree while designing the exclusion from private-law transactions. Relying on the criterion of ownership is simpler and for this reason is more often postulated in literature on the subject. Wojciech Kowalski in his comments *de lege ferenda*, made before the National Register of Lost Cultural Property was established in Poland, argued the case for the *res extra commercium* regime to embrace: "all movable state-owned historic objects, hence including in the first place museum collections and collections of diverse state institutions, for instance those of universities and the Polish Academy of Sciences, and historic objects used to furnish offices, for instances, the Chancelleries of the President and of the Prime Minister, as well as ministries and provincial offices. The regime would also embrace archaeological finds and excavations".[259] In turn, the protection of the second degree, that is exemption from the Polish Civil Code, Art. 169, would cover historic objects gathered in non-state public collections and those entered into a register of monuments. Thus, the construction would resemble that known from the Unclaimed Property Act. The other objects, outside of these categories, would be protected only by the provisions of the ratified UNIDROIT Convention. A proposition going further ahead was formulated by us and relied on the conception of successor interest protection. What this involves is a shift of emphasis from "owner" to "historic object preservation" and striking a balance between the holder and universal interest (both national and international).[260]

Consequently, on the national level, the *res extra commercium* regime should embrace the most important objects and if they were a private property, they should be bought out and included in the public domain.[261] In other words, we

258 Some of those inconveniences may be overcome by, for example, several museums exchanging deposited objects for use.

259 W. Kowalski, *Nabycie własności...*, pp. 263–264.

260 A. Jagielska-Burduk, op. cit., pp. 281–286 and 304–305.

261 The way in which negotiations with the owner are carried out cannot be based on *quasi* nationalistic mechanisms. In the event there is consent for a buy out, an object cannot be given the status of an object entitled to higher protection available under *res extra commercium.*

suggest that objects should be preliminarily divided using the criterion of "value", and those, which are privately owned, should be bought out. Once cultural property objects are divided, the criterion of "ownership" ought to be applied. Hence, to the *res extra commercium* regime, the most valuable and only state-owned objects would be subject.[262]

The Polish legislator has skirted such constructions by extending the second degree of protection mentioned by Kowalski to categories one and two. Hence, a less radical path has been chosen without going into discussion about extending a special legal regime to not only "state-owned objects" but also, and against their owner's will, more valuable ones.[263] Does it mean that the problem of *res extra commercium* has been associated so far primarily with "ownership" and not "value"? Poland has only seemingly not seen a serious discussion of this topic yet. The first trials, so to speak, took place in the course of work on amendments to the APGM. Originally, the work aimed at introducing a new form of historic object protection, namely an entry into the List of National Treasures (LNT), and creating a possibility of entering a movable privately-owned object into a register of monuments by a voivodeship inspector of monuments on his own initiative.[264]Finally, in the 2015 Act to amend the APGM and the Act on Museums,[265] only the new form of protection was kept, i.e. the LNT. However, due to many doubts concerning the restriction of ownership, the president has sent the Act to the Constitutional Tribunal Court for review. It is worth reflecting here if the LNT touches upon the question of *res extra commercium* at all. Here, the legislator has neither defined a national treasure nor has it directly indicated what objects are meant, leaving this to the decision of the Minister of Culture and National Heritage.[266] The LNT was to include movable cultural property of a special value for

262 A. Jagielska-Burduk, op. cit., pp. 304–305.

263 The problem with movable monuments owned by churches should be stressed here, and at the same distinguished because these objects may be categorised as objects in which the trading is excluded or at least significantly restricted under canon law.

264 See P. Dobosz, *Koncepcja Listy Skarbów Dziedzictwa w systemie prawa ochrony zabytków w Polsce*, in: *Kultura w praktyce. Zagadnienia prawne*, Vol. 2: *Wokół problematyki prawnej zabytków i rynku sztuki*, (ed.) A. Jagielska-Burduk, W. Szafrański, Poznań 2013, pp. 199–224.

265 Ustawa z dnia 10 lipca 2015 r. o zmianie ustawy o ochronie zabytków i opiece nad zabytkami oraz ustawy o muzeach [Act to amend the APGM and the Act on Museums], The text of the Act available from http://orka.sejm.gov.pl/proc7.nsf/ustawy/3112_u.htm (accessed: 20.07.2015).

266 As the General Inspector of Monuments ensured in the course of the legislative work we resorted to expert knowledge, obtained mainly from the Monument Protection

national heritage, belonging to the category of monuments, in respect of which restitution proceedings may be conducted. The category will change when Directive 2014/60/EU mentioned earlier is implemented into the national legal system and the category of national cultural property is established.[267]

This shows that Poland is witnessing now an intensification of work aimed at changing the heritage protection system. The change is not only forced on the country by external factors, but it is also spawned by the ideas of domestic political decision-makers who often lack a comprehensive view of the entire system and do not inform the general public about the directions of its changes. Under the amending Act, into a register of monuments, objects put on the LNT were not to be entered. Since there are no clear criteria what a heritage treasure is, it is possible that most objects which were to be put on the LNT are already entered into a register of monuments or a museum inventory, but it is also possible that there are others which do not feature on either.[268] Putting a historic object on the LNT is done at its owner's request or on the initiative of the Minister of Culture and National Heritage even when its private owner objects. The entire LNT, it could be said, is marred by the rather imprecise criterion of "particular significance", and not ownership, used when conferring a special status on such cultural property.[269] Although this is not the *res extra commercium* regime, the doubts that arise today in respect of the "particular significance" objects that are privately owned and could potentially be put on the LNT (as for instance Lady with an Ermine by Leonardo da Vinci or Landscape with the Good Samaritan by Rembrandt) draw attention to two aspects which are not contradictory:

- it is counterproductive to confer a special status, including that of *res extra commercium*, on objects held in private collections without the consent of their owners, even by reason of their particular significance. Any such attempts not only cause a media brouhaha and sense of grievance on the part of owners,

---

Council.

267 The consequences of the ratification of the UNIDROIT Convention of 1995 should be taken into account here.

268 In particular those that are owned by private persons because in such a case an entry in the register of monuments is in principle made at the request of the owner. Thus, potentially, such an entry on the List of National Treasures will be the first one and the first step in extending over them special protection, and imposing limits on their ownership.

269 An attempt to regulate the List of National Treasures belongs to one of the most interesting cases in Polish legislation regarding heritage protection – imposing an extraordinary legal regime in which the category of a "value" decidedly prevails over "ownership".

but also raise questions in the first place as to the constitutionality of such measures on account of the considerable restriction of proprietary rights,
- any "higher regime" for cultural property, especially that of exclusion from private-law transactions, if planned in respect of state-owned movable cultural property, should be also made available for private owners of "exceptional value" objects. Preserving optionality is desirable. Showing the advantages of accepting a "higher regime" leaves to a private owner the decision whether a higher degree of protection and other benefits (as for instance in the case of the LNT – special subsidies to cover the costs of maintenance or restoration or safety devices to be installed in the room where the object will be kept) mean more to him than leaving the possibility of entering into private-law transactions.

Finally, not only the category itself but also the number of objects covered by the status of *res extra commercium* ought to be discussed along with any changes in time in this respect (Fig. 2). In Poland, after the regaining of independence in 1918 and until 1962, the status of *res extra commercium* practically was not applied to any objects. Under the legal system currently in force, the number of such objects, when compared to all objects making up the protected heritage, is not large in the first place (because it covers part of archival materials – belonging to proper collections – and archaeological artefacts) and, secondly, it is not constant and cannot be precisely determined (because archival materials covered by the regime grow and the number of archaeological artefacts cannot be determined). For the purpose of this discussion, such objects could be called *res extra commercium in spe*; although they do exist, they are not formally covered by the status in question, but will be in the future (without changing the legal category).

Hence, this set of objects would include items that will only be procured as a result of archaeological investigations and archaeological artefacts discovered or found by chance (in the diagram they are marked with a dotted line which illustrates the fact that their number cannot be determined exactly and is, therefore, changeable). With time, the number of *res extra commercium* objects will grow, reflecting the growth in the category of objects excluded from private-law transactions. This, however, will be a result of measures forced upon Poland by international law (following from the ratification of conventions). The number may considerably exceed a certain ceiling only when all state-owned historic objects are considered excluded from private-law transactions (or when a construction resembling public domain is established) or when additionally, this category is extended to privately-owned objects of exceptional/special value at the request/with the consent of their owners. The exclusion of state-owned cultural property from private-law transactions must not be automatically identified with the construction of a public domain. For it is possible to design a *res extra commercium* regime, relying solely on the criterion of ownership.[270]

Fig. 2. How the number of objects covered by the res extra commercium *regime has changed in time, compared to the total number of protected objects in Poland.*

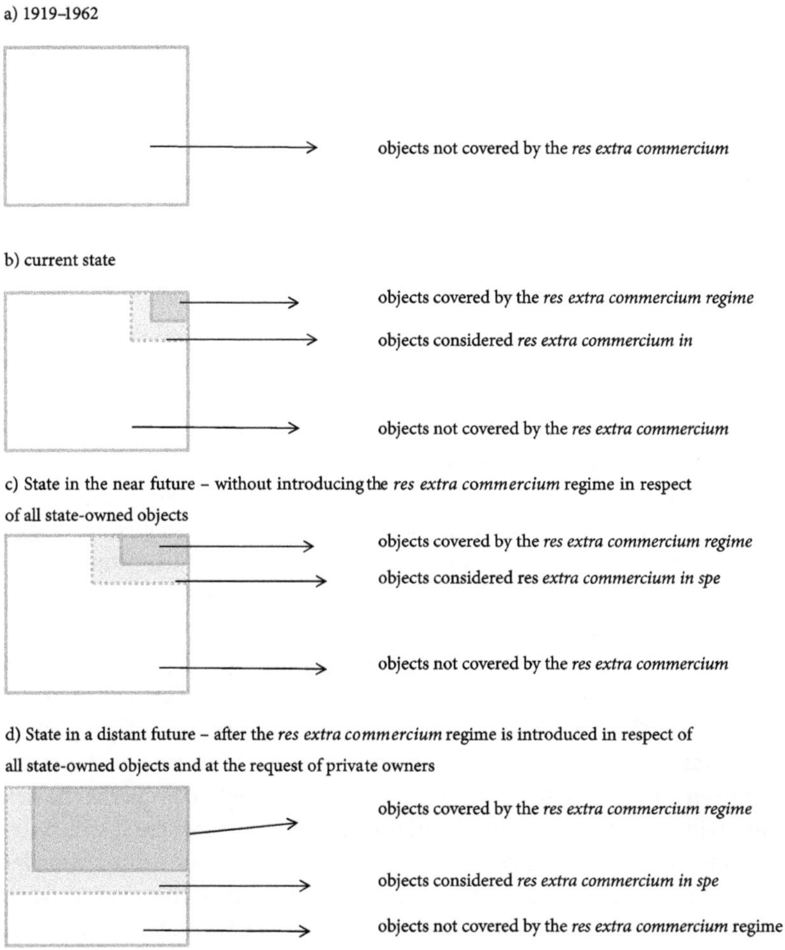

Source: author's description (W.Sz.)

270 While the public domain that follows the French, Belgian or Italian models, is based on the criterion of ownership understood as public value is and related to public service, public benefit or acting in public interest.

When constructing the status of *res extra commercium*, a thought should be given to not only its application, specifically to the question of how effective the prohibition is, but also lost opportunities and additional benefits following from the introduction of the regime. It often happens that such measures are opposed by associations of antiquarians and art dealers as for instance in the case of the National Cultural Property Protection Act in Germany in 1997.[271] The impact of the *res extra commercium* regime on the art market depends on how broadly defined the regime is. If only state-owned cultural property is encompassed by it, then in the case of Poland, there will be little difference (differently than in Western European countries). This follows from the fact that although it is lawful to sell objects no longer considered museum pieces, hardly any sales are made. Polish museums practically have not attempted to sell any former museum pieces.

The introduction of the *res extra commercium* regime can take the following three paths:

a) PRIVATE-LAW PATH: creating a special status for certain cultural property grounded in private law is the simplest and most effective solution. A public owner of such cultural property will be forever immune against losing the ownership of it, because the very private-law construction of the *res extra commercium* regime precludes acquisitive prescription or a bona fide purchase. To create such a status in private law would entail enacting provisions within civil law that would make a bona fide purchase, acquisitive prescription and limitation of actions ineffectual in relation to such property.
   As usual in such cases, however, a problem will arise how to determine which objects are to be excluded from private-law transactions. This is so because any detailed definition whose length is not unnecessarily excessive is practically extremely difficult to write unless the scope of exclusion coincides with state ownership or encompasses very specific categories of property (e.g. museum pieces). Otherwise, if an attempt is made to extend the *res extra commercium* regime to a less specific category of public property, the definition will cease to be clear and will provoke situations where it still could be disputable whether a given object is covered by the *res extra commercium* regime or not. For at the same time, the introduction of this regime naturally entails the liberalization of the provisions on purchase under voidable title of objects not covered by the regime (frequently privately owned without any special status[272]).

271 Compare A. Weidner, op. cit., p. 307.

272 For example, an effect of entering objects into inventories of private museums.

b) PUBLIC LAW PATH: finding that cultural property is public would require the prerequisite of a new status of specific cultural property items and their subordination to the public power over an object by virtue of an administrative act. These could be then both state-owned cultural property items and others owned by private people (however, owing to possible constitutional doubts, the consent of such people should be required). Also in this case, inventories of such objects would be necessary as it would be necessary to properly designate them and publicly announce their new status. Such property items would not be *res extra commercium* outright, but as long as they would not be deprived of the characteristics of a public object, they would have to be restored to their owners and thus would not be subject to sale, assignment, acquisitive prescription, etc.[273] A desirable flexibility of this path carries, however, certain disadvantages. Namely, a public law claim for the restitution of a thing would be effective at home, but rather debatable abroad, because a state may exercise its state power only within its borders.
c) MIXED PATH: combines the elements of the previous two paths. As in the case of the public law path, it is necessary to pass a general statute, e.g. on national cultural property. The statute would centre on defining cultural property or objects having cultural, historic, archaeological, artistic or research value and serving public purposes. This could be possible employing the construction of a public institution (and not ownership) – or property designated for public use as part of cultural or research tasks of a public institution. It would not matter whether a given cultural property object is owned by this institution or by a private person. In the latter case, however, it would be necessary to obtain the relevant consent so as to ascertain the public character of the item in question.[274] Such public institutions would need to have their inventories which would have to be available for inspection to the general public. The ascertainment of the public nature of a thing would coincide with its entry into the inventory and the public announcement where the inventory could be inspected. Such cultural property objects serving public purposes and accorded a special treatment as public things could not be exempted from fulfilling the purposes in the area of public benefit, which would justify a major interference with ownership. Defined in this way, cultural property would be covered by a special status afforded to it by

273 This results from the fact that the a public-private claim to release a thing would not be capable of being counterclaimed with private-public claims.

274 A consent could be granted provided that it is granted under condition subsequent, or with a reservation that it may be withdrawn.

private law as well. Public-law power over a thing would be superimposed on private-law relations and thereby a given public institution would always enjoy a public-law cause of action for its restitution, which would not be time-barred. Such public cultural property could be sold, exchanged, etc.; the only exception being the acquisition of ownership without the consent of entities entitled to its disposal. On account of the public purpose, cultural property included in this category is supposed to serve, its sale would be highly restricted. Furthermore, the duty to protect cultural property would be maintained. In this way, alienation of public cultural property would be highly restricted and actually would come down to a general policy of collection management. With some reservations, it does not exclude even the sale of museum pieces. It is these characteristics and the preservation of the legal possibilities of collection de-accession that the mixed version features and not the classic, of the *res extra commercium* regime.

Each path has its pros and cons which can be seen already at the stage of bill drafting especially when it comes to defining the categories of property to be covered by this exceptional regime. The classic – private-law path – is the most desirable but the least popular with countries now. In practice, it is only this path that ensures better effectiveness of claims for restitution of such property in case it is unlawfully removed abroad. Furthermore, this path makes the construction of exclusion from private-law transactions more popular, which may be less important today but could become crucial in the long run. This, in turn, will be favourable to the final acceptance directly (and not only indirectly) of specific categories of cultural property as *res extra commercium* by international law.

From the formal point of view, the "future" of the *res extra commercium* regime in the system of heritage protection in Poland may unfold in three directions:

a) resignation from incorporating this category into the system. This, however, would result in abolishing currently existing categories established in respect of archaeological artefacts and certain types of archival materials, as well as preventing the ratification of the UNESCO Convention on the Protection of the Underwater Cultural Heritage as it unequivocally calls for the introduction of a prohibition to trade in such objects.
b) maintenance of "zero option", i.e. making no significant changes with the exception of those forced on Poland by international or EU law. Apart from the UNESCO Convention on the Protection of the Underwater Cultural Heritage, other legislation, including even Directive 2014/60/EU, does not call for

the introduction of the *res extra commercium* category, leaving it to the decision of individual countries.

c) enlargement of the *res extra commercium* category, independently of the implementation of supranational measures to the national legal system. Here, two paths are possible:
   - the progressive "leapfrog" tactic or the introduction of the *res extra commercium* category in stages, with respect to various categories of cultural property, and only the consecutive unification of exclusion from private-law transactions;
   - an uncompromising "sudden strike" – taking a political decision leading to new legislation providing for the *res extra commercium* regime with respect to all historic objects owned by the State Treasury (or even by local governments).

In the latter case, the "criterion of ownership" may be replaced by the "criterion of importance" of objects covered by the regime. The replacement may give rise to a number of doubts concerning both the grounds for excluding privately-owned objects from private-law transactions and the actual possibilities of accurately assessing the criterion of value (exceptionality) in the absence of special catalogues or lists of such objects. Of course, in this case, there will be more doubts and borderline situations than in the case of adopting the ownership criterion. This path may involve settling the question whether the restrictions of general principles of private-law transactions should also affect private property not shown in any register and cultural property belonging to non-state public collections. An answer in the affirmative would lead to far more advanced changes and, in the opinion of this author (W.Sz.), considerably affect the market. The more so as objects which, for instance, today are considered modern art and are freely bought and sold, often ending up in private hands, will become monuments with time and that of considerable value.

Certainly, neither of the two paths outlined above, being concrete options for the heritage protection system, will be followed. Poland is practically doomed to a third path, because no political decision-maker will dare to "lower" heritage protection by resigning from the *res extra commercium* regime or even block the encroaching of this regime upon successive heritage components. It is said that the regime is expanding, because it is necessary to bring order to the degrees of protection, standardise its principles with respect to state-owned cultural heritage objects and follow international measures and those of other countries moving in this direction. Furthermore, in Poland, on account of the universal awareness of heritage war losses, the introduction of the *res extra commercium* category and exclusion from private-law transactions will sooner meet with the approval of the general public than giving up such "support" for the heritage protection system. In the media, too, it is easier to justify such an idea, by leading both a positive campaign ("it is necessary to protect important components of our heritage") and negative one ("they intend to sell out our national heritage"). For people who have little knowledge about the heritage protection system but who represent a major segment of the electorate taken into account in political decision-making, the details of protection and the directions the *res extra commercium* category expands are of secondary importance in contrast to the identification with state-owned objects, e.g. museum pieces understood as "public property" that is "and mine".

In 1958, Stanisław Nahlik wrote that the future of international law with regard to heritage protection lay in the restrictions of transactions in cultural property by establishing the *res extra commercium* regime.[275] What raises controversies, though, is the correlation between the categories of cultural property covered by the regime and how broad they ought to be. Although the present authors do not advocate a significant expansion of the *res extra commercium* regime, its introduction as an element in heritage protection is not merely jurists' whim but an inevitable step, following from the spread of the regime as an effective instrument in heritage protection. Ultimately, this very instrument will be employed not only by international law but above all by national legal systems, possibly followed by EU law to a greater degree when this path is universally accepted by individual Member States.

II.2 Legal institutions and the separation of property in cultural heritage management

Enterprises and foundations

With regard to cultural heritage academic legal studies have distinguished foundations, and funds and enterprises operating within them. These entities operated on the basis of assets drawn from a given estate. Funds usually undertook their statutory tasks by increasing expenditure sourced from, for example, a scholarship fund, while enterprises, apart from pursuing the goals that underlay their formation, carried out other activities and directed proceeds earned from

275 S. Nahlik, op. cit., p. 390.

them to different organisations, such as hospitals or universities.[276] Attempts in legal doctrine to distinguish new types of legal persons alongside already existing foundations failed due to the overlapping meanings and scope of these concepts with the already existing ones, and were likewise unsuccessful in practice because of similarities in their organisation and operation.[277]

The idea that underlay the setting up of foundations and private enterprises in the 19th century was to separate certain assets from private property in order to fulfil a social purpose determined by their founders. Regarding the ownership status of such assets, they were separated from the founder and formed a legally and financially distinct entity. While in the 19th century the purpose of many foundations in Poland was to maintain essential knowledge of Polish culture and art, in the 1990s, the foundation was to play a bridging role connecting the period of nationalisation and declining private initiative in the cultural area as a consequence of the abolishment of the entail with the new political and legal regime. Today, foundations are predominantly focused on achieving the most efficient management of a collection, both legal and economic. This goal is being successfully realised by for example Banco Santander Foundation, or the Art Stations Foundation operating in Poland.

The perception of a foundation in the public mind is that it is a creditworthy entity carrying out operations focused on achieving the common good. Polish foundations such as the Princes Czartoryski Foundation, The Kórnik Foundation or the Ossolineum National Enterprise exist in the social consciousness as public institutions, notwithstanding the fact that the last two are entities of public law, despite their initially private origin. Similar to these, are associations operating as collections or museums, for example the Museum of Technology and Industry of the Chief Technical Organisation or the Poznań Society of Friends of Sciences. Their operations, although financially supported by the State for specific public tasks, are of a private character. The analysis presented below of the relationship between a founder and a relevant enterprise or foundation will show the movement of individual items of a collection and the way in which assets that constitute cultural heritage are separated and placed within a foundation.

A foundation may also be a way of ensuring the preservation of those elements of cultural heritage which used to be privately owned but whose owners have for various reasons (historical, political, social) been deprived of their

276 F. Zoll, *Prawo prywatne w zarysie przedstawione na podstawie ustaw austriackich*, Kraków 1910, p. 17.

277 E. Ochendowski, *Zakład administracyjny jako podmiot administracji państwowej*, Poznań 1969, p. 109.

property. Therefore it is important to depict the web of historical circumstances pertaining to cultural heritage and the relationship between a founder and an entity which the founder has created as a separate unit and to which he has transferred certain elements of heritage. Sometimes such a unit only acts as an "operator" with a no more than a titular right to those elements.

Foundations in Poland are regulated by the Act of 6 April 1984 on foundations.[278] In Polish legal terminology the concept of an enterprise (*zakład*) is related to administrative law. Pursuant to Article 1 of the Act, a foundation may be created for the purpose of fulfilling social purposes or economically useful purposes only on condition that they are in accordance with the basic interests of the Republic of Poland. A list of allowable purposes includes culture, art and monument preservation and protection. The Act provides for substantial freedom for the founder of a foundation to decide upon the name of the foundation, its seat and assets, purposes, rules, the form and scope of its activities, the composition and organisation of its management and appointment of its members as well as the rights and duties of the organisation and its individual members. The charter of a foundation may also include other provisions regulating the foundation, among others the running of its business activities. From the point of view of art collection management, provisions governing the integrity of a collection, its acquisitions policy and maintenance are of special importance and they may well apply to other elements of heritage such as buildings or parks.

Today, an enterprise, or more accurately an enterprise under administrative law, is related to the public sector. The function of such an enterprise with a cultural heritage management function is now being undertaken by museums. It is thus recognised that museums constitute untypical administrative enterprises which, apart from providing services, carry out other activities, beyond those within the scope of administrative service providers.

As proposed in the literature, museums are open enterprises operating in the field of art and culture but are not limited to those activities.[279]

In order to demonstrate the continuity mechanism as well as the financial aspects of the operations of a foundation acting as a service provider and at the same time manager of an art collection, it may be worthwhile to analyse the Library of the Ossolineum Enterprise and the Princes Czartoryski Foundation.

---

278 Ustawa z dnia 6 kwietnia 1984 r. o fundacjach [Act of 6 April 1984 on Foundations], Dz. U. 1984 No. 21 item 97 as later amended.

279 Literature containing an analysis of a museum as an administrative establishment is exhaustive and hence a similar analysis has been abandoned here. For more, compare: K. Zalasińska, *Muzea publiczne. Studium administracyjnoprawne*, Warszawa 2013.

The history of these entities and their legal and financial problems show how military conflicts or changes of state political regimes prevent the development of a safe mechanism of cultural heritage management. Foundations change and adapt to the times in which they function, but their public purpose (promotion of science, culture and art) remains unchanged.

The library which subsequently became the core of the Ossolineum National Enterprise was initially planned to be based in Kraków. It took almost twenty three years (from about 1800) to decide upon the proper legal form of the planned enterprise and to find appropriate partners for such a major undertaking (it was planned to be based on the collections accumulated by Józef Ossoliński and be open to the public). This public status would have been achieved if the library had been put under city council management. However, the public status of the library would have, in the view of the owner of the collection, presented a risk to the indivisibility of the collection in the event of a possible invasion by foreign states.[280] In consequence, all other proposed solutions as to its legal form were based on private law. An attempt was then made to include the library in the Zamojski entail and place the library in Zamość. To that end, an arrangement between count Stanisław Zamojski and Józef Ossoliński was agreed in 1804.[281] Józef Ossoliński examined various forms of library that would be open to the general public, but would remain his private property. The book collection was to complement the entailed library but constitute at the same time a separate entity independent of the entailed library and the academic library of the Zamoyska Academy. The former, should the entail cease to exist, was to become the "public property of the country and the Nation, achieved in such a manner, that it be placed under the Highest Care of the government".[282] The main objective of the founder was to "secure the collection from being dispersed.[283] There were two attempts to draft a charter in proper wording. In the preamble the founder of the library to be founded initially in Tarnów stated that his choice of the legal form of the library was dictated by the fact that he was childless and had no heirs.

280 W. Jabłońska, *Ustawy fundacyjne Józefa Maksymiliana Ossolińskiego*, "Ze Skarbca Kultury" 1977, Issue 28, pp. 130–131.

281 Agreement between Józef Maksymilian Ossoliński and Count Stanisław Zamoyski regarding establishment of the Ossoliński Library in Zamość of 17 August 1804, in: W. Bruchnalski, *Zakładu Narodowego im. Ossolińskich Ustawy, przywileje i rzeczy jego dziejów dotyczące*, Lwów 1927, p. 1 et seq.

282 Ibid. pp. 1–5.

283 *Original charter establishing the Ossoliński Library in Tarnów, 1808*, in: W. Bruchnalski, *Zakładu Narodowego im. Ossolińskich…*, p. 17 et seq.

Thus, in his will he proposed a curator whom he obliged to complete a 6-month apprenticeship in the library upon his appointment. Other duties of the library curator included the formal taking up of the function and taking all necessary and available protective measures in the event of a war or other "commotion".[284] The curator managed the literary as well as the asset fund, acted as the employer of the Library's director and its personnel.[285] He could perform all the above duties personally or through a proxy. Among solutions proposed but never adopted since they met with the objections of the founder was one which provided that the Library Fund was to be the owner of all the founder's estate after death (§ I).

Eventually, in May 1817 a decree issued by the Court Chancellery approved the foundation of the National Library in Lvov, a decision subsequently endorsed by Emperor Franz I of Austria. The enterprise was exempted from paying stamp duty, death duty and inheritance tax.[286] With regard to the land title it was agreed to transfer it to the Library's curator. The proceeds from the land in the amount of 6 000 guldens, equivalent to 24 000 Polish zloty, were to be used for Library purposes and the rest to remain at the curator's disposal. The amount was to be reviewed every 50 years based on the current value of the money and grain (§ 6). An important provision of § 8 contained the founder's stipulation that the Library's equity remains private property managed by families named in the codicil. The Curatorship of the Library was linked to the ownership of property due to the curator, determined according to strictly specified principles. Anticipating potential damage to the library collection, the founder also provided for the setting up of a mechanism financing the recovery of up to twenty thousand volumes from the proceeds obtained from the land (in which case the funds left at the curator's disposal and discretion would have been significantly reduced (§ 9).

In the original proposal formulated by the founder, upon taking up appointment the curator was obliged to spend 3 months familiarising himself with the work of the Library. That was only half of the 'orientation' time required in the 1808 Charter. Every other legislative act establishing a library also provided for an auditing organ and for the Library in Tarnów it was composed of a six-member office (*eforat*). In the case of the Lvov Library it was a State Commission (*Deputacja Stanowa*) with which the curator was to lodge an annual report. If the

---

284 Ibid. p. 21.

285 W. Jabłońska, op. cit., pp. 139–140.

286 *Emperor's privilege exempting the Ossoliński Enterprise from the stamp duty, death tax and inheritance tax of 30 June 1817*, in: W. Bruchnalski, *Zakładu Narodowego im. Ossolińskich…*, p. 12; J. Trzynadlowski, *Zakład Narodowy imienia Ossolińskich 1817–1967. Zarys dziejów*, Wrocław – Warszawa – Kraków 1967, p. 34.

Office were "non-existent" the report would have to be substituted by the Lvov City Council (§ 57). The manner in which families, curators and their successors were to be appointed was very similar in wording to the corresponding provisions found in the charters of Roman *fideicommissum hereditatis*. Both obliged curators to exercise due care to ensure the safety and security of the collection, and one of the requests was to provide adequate fire-protection of the building in which the collection was housed (§ 11).

Within the Ossolineum Enterprise, whose organisational structure and type of services were shaped to satisfy the demands of future readers, since 1823 there functioned the Lubomirski Museum.[287] Its resources consisted of Prince Henryk Lubomirski's collection[288] which, immediately upon the signature of a relevant agreement were moved to the Ossolineum. Some, however, (in 1870) were transferred to Lvov.[289] The agreement included a clause that allowed the donor to leave selected items of the collection to himself and his heirs in Przeworsk. It should be added here that this type of solution was used when collections were given for public purposes and the public allowed access. For example, when Edward Rastawiecki was transferring his collection to the Poznań Society of Friends of Sciences, he made a provision that part of his collection would stay with him till his death.[290] Following Rastawiecki's death, the collection was included in the Ossolineum collection with the reservation that it be displayed as a separate collection[291] as Musaei Lubomirsciani, in a separate exhibition hall. The cost of the exhibition was to be covered by Prince Lubomirski.

Following the inclusion of the Lubomirski Museum in the Ossolineum, the curatorship was divided into an economic and a literary part, the latter being connected with the Przeworsk estate (§ 3[292]). Literary curatorship was to be conducted by Prince Lubomirski and his successors in the order determined in the entail document. The literary curator was not paid for his services but enjoyed discretion in the management of the resources received from the economic

---

287 Agreement concluded by Count Ossoliński and Prince Henryk Lubomirski of 25 December 1923, in: W. Bruchnalski, *Zakładu Narodowego im. Ossolińskich…*, p. 188 et seq.

288 A. Fischer, *Zakład Narodowy imienia Ossolińskich (Ossolineum), 1817–1917*, Lwów 1917, p. 79.

289 Ibid.

290 A. Jagielska-Burduk, W. Szafrański, M. A. Górska, *Wirtualna Galeria im. Mielżyńskich. Historia – idea – prawo*, Poznań 2013, p. 13.

291 A. Fischer, op. cit., p. 28.

292 Agreement concluded by Count Ossoliński…, p. 188 et seq.

curator for the library. His duties included administration of the building housing the library. In the event of the extinguishing of the Lubomirski line and the entail ceasing, the property of the entail was to be included in the literary curatorship and the management to be vested in Ossoliński's successors (descendants). The economic curatorship was to be handed down as provided for in the codicil. The Przeworsk entail was approved as late as 1866. The wording of the entail documents made many references to legislative acts related to its inclusion in the Ossoliński Enterprise. The division into the literary and economic curatorship was confirmed and the establishment of the Lubomirski Museum endowed with an art collection. However, it was also made clear that part of the collection was to remain in Przeworsk, in the hands of the original owners, while all new acquisitions purchased with funds from the reserves were to enrich and enlarge the Museum collection. The entailed estate, apart from the real estate was to include valuables and other movables specified in the list attached to the document, as well as the "collection of books, medals, paintings, art and antiquities capable of being counted and added to the inventory".[293] Undoubtedly, the initiators of the Przeworsk entail understood that the legal form of the entail guaranteed a more stable solution than the Enterprise established by Józef Ossoliński, as could be best proved by the wording of the draft charter of the entail, stating that in the event "of the Ossoliński National Enterprise being altered by the Country's Authorities" (in the document establishing the entail the word used was "abolished" in the meaning of liquidated) or if its funds be used otherwise than for the purpose specified by the founder, the curator's powers were to be limited or cancelled, and in such an event the right to join the entail to the enterprise waived or, where the two have already been joined, terminated. The provisions of the document establishing the entail detailed the use of its funds for purposes other than defined as consequently requiring a valid judicial order, likewise the limiting of the literary curator's rights.

The personnel of the Enterprise did not consist of qualified staff but was rather composed of enthusiasts. The Enterprise operated based on its land property, the character of which was also being transformed from rural to urban. There was also the Ossoliński Publishing House which generated additional profit.[294]

---

293 Document establishing the Przeworska Entail of Princes Lubomirski, Vienna 10 July 1866, in: W. Bruchnalski, *Zakładu Narodowego im. Ossolińskich…*, p. 493.

294 M. Gębarowicz, *Zbiory muzealne w Zakładzie Narodowym im. Ossolińskich*, in: *Ossolineum. Księga pamiątkowa w 150-lecie Zakładu Narodowego imienia Ossolińskich*, (ed.) B. Olszewicz, Wrocław 1967, pp. 139–140.

The collection was being enlarged by gifts and donations, and also items were purchased based on specially drawn up sale agreements.

The establishment of the Enterprise by Józef Maksymilian Ossoliński himself during his lifetime meant that the management of the collection was parallel to and connected with the founder's own activities which, among other things, enhanced the collection with new purchases financed from his private resources.[295] The Library's finances were also largely based on resources granted to it by the founder as well as donations or gifts from other people. Additionally, each curator was obliged to contribute to the enlargement of the collection. There were specific dispositions regarding the amounts devoted to maintaining the personnel, the buildings and the collections. Other (state-owned) museums run at the same time were in competition with the Enterprise, but there were still numbers of private owners[296] who would themselves decide to enter into loan or lease agreements with the Museum, or even conclude donation agreements with all the subsequent legal consequences.

Attempts were made to include in the name of the Library the adjective "national". In an official letter written by Prince Henryk Lubomirski petitioning for the right to emphasise ties with the nation and public service, we read that some public institutions had already referred to the Library as national, in acknowledgement of its national character. It was also emphasised, in the same letter, that the private-public status of the collection did nothing to exclude the public character of the library, nor did the "retaining of ownership or perpetuating the name of counts Ossoliński and Princes Lubomirski deprive the collection of being so honoured (called national) because nothing would change its purpose".[297] The answer that came was negative, the petition was dropped, but it was nevertheless concluded that the Library could rely on the customary perception of it as a national enterprise. Obviously an attempt to achieve official status as 'national' was also of symbolic character, apart from an effort to secure for the Library some concessions from the governing authorities.

All in all, the operations of the Ossolineum came close to the model of cultural centres promoted today, i.e. it combined the activities of a museum, a library and a publishing house. Its founder also pursued a policy of attracting scholars whose

295 A. Fischer, op. cit., p. 31.

296 M. Gębarowicz, op. cit., p. 136.

297 Letter sent by Prince Lubomirski to the Department of States (*Wydział Stanów)* asking for suport in the efforts to win for the Ossoliński scientific enterprise a universal title of "national", Lvov 16 June 1928, in: W. Bruchnalski, *Zakładu Narodowego im. Ossolińskich…*, p. 402.

interests focused on Polish history and literature.[298] As in the case of the entail, different solutions were considered, in order to decide which option would be best from the point of view of securing the safety of the public and private property. The starting point for these deliberations were past (historical) cases when state property was repossessed in time of war.[299] The choice of the mechanism was not only considered as one that interfered with the structure of family affairs, but also as limiting such intervention by external entities. Such a choice of legal solution was undoubtedly the result of an analysis of the external environment and the political situation. The link between the Library with the Przeworsk entail constituted, both security for the literary part, and also an important element of the entail, which determined its participation in public life for the public benefit.

Pursuant to the decree of 24 April 1952 on the liquidation of foundations,[300] the Ossolineum was liquidated and its property passed on to the State. More than 40 years later, by virtue of the Act of 5 January 1995, a new entity, the Ossoliński National Enterprise,[301] was established. The intention was to create a legal successor to the former Enterprise, although operating as a foundation subject to public law. The Preamble of the Act on the Foundation read: "the Ossoliński National Enterprise was inspired and has continued to be inspired by the statement of Józef Maksymilian Ossoliński made on 17 July 1804 according to which upon the death of the Founder all the property became 'the public property of the Country and the Nation'". Pursuant to Article 5 of the above Act, the Enterprise was assigned assets covering (on the date when the Act came into force) The Ossoliński National Enterprise – the Polish Academy of Sciences Library in Wrocław. One unit, the Publishing House, was excluded from the Enterprise. The Act also specified the assets and the financing of the Enterprise. Regarding the latter, the maintenance, the building up and accessibility of the collections (termed in the Act as "state" – "państwowe") of the Ossolineum National Library and the Princes

298 A. Fischer, op. cit., p. 28.

299 M. Gałyga, *Status Zakładu Narodowego im. Ossolińskich w okresie zaborów i w latach międzywojennych*, "Czasopismo Zakładu Narodowego imienia Ossolińskich" 1992, Issue 1, p. 24.

300 Dekret z dnia 24 kwietnia 1952 r. o zniesieniu fundacji [Decree of 24 April 1952 on the liquidation of foundations], Dz. U. 1952, No. 25, item 170 and 171.

301 Ustawa z dnia 5 stycznia 1995 r. o fundacji – Zakład Narodowy imienia Ossolińskich [Act of 5 January 1995 on the Foundation – the Ossoliński National Enterprise], Dz. U. 1995, No. 23 item 121 as later amended.

Lubomirski Museum were to be co-financed with a permanent subsidy.[302] Other financing resources were to include proceeds from the Enterprise's profits, income from its business activities, donations, legacies and bequests.

The legal form of the Foundation adopted in the Act was unclear. On the one hand it was a new legal entity, on the other hand, though, it was a partial legal form of the former entity that existed before WWII. Moreover, the Act stated that "the Foundation should be reactivated and all its property in the country should be returned to it while the Foundation itself should also be enabled to claim the recovery of its property outside Polish territory.[303] As can be seen, not all the goals determined by the founder were to be realised since the idea of the indivisibility of the art collection or the building up of resources failed to be continued.

The provisions of the Act of 5 July 2007 amending the earlier Act on the Foundation – the Ossoliński National Enterprise[304] introduced a number of amendments to the Act which reactivated the Enterprise. One concerned the issue of legal succession. It was shown that the Enterprise was the legal successor of the foundation established by Józef Maksymilian Ossoliński. All references to the provisions of the decree of 24 April 1952 on the liquidation of foundations and the decree of the 31 December 1956 on the completion of the provisions liquidating the Enterprise were deleted.[305] It was deemed that the limited succession provided for in the original text of the Act made its scope unclear, which consequently influenced the activities of the Enterprise which sought to recover the assets dispersed in various Polish and foreign museums. It happened too, that when claims were made for the return of individual items of the collection to the Enterprise, the legal capacity of the Enterprise to recover them was questioned. There are, however, institutions in possession of items from the collection that acknowledge the legal succession and are willing to work out solutions that will make the use of items from the Enterprise's collection possible.

---

302 From information received, in 2015 the Enterprise employed about 160 staff which means that apart from its statutory activities it also fulfils the duties of an employer.

303 H. Cioch, *Prawo fundacyjne*, Warszawa 2011, p. 136.

304 Ustawa z dnia 5 lipca 2007 r. o zmianie ustawy o fundacji – Zakład Narodowy imienia Ossolińskich [Act of 5 July 2007 amending the Act on the Foundation – Zakład Narodowy imienia Ossolińskich], Dz. U. 2007, No. 147, item 1029.

305 Dekret z dnia 31 grudnia 1956 r. o uzupełnieniu przepisów o zniesieniu fundacji [Decree of 31 December 1956 on the completion of the provisions liquidating foundations], Dz. U. 1957, No. 1, item 3.

The policy which aimed at bringing together the items from the Ossolinski collection was to be supported by a statutory piece of legislation which stated that the Ossolinski National Enterprise was the only successor of the pre-war Enterprise. It is also worth noting that the restoration of the whole collection did not only mean the recovery of the lost items but also the accessibility to the public of those left in the Ukraine. One of the tasks undertaken to that end in 2004 was the digitalisation of the collection. According to the count in 2015 a total of 4.5 million scans have already been made and the co-operation agreements between the Lvov Library and the Enterprise are regularly renewed.

Pursuant to the provisions of Article 13 of the Act on the Foundation of the Ossoliński National Enterprise, to all matters not regulated in it, the provisions of the Act on Foundations of 6 April 1984 shall apply.[306] Thus, apart from the specific regulations contained in the Act, the Foundation the Ossolinski National Enterprise is subject to the provisions of the Act on Foundations. In the rationale explaining this approach, reference was made to the document signed on 17 September 2002 by the director of the Enterprise and the heirs of Prince Andrzej Lubomirski in which both parties undertook to collaborate in the efforts to restore the Lubomirski Museum within the structures of the Ossolineum Enterprise and to return it to its former splendour as well as to take measures aimed at the recovery of items originally in the Lubomirski Museum collection.[307] The work of the Enterprise in areas such as the determination of the location of individual items of the collection and their ownership status is considerable but unfortunately, despite explicit provisions in the founding acts or the will expressed in the preamble to the Act establishing the enterprise as a public law foundation, not all entities are prepared to respect the ownership *status quo* of the collection, which as a result of Poland's history, is not reflected in the physical possession of its items.[308]

---

306 Ustawa z dnia 6 kwietnia 1984 r. o fundacjach [Act of 6 April 1984 on Foundations], uniform text]Dz. U. 1991, No. 46, item 203 as later amended.

307 *The fate of Lubomirski Dürers. Recovering the Treasures of the Ossoliński National Institute,* Solemn undertaking of 17 September 2002, (eds.) A. Juzwenko, T. Mirecki, Wrocław 2004, p. 22.

308 Rationale. The amended Act of 5 January 1995 on the Foundation – the Ossoliński National Enterprise (Ustawa z dnia 5 stycznia 1995 r. o fundacji – Zakład Narodowy imienia Ossolińskich, Dz. U. No. 23, item 121 and of 2002 No. 153, item 1271) resulted from the need to make substantive and organisational amendments, print 1624.

It was only in January 2015 that, following an agreement between the Ossolinski National Enterprise and the Museum of Literature in Warsaw, many of the state cultural institutions eventually recognised the Enterprise as the factual legal successor. Following an agreement between all interested parties already entered into in 2001, The Museum of Literature finally applied to the Ministry of Culture and National Heritage requesting it to remove the paintings from the Inventory of Musem Collections since they constituted a part of the Ossoliński collection. A relevant decision was issued in 2013.[309] However, some of the exhibits will remain in the Museum pursuant to a civil law agreement entered into with the Ossoliński Enterprise.

The Act of 5 July 2007 amending the Act on the Ossoliński Foundation granted the remaining part of the Ossoliński property to the Ossoliński Enterprise[310] as a manifestation of the will to finalise the unification of the Ossolinski heritage and to "complete the long process of bringing together the property of Józef Maksymilian Ossoliński granted to the Polish nation at the hardest time of its stateless status, and subsequently divided in 1952 into two separate institutions".[311] Additionally, the Enterprise was to receive certain property assets from the Ossolinski Publishing House, once it was partially privatised. These assets were to take the form of dividend deriving from the shares in the Publishing House due to the State Treasury, which the Treasury was to pass over to the Ossoliński Enterprise. This is an example of the history and heritage of a private foundation continued in the form of a public law foundation financed by annual subsidies assigned to carry out its statutory tasks. The Ministry responsible for the Foundation's activities is the Ministry of Culture and National Heritage which has replaced the Ministry of Science and Higher Education as an administrator of budgetary funds. The state subsidy is determined annually as part of the state budget which guarantees a fixed amount

309 *Po 75 latach obrazy z Muzeum Lubomirskich wracają do zbiorów Ossolineum*, http://ossolineum.pl/index.php/po-75-latach-obrazy-z-muzeum-lubomirskich-wracaja-do-zbiorow-ossolineum/ (accessed: 10.06.2015).

310 Ustawa z dnia 5 lipca 2007 r. o zmianie ustawy o fundacji – Zakład Narodowy imienia Ossolińskich [Act of 5 July 2007 amending the Act on the Foundation – Zakład Narodowy imienia Ossolińskich], Dz. U. 2007, No. 147, item 1029.

311 Draft act on the amendments to the act on the foundation – the Ossoliński National Enterprise, Seym of the Republic of Poland, the fifth term of office, Warszawa 23 May 2007, print 1788.

of financing of the Enterprise and its operations, while the form of ownership of the heritage and the continuation of the private enterprise is now public.[312]

Private foundations are a common legal form of bodies engaged in activities in the cultural sphere, especially when the integrality of an art collection is at stake. This is because charters of foundations may contain explicit provisions aimed at securing the inalienability of a collection, while the foundation itself may also be managed in a certain way precisely specified in its charter. The legal form of foundations has been undergoing a certain evolution and its role in the management of the cultural heritage has been increasing. Today, the activities of foundations are regulated in the Act on Foundations.[313] Pursuant to Article 1 of this Act, a foundation may be created for purposes that comply with the fundamental social or economic interests of the Republic of Poland. These include interests inseparably connected with cultural heritage, such as the development of the economy and science, education, art and culture, environmental protection and monument preservation. Foundations may be founded by private individuals or legal persons, or a combination of several of them, by way of a deed (notarial act) or a relevant provision in a will[314] and operate pursuant to rules included in a charter adopted by the founder. The name, seat, assets, purpose and scope of activities to be carried out by the foundation, as well as the composition of its management, its organisation and duties, competences of its members are specified.[315] The founder may provide in the charter for the form of his/her future relationship with the foundation and reserve for himself/herself the right to decide upon its future operations, or include a provision that certain changes in the operations of a foundation

---

312 Unfortunately, the legal form of the Establishment does not allow it to tender since a public law foundation may not be a beneficiary of funds dedicated to entities from a third sector.

313 More on foundations in: P. Suski, *Stowarzyszenia i fundacje*, Warszawa 2011; H. Cioch, *Prawo fundacyjne…*

314 M. Mrówczyński, *Uwarunkowania prawne tworzenia instytucji kultury oraz stowarzyszeń i fundacji prowadzących działalność kulturalną*, in: *Kultura w praktyce. Zagadnienia prawne*, Vol. 2: *Wokół problematyki prawnej zabytków i rynku sztuki*, (eds.) A. Jagielska-Burduk, W. Szafrański, Poznań 2013, p. 80.

315 Verdict of the Appellate Court in Poznań of 18 July 2013, file I ACa 541/13, LEX No. 1363342.

will be contingent upon his/her consent.[316] The founder may also be authorised to alter the charter.[317]

Another reservation that can be made in the charter regards a decision to enlarge or restrict the scope of operations of a foundation or to change completely its statutory activities, which may be made contingent upon the consent of the founder or a person appointed by the founder. If this possibility were made common knowledge, the foundation as a legal form established to support the management of cultural heritage would attract more interest. It should also be stressed that a founder may co-participate in the management of his foundation and as such exercise a wide range of competences. It has been stressed in literature that legislation regarding foundations is relatively basic[318] and the Act on foundations fails to regulate issues related to the founder.[319] Pursuant to the Act the founder may, apart from determining which assets (both movable and immovable) are to be transferred to the foundation, establish contacts with the foundation based upon civil law contracts. A clear cut separation of the founder from the ownership of the foundation property provided for in the Act is responsible for a lack of interest on the part of private entities in managing these assets. And yet, a situation may be envisaged where a foundation established by an owner of a certain portion of heritage has possession of a historic object and

---

316 See the ratio presented in the Resolution of the Supreme Court of 12 April 2007, file III CZP 26/07, LEX 236109: "A possibility of an amendment of such decisions, including decisions concerning the name of the foundation or its carrying out a business activity related to its statutory matters cannot be excluded by amending the charter because since the founding act is an act of law, the interpretation of the statements of will in assessing such possibility will be a decisive factor (Article 65 k.c.). Thus if the interpretation of the statements of will included in the charter and in the founding act allows in a given case for such a possibility, a possibility of a change or amendment of those provisions that exceed the obligatory wording of a founding act specified in Article 3 clause 2 letter f cannot be excluded *a limine*." Such solution was adopted in Article 20 of the Princes Czartoryski Foundation Charter reading: "An amendment to the Charter shall be made by a resolution of the Foundation Council adopted pursuant to Article 14 clause 8 of the Charter and following a consent expressed by the Founder of his Successor."

317 Resolution of the Supreme Court of 24 November 2006, file III CZP 114/06, LEX 198925.

318 M. Mrówczyński, op. cit., p. 83.

319 H. Cioch, *Wpływ orzecznictwa na rozwój prawa fundacyjnego*, in: *Aurea praxis, aurea theoria. Księga pamiątkowa ku czci Profesora Tadeusza Erecińskiego*, (eds.) J. Gudowski, K. Weitz, Vol. 2, Warszawa 2011, p. 2199.

certain collections which, based upon a civil law agreement, it will have to manage. Pursuant to Article 5 clause 2 of the Act on foundations, a founder may decide which minister will be relevant for a given range of activities of the foundation and submit this information to the Registry court.[320]

While the Ossoliński Foundation operates as a public law enterprise, some other foundations operate as private entities. To these belongs the Princes Czartoryski Foundation created in 1991 when the transformation of the political and legal systems allowed the choice of the modern legal form of a foundation originating in the Sieniawa entail already established in the 19th century in the form of a *fideicommissum*.[321] Its collection included Leonardo da Vinci's Lady with an Ermine, one of the most valuable artworks in Poland. The purpose of the Princess Czartoryski Foundation is expressed in Article 6 of its charter which provides that the Foundation is created to preserve the Princess Czartoryski Museum and Library in Kraków as well as the real property constituting the assets of the Foundation in Kraków and Sieniawa, as they are all perceived as an integral and inseparable entity. At the same time the Foundation is to make the collections open and accessible to the public. The terms "integrity of the collections" and "protection of the collection" used in the charter are worthy of note here. Protection as understood today in the frame of the current Act on the Protection and Guardianship of Monuments is an activity in the area of cultural heritage exercised by public entities.

Sometimes, however, protection may not only concern the tangible assets, but may include or apply to the maintenance of a certain *status quo*, where the private and the public elements meet. And indeed, the role of "the advocate of private property", in fact its own collections, was played by the Foundation in the course of discussions on the amendments to the Act on the Protection and Guardianship of Monuments. The work on the amended Act was in practice being carried out by the Ministry of Culture and National Heritage which also prepared a document regulating a new method of entering objects of cultural heritage on the List of National Treasures. No consultations or negotiations with the Princes Czartoryski Foundation or any other private owners or traders in art objects took place, even though the Ministry had planned to include at least two items from the Czartoryski collection in the List. The Princes Czartoryski Foundation's attempts to be included in the legislative work on the new regulation

320 In the documents analysed, the founder's reference to a relevant minister is also included in the wording of the charter.

321 W. Kowalski, *Ochrona integralności zespołów zabytkowych w Polsce – podstawy prawne i praktyka*, "Ochrona Zabytków" 1995, No. 3, p. 251.

failed and it was only after the media published a number of articles describing the situation, and that happened only when the draft legislation was about to be read in the Upper House of the Parliament (the Senate) that the Foundation was included in the parliamentary debate. And so, the Princess Czartoryski Foundation Chairman, Marian Wołkowski-Wolski proposed among other things that at least the entry of an object on the List of National Treasures required the prior consent of its legitimate owner. In doing so, he represented the interests of all private owners of objects or property of historical value as well as other foundations and associations. What should also be noted here is the provision determining the inalienability of the assets specified as a collection belonging to the Princess Czartoryski Museum and Library (as at the inventory of 1939). Such and similar provisions can be traced in charters and other historical documents of other foundations and associations.

Creating a foundation was one of the solutions that private owners resorted to when items of their own property were included in a museum inventory.[322] This gave rise to the Raczyński Foundation at the National Museum in Poznań as well, which was established in 1991. As there was no legislative act that would regulate reprivatisation questions in Poland, the foundation became an example of a middle of the road solution, balancing two interests, the private and the public. At the same time it was an answer to the lack of a systemic resolution of the problem. Unfortunately, not all private owners of objects exhibited in museums sought such a compromise; others, unwilling to create a foundation or chose to settle the matter by taking legal action. Still others opted for an out of court settlement but spent too long negotiating other forms of management of their possession and eventually lost the right to claim the possession back under the limitations principle.

The creation of the Raczyński Library was a solution chosen in respect of the ownership issue of a collection housed at the Wielkopolskie Museum before WWII. It is worth adding here that the taking over of a part of the gallery and furnishings by way of implementing a nationalisation process under a regulatory decision[323] issued in connection with a decree on the enforcement of an

---

322 F. Cemka, *Informacja o pracach związanych z ustawą o reprywatyzacji muzealiów w Polsce*, in: *Zbiory publiczne a kolekcjonerstwo prywatne. Problematyka ochrony dziedzictwa kulturowego w przeszłości i dzisiaj*, (ed.) J. Lipińska, Warszawa 2000, p. 14.

323 Rozporządzenie Ministra Rolnictwa i Reform Rolnych z dnia 1 marca 1945 r. w sprawie wykonania dekretu Polskiego Komitetu Wyzwolenia Narodowego z dnia 6 września 1944 r. o przeprowadzeniu reformy rolnej [Decision of the Minister of Agriculture and Agricultural Reform of 1 March 1945 on the execution of the Decree

agricultural reform,[324] did not only constitute a violation of the law and was outside the scope of the purpose of the agricultural reform, but led to a gap existing till today, regarding the collector – museum relationship, which is also a turning point in the history of Polish museology.

From the very inception of the Raczyński Foundation, the Raczyński collection was managed by private entities, but in close collaboration with public ones. Although it was created as a family foundation, it contains the public element referred to above, which can be seen when it comes to the Foundation's management (the Chairman of the Foundation and the Foundation's headquarters, which is, pursuant to the wording of § 1 of its charter, the National Museum in Poznań).[325] The provision of § 10 of the Foundation's charter provides that each director of the National Museum in Poznań shall act as President of the Foundation. This "personal union" reflects the intention of the founders of the Foundation that the latter collaborate with the Museum. There is a problem though because in the current situatio, the same person performs two functions (those of President of the Foundation and Director of the Museum), which from the point of view of management are the most important functions in these two institutions. This, however, is mitigated to some extent by the fact that the President of the Foundation may represent it in conjunction with another member of the board. And yet, a proposal to separate the holders of these two functions personally had already been put forward in 2000.[326] Pursuant to Article 5 *in fine* of the Act on Foundations, a foundation charter may provide for the creation of other organs of a foundation, other than its board. In the case discussed this organ is the Supervisory Board of the Foundation which plays an advisory and supervisory role to the (Management) Board. The tasks of the Supervisory Board include issuing opinions on the Management's annual reports and, at the request

---

of the Polish National Liberation Committee of 6 September 1944 on the enforcement of an agricultural reform], Dz. U. 1945, No. 10, item 51 as later amended.

324 Dekret PKWN z dnia 6 września 1944 r. o przeprowadzeniu reformy rolnej [Decree of the Polish National Liberation Committee of 6 September 1944 on the enforcement of the agricultural reform], Dz. U. 1945, No. 3, item 13 as later amended.

325 The seat of a foundation referred to in the charter should be a place (town). According to Article 41 of the civil code is the Act or a provision based on such Act do not provide otherwise, the registered office/seat of a legal person is the place at which its managing organ has its seat. In the case of the Raczyński Foundation, the charter incorrectly refers to the National Museum in Poznań (a cultural institution) as the Foundations seat, rather than the city of Poznań.

326 K. Kalinowski, *Fundacja im. Raczyńskich przy Muzeum Narodowym w Poznaniu – model nowej własności historycznej kolekcji*, in: *Zbiory publiczne…*, p. 25.

of the Management, giving an opinion on plans and draft projects of its planned activities. Once again, as can be seen, the composition of the supervisory organ mentioned in the charter is based on a close relationship between the Foundation and the Museum, as the Director of the National Museum (and thus the President of the Management Board of the Foundation), is also a member of the Supervisory Board. Among other functions carried out by the Foundation is one aimed at restoring its former spatial, legal and economic status.[327] A certain inconsistency may be noted when it comes to the functioning of the Supervisory Board in practice, since its meetings may be initiated by the Chairman of the Supervisory Board or President of the Foundation's Management Board (who is also a member of the Supervisory Board). On the positive side, a very good solution is membership of the Supervisory Board of officials connected with certain state entities and NGOs. These people are generally recognised as being influential as regards cultural matters and hold positions that commonly enjoy public confidence.[328]

The fact that the management of the Raczyński collections was widely left to the competences of the National Museum seems to confirm the belief that the activity of a private foundation had been reduced to the rather artificial ownership of the separated part of the collection. Such a solution appears to be compatible with the intention of the founder who most certainly envisaged the close collaboration of interested entities. It may indeed be treated as a bridge solution that formalises in a certain way the legal position of the collection and seemed to be the best possible solution available at the time. What is more, such a solution would not have been possible if it had not been for the will and intention on the part of the founder of the collection who at the time of its establishment was ninety nine years of age.[329] The financial participation of the National Museum in Poznań in the maintenance of the collection was already inscribed in the charter

327 Compare: M. Pietraszak-Dmowski, *Fundacja im. Raczyńskich przy Muzeum Narodowym w Poznaniu*, "Kronika Wielkopolski" 1993, No. 1, p. 80.

328 Pursuant to § 16 of the charter, the composition of the Supervisory Board is as follows: President of the Management Board of the Foundation, representative of the Raczyński family appointed by the Founder and his Legal Successor, President of the Poznań Society of Friends of Sciences, President of the Poznań branch of the Polish Academy of Sciences, Rector of the Adam Mickiewicz University in Poznań, Director of the State Art Collection at the Wawel in Kraków, Director of the Institute of the History of Art in Poznań, Director of the Royal Castle in Warszawa, Director of the National Museum in Kraków.

329 Compare M. Pietraszak-Dmowski, op. cit., pp. 76–78.

of the Foundation at its very inception. Pursuant to § 5 of the Charter, all costs related to the maintenance of the collection and the palace in Rogalin are covered by the National Museum in Poznań. This reservation is of key importance and reflects the financing of the activities carried out by the Foundation. At the same time it also justifies certain provisions of its charter, to equip a private collection with a 'public prosthesis'.

Pursuant to the binding agreements "the care of the collection in its entirety has been vested in the National Museum [...] which is authorised to manage the collection regarding lending, conservation, or licensing its reproduction, albeit in consultation with the Management Board of the Foundation".[330] A collaboration agreement and a deposit contract have been entered into.[331] In the event of objects being lent to other entities, a fee of 1% of the market value of the object (as determined in the insurance policy agreement) is charged. The Foundation, on the other hand, receives part of the revenue generated by tickets sold to the Palace complex in Rogalin. Pursuant to § 5 of the collaboration agreement between the Museum and the Foundation, the latter has the right to refuse its consent regarding the organisation by the Museum of an event deemed unfit for the character of the Palace complex or one which would jeopardise the collection.

Pursuant to § 3 point 6 of its charter, the Foundation conducts business activities as an agricultural holding, an agricultural and food-processing farm as well as a publisher and trader in publications. This model of doing business and generating income, based on agricultural property, is similar to the original organisational structure of the Ossoliński Enterprise. It may even be said that it follows an earlier model with its business part existing alongside the part carrying out the statutory purposes of the Enterprise. However, the actual business operator is not the Foundation, but an entity under the trading name of *Majątek Rogalin* (Rogalin Property) owned by the Foundation and acting as its external operator. In this respect, the operations of the Raczyński collection are similar to the original model in which the cultural function was performed by the art gallery (built in Rogalin in 1912) and the real estate separated from the gallery and pursuing the economic function.

The Founder of the Foundation Edward Raczyński said: "Rogalin [Property] will support the Gallery and the Gallery will support Rogalin [Property]."[332]

330 W. Suchocki, *Fundacja im. Raczyńskich przy Muzeum Narodowym w Poznaniu*, in: *Własność a dobra kultury*, (eds.) G. Czubek, P. Kosiewski, Warszawa 2006, p. 88.

331 The deposit contract and the collaboration agreement were entered into on 26 October 2002 in the wording as earlier agreed.

332 E. Raczyński, *Rogalin i jego mieszkańcy*, Poznań 1991, p. 208.

These words are the best illustration of the mutual benefits arising from the coexistence of the two entities. Rogalin Property is to serve the collection of artworks and the two are to complement each other. The maintenance of the organisation and landscape that surrounds the palace is of predominant importance as it is essential that the spatial environment remains intact and no industrial investments make their presence felt there. This seems to be the key to ensuring the tradition and atmosphere of the place. Rogalin Property currently leases the former property of the Raczyński family from the Agency for the Agricultural Property to which the real property currently belongs.[333] The company's [Rogalin Property's] role continues to be that of facilitating landscape protection, nature conservation and, first and utmost, preservation of the historic significance of the site. In a certain way, the activities pursued by the Wielkopolska monument conservationist who initiated the procedure of entering the historic spatial arrangements of Rogalin real estate in the Register of Historic Monuments are compatible with the statutory assumptions of the company Rogalin Property. However, the decision issued in that regard on 10 December 2014[334] was appealed against by a number of opponents and has therefore not yet come into force.

The reference to the integrity of the property made in the Foundation charter means that it cannot be sold, even if the proceeds from such a sale were to be used for the statutory activity of the Foundation.[335] This provision acquires another dimension in the context of museum collection management and is intended (in the view of some) to act as an instrument blocking the de-accession of the collection observed in some other countries.[336] The requirement to maintain the integrity of the collection applies only to the part brought into the Foundation by the Founder, Edward Raczyński, and the Obrzycko line of the family. It does not apply to the paintings and others objects of art originating in the collections of Wincenty Raczyński and his family (§ 4 letter B point 3 of the charter). The Founder's intention to provide for the inalienability and integrity of the collection was to secure a potential buy-out of the property of Rogalin.

---

333 In 2013 the Foundation applied for a donation to be made by the Real Property Agency requesting a piece of land to be given to the Foundation to help it to exercise its statutory goals.

334 Number of register 945 – Wlkp-A. K.

335 K. Kalinowski, op. cit., p. 25.

336 N. Fyderek, W. Szafrański, *Sprzedaż muzealiów – niewykorzystana szansa czy brak konieczności*, w: *Kultura w praktyce. Zagadnienia prawne*, Vol. 3: *Muzea a rynek sztuki. Aspekty prawne*, (eds.) A. Jagielska-Burduk, W. Szafrański, Poznań 2014, pp. 11–51.

In its recent decisions, while agreeing to the removal of a given object of art from the inventory of museum objects, the Ministry of Culture and National Heritage has always recommended that a civil law agreement be entered into by a museum and the owner of a given object.[337] Such an approach suggests that at least at the ministerial level there is the view that ownership of private property should be respected. Obviously, the decision itself to remove an object of art from the inventory and the Ministry's recommendations that museums should enter into agreements with owners of objects if they wish to exhibit them will not improve matters in that respect immediately, but it is a step in the right direction. The desired model of the relationship between an object owner and a museum is not only subject to legal regulations, but ethical norms as well that bind museums and their managers. The ministerial recommendations like the one mentioned above belong to such ethical norms and are often very precise. In the case of the Raczyński Foundation, the decision to withdraw objects from the inventory of museum objects came second, after the creation of the Foundation.[338] This sequence of actions reflects the Founder's desire to keep the collection in Poland.[339] The negotiations ended successfully and the collection, one of the most important of Polish museum collections, has eventually stayed in the museum, retaining, however, its private ownership status.

Also interesting are foundations created by collectors in recent years. An example of these is the Art Stations Foundation founded by Grażyna Kulczyk or the Kraków Nowosielski Foundation set up by relations of the artist. While the former is a reflection of Grażyna Kulczyk's ideas and passion and enjoys the status of a public benefit organisation, the latter is linked to Galeria Starmach and its owners wish to cointinue Jerzy Nowosielski's work and maintain a database with information on the collection of his works.

The Art Stations Foundation is active in many cultural areas where it either carries out statutory activities as defined in § 6 clause 1 of its charter or engages in its business activities. These activities show how a private institution may successfully combine a number of different forms of cultural activity. Wishing to identify the Foundation's tasks that focus on a broad understanding of cultural heritage management, and without going into a detailed analysis of the meaning of the concepts used in the wording of its charter, the following tasks pursued by

---

337 Decision of 14 November 2013 on permission to delete the collection of the Poznań Society of Friends of Sciences from the inventory of museum objects.

338 Decision of the Minister of Culture and Art to delete a collection from the inventory of museum objects dated 26 June 1995, source: K. Kalinowski, op. cit., p. 24.

339 See M. Pietraszak-Dmowski, op. cit., p. 75 et seq.

the Foundation may be identified: enlarging the collection (accessing Polish and foreign objects of art, purchasing and disposing of art objects, including their acquisition by way of auction, tender or bargaining, maintenance of the resources (collections) including protection of historic cultural and art objects and monument preservation, and improving accessibility organising or helping to organise art exhibitions and fairs).

The Foundation came into being in 2004 and since then has successfully implemented the 50/50 principle, combining in equal proportions art and business. Its operations focus on two activity programmes centred on contemporary and performative art. According to its charter, the Foundation may undertake different types of activities in the field of culture, including running museums, libraries, archives, cultural centres and other cultural bodies. Cultural centres of a multi- profile character, engaged in a variety of types of cultural activity, seem to be the inevitable future of culture management. They help to use the human resources potential better and lead to a better use of the funds assigned for investment in infrastructure.[340] Pursuant to § 8 clause 2 of its charter, the Foundation may engage in business activity itself or may carry it out through separate entities. Their creation and liquidation as well as operating principles are determined by the Foundation Council on a motion put forward by the Foundation's Management Board, following a recommendation by the Programme Council. Thus it appears that the Foundation serves as a springboard for appointing entities related to the Foundation at least in the area of its declared business activities. The wide diversification of business referred to in § 8 clause 1 of the charter, largely identical with the Founder's business, makes the Foundation's activities creditworthy and financially stable.

The Nowosielski Foundation, on the other hand, is linked to the Starmach Gallery and its owners. Its purpose is to continue Jerzy Nowosielski's art and keep a database on the collection. Foundations related to an artist are important from the point of view of the Polish art market because they help transparency. Their role is similar to that performed by agencies engaged in certifying objects of art or publishers of art catalogues as contributors to the reliability of trading in an artist's *catalogue raisonne* works.[341] A good example of this is

340 A. Jagielska-Burduk, W. Szafrański, *Sektor kultury – działalność kulturalna. Wokół problematyki prawnej*, in: *Kultura w praktyce. Zagadnienia Prawne*, Vol. 1, (eds.) A. Jagielska-Burduk, W. Szafrański, Poznań 2012, p. 18.

341 M. Findlay, *Calague raisonné*, in: *Ekspert kontra dzieło sztuki. Rozpoznanie falsyfikatów oraz fałszywych atrybucji w sztukach plastycznych*, (ed.) R. D. Spencer, Warszawa 2009, p. 99.

the Andrzej Wróblewski Foundation which owns the copyright to almost all his works. Through its activity the Foundation not only ensures that Wróblewski's work is not forgotten, but by collaborating in the organisation of exhibitions of his works and the publication of information, it also increases the artist's recognition abroad. At the same time the Foundation spends much time segregating and ordering the work of Wróblewski, an activity that gives it indirectly the status of a 'certifying' agency, authenticating the works of its patron. A similar role in Western Europe is played by the International Foundation for Art Research.[342] Another organisation which to some extent had a similar role was the Pollock-Krasner Foundation Inc., vested with the task of developing Jackson-Pollock's *catalogue raisonne*.[343]

For the participant in activities conducted by a foundation, its ownership structure is irrelevant. It only becomes of importance when the management of an art collection is in question. In a sense, a private collection may be 'serviced' by a dedicated professional entity, although the latter must, in one way or another, be related to the founder. Collection management, however, does not merely mean transferring objects and cultural heritage from one collection to another or separating them to form another collection. It also means using various available legal mechanisms for the purposes of the protection and publicising of a given collection.

Foundations operating in the cultural sector today do not use up all the possibilities which are currently available to them, or rather to persons related to them. Such possibilities arise from the knowledge and understanding of the art sector and its specifics. This is a shame because within or through a foundation, a collector could not only realise his/her cultural plans of collaborating with domestic and foreign entities, but could also use the services or skills of a dedicated foundation which may also act as a professional manager of artworks. And indeed there is no reason why the professional management of objects of art could not constitute one of the objectives of the business conducted by a foundation. Revenues from this type of business could be used for its statutory activities, while services provided externally by experts collaborating with the foundation would enhance its market position.

From the perspective of time, a foundation constitutes a certain link between generations. It expresses the founder's will extending over two or more

342 International Foundation for Art Research – IFAR.

343 The foundation has now stopped issuing opinions about the authenticity or non-authenticity of works.

generations, and aims at achieving a certain purpose determined for certain objects (which, at the same time, belong to a cultural heritage). It is therefore important that there are clear procedural principles which must be followed if a foundation were to be dissolved or its remaining property transferred to another institution of a similar character, or to the care of the State Treasury. A foundation must operate in a manner enabling the fulfilment of its founder's mission, or the continuation of a renewed mission determined by the founder's legal successors. Historically, foundations stemmed from an entail or were created in the 90s of the 20th century to 'take over' the care of collections deposited before WWI. Their mission most frequently called for the indivisibility and integrity of the collection as a whole. Unfortunately, the maintenance of the inseparability of a collection which is frequently composed of objects of varied artistic or historic value is sometimes a difficult or too challenging a task.

The main focus of any foundation ought to be the preservation of cultural heritage for future generations and the dissemination of information on the protected works of art. Where such items are important for the whole national cultural heritage, assistance for their maintenance should also be available from the State. However, while the integrity of a collection is important from the founder's point of view, it is the managers of the collections, i.e. foundations to which collections were transferred, who should be made responsible for the consequences of such decisions.[344] The integrity of a collection is nevertheless an internal matter and cannot be an argument when seeking financing from public funds, if a foundation lacks own funds to provide for its current needs. This is well understood nowadays and therefore charters of foundations created in modern times, when they are based on newly created objects of art, do not contain any references to the inseparability of the collection. Collections are flexible and their objects are transferable. There are also different forms of relation between the foundation and the founder, most of them are based on a civil law agreement, or reflect regulations specified by foundations regarding ownership of objects held in their possession.

Protection of property and succession, important in the private sector, is as important when it comes to cultural heritage. No wonder then that already in the 19th century prospective founders made projections of the legal and economic consequences of possible future decisions and their impact on the stability and durability of a planned foundation, or its possible liquidation. Foundation

---

344 Thus it may be believed that certain provisions regarding donations are not binding any longer due to a substantial change in circumstances.

charters consequently specified liquidation procedures, which was also possible to do by virtue of a decision issued by a registry court. The liquidation principles vary. The charter of the Princes Czartoryski Foundation provided for the hereditary character of the Foundation, while the Arts Stations Foundation envisages the acquisition of the assets by the founder's legal successors, and their further use for purposes specified in the charter. In the case of foundations involved in cultural heritage management, their durability should be given special attention.

Thus, it may be worthwhile considering the appointment of an institution of guarantors to ensure the fulfilment of the founder's will in respect of cultural heritage. The most frequent instrument of control encountered in foundation charters is a collegiate organ called the Foundation Council. This organ is related to the founder or his/her legal successors. Another important aspect from the point of view of reporting and control is reference to a minister relevant to a given foundation or its operations. Such an organ of control, or supervision may not, however, influence the choice of mechanisms of heritage management, or the choice of the most effective ways of disposing of the heritage. Although it is usually the manager who is responsible for deciding upon a solution, the disinterested opinion of an independent expert may be recommended. Those in possession of cultural heritage frequently lack the financial assets to either keep it or to verify existing solutions in respect of the heritage by paying for an expert opinion. An institution intended to evaluate the adopted solutions should have in its composition representatives of both the public and the private sector, while the costs arising from its work should be covered from specifically assigned funds of the budget of the Ministry of Culture and National Heritage.

Summing up, there are two reasons why a collection is moved to a foundation: either a collector decides to move all or part of the collection to a foundation and vest its management with a foundation or appointed agent, or a decision to transfer property to a foundation is a solution adopted in order to solve the ownership status of artworks taken over by the State Treasury. Today, the predominant task of a foundation is to prevent a collection from being dispersed. Unfortunately there are still insufficient legal regulations governing the building up of a collection, and as a result uncertainty as to the succession regulations.[345] A collector builds up a collection in order to save it from disappearance. "What is collecting, after all, if not a fight against dispersal, a process in which fascination,

345 R. Dembska, *Problemy dziedziczenia kolekcji w świetle polskiego prawa spadkowego*, in: *Wokół problematyki prawnej zabytków i dzieł sztuki*, (ed.) W. Szafrański, Poznań 2007, pp. 125–129.

co-incidence and certainty, growing over the years begin to form a certain, albeit imperfect, entity." After all, collecting is, first and foremost, a struggle against dispersal and excess".[346] A foundation may also be another stage in the collecting of objects, before embarking on a new one, an attempt to make the collection available to the public, or it may be a manifestation of a collector's intention to co-participate in the shaping of the art world. When a collection is homogeneous, it may successfully become a copyright manager, certifying objects of art and undertaking activities aiming to publicise an artist's works.

In a foundation, as well as in an Enterprise, the strongest bond is its organisation. Another very important element is a desire to maintain a collection intact and to retain private ownership of historic monuments or real property. Such an approach has its historical rationale in the case of an Enterprise, and reflects social and economic reasons in the case of a private law foundation. The principle of securing the cultural heritage includes restricted rights to its free disposal. All these make a foundation (and in the past an Enterprise) a strong pillar of contemporary and future cultural heritage management. Against the background of other scenarios of collection management, a foundation is the most appropriate way of realising the vision of a private individual i.e. the owner of the heritage. However, ensuring its organisational continuity requires financial back-up and in the case of larger organisations also the employment of staff, which means that despite its obvious good points, a foundation is seldom the choice of collectors or owners of artworks.

Fideicommissum *(entail)*

In modern history, the institution of a *fideicommissum* in many European states and the almost equivalent entail in Poland played an important role. Polish families considered placing their property "under the care of a special protective law"[347] as a proper way of maintaining their property. By creating these institutions owners of cultural heritage participated, in a way, in the development of a cultural policy to be followed by private individuals. It may even be said that these forms of securing the protection of private collections were among the first manifestations of an organised process of collecting objects of historical and cultural importance. These collections were important in their time and influenced future generations as being the first attempts make private collections available

346 J. Stelmach, *Uporczywe upodobanie. Zapiski kolekcjonera*, Olszanica 2012, p. 19.

347 E. Maliszewski, *Ordynacye polskie (Dokończenie)*, "Ziemia. Tygodnik Krajoznawczy Ilustrowany", 7 May 1910, p. 292.

to the public, giving rise to the development of private and public museology and art collecting. The mechanism of conscious cultural heritage management which subsequently developed was based on those first legal institutions primarily created to confirm the importance of a given family, and help it to maintain social position and prestige. The institutions of *fideicommissum,* and an entail are almost identical, showing many similarities and similar solutions. A family *fideicommissum* and an entail, as well as other entities such as a trust substitution, or a *primogeniture* were "institutions essentially identical although taking different forms depending on the time, place and circumstances in which they originated".[348]

As studies point out, "*fideicommissum* denoted a broader meaning than an entail, as it included *primogeniture* as well as *ultimogeniture*".[349] The term 'entail' that originally denoted an act establishing the special status of a certain part of a property or estate was later also understood as a specific piece of property determined in the charter of an entail, e.g. the Gołuchów entail[350]. A family estate, on the other hand, or an entail estate, was meant to denote "a property which pursuant to a legal act drawn up by its founder, ought to remain indivisible and inalienable, and which all members of a given family were to use in the order specified in charters".[351] Pursuant to the wording of Article 1 clause 2 of the Act of 13 July 1939 on the liquidation of family entails[352] a family entail was understood as any disposition by virtue of which a specified part of a family estate was to constitute an inalienable property of the family and be maintained for all, or at least most future generations, through either an appointed supervisory authority exercising competences over the estate, or by restricting the owner's rights to dispose of the property and creating entails, *fideicommissum, primogeniture* as well as *ultimogeniture.*

In Poland, the term *fideicommissum,* which originated in Germany, was often used interchangeably with an entail. Polish entails originally aimed at separating a piece of land from the whole estate, to serve economic or political purposes.

---

348 K. Sójka-Zielińska, *Fideikomisy familijne w prawie pruskim (w. XIX i pocz. w. XX)*, Warszawa 1962, p. 8.

349 A. Mełeń, *Ordynacje w dawnej Polsce*, Lwów 1929, p. 22.

350 Ibid. p. 21.

351 *Encyklopedia podręczna prawa prywatnego*, założona przez H. Konica, [Reference Encyclopaedia of Private Law by H. Konic], (eds.) F. Zoll, J. Wasilkowski, Vol. 2, Warszawa 1936, p. 1222.

352 Ustawa z dnia 13 lipca 1939 r. o znoszeniu ordynacji rodowych [Act of 13 July 1939 on the liquidation of family entails], Dz. U. 1939, No. 63, item 417.

As the cultural identity and wealth of landowners increased, the separated parts of real estate had been enriched with movables as well, such as objects of art, or, ultimately, museum collections. This trend continued over the years and was intended to create "*splendour familiae* to be achieved by pursuing numerous individual tasks. For example, the document creating the Gołuchów entail emphasised the political role of the family expressed in the following wording: "By creating an entail we create a guarantee that certain historic families burdened with **higher duties** (authors' emphasis) whom society sees as leaders, will not lose their economic base, so indispensable for taking up an appropriate position or office. Society considers it the duty of large landowners to create *primogenitures* and secure our ownership of these lands."[353] The "higher duties" mentioned above were not only placed in an economic context, but also in the service of cultural development.[354] Not all such initiatives were successful and not all entails lasted long.[355] The creation procedure required double approval issued by a state authority, one called a permit and the other endorsement (*pozwolenie* and *aprobacja*). The former was granted by the king and then by the Sejm whereas the latter was issued by the Sejm following the adoption of a legislative act establishing an entail. It is worth noting that the procedure requiring a preliminary permit (promise) before an entail was created was of a similar significance as the contemporary promise issued under administrative law.[356] Sometimes the required endorsement of the validity of an entail was merely implied and then taken for granted.

Another important requirement was that the provisions of the founding act quoted in the permit complied with the purpose of the institution itself. However, final endorsement could be granted exceptionally event if an entail was created somewhat differently than strictly according to the wording of the permit.[357] The entail would consist of immovables and movables. Among the latter were, apart from the equity, also items of heritage such as: "family treasures (jewelry, valuable clothes) weapons, collections (of objects of art), libraries, or even elements

353 Document on the creation of an entail of Princes J. O. Czartoryski Family, BPP, ms. 845, sheet 14 verte.

354 More in: P. Dąbkowski, *Prawo prywatne polskie*, Vol. I, Lwów 1910, pp. 36–39.

355 E. Maliszewski, op. cit., p. 278.

356 M. Stahl, *Przyrzeczenie publiczne (administracyjne)*, in: *Prawo administracyjne. Pojęcia, instytucje, zasady w teorii i orzecznictwie*, (ed.) M. Stahl, Warszawa 2013, pp. 482–486.

357 A. Mełeń, op. cit., pp. 19–32.

of furniture from family palaces".[358] One restriction was that an entail could not consist of movables only. The movables had to be listed separately. The draft of the Gołuchów entail founding act provided that "an accurate inventory of all movables was needed if they are to be included in the *primogeniture*".[359] This requirement was necessary since the main purpose of entails set up during the partition was to protect Polish property from being confiscated (by the partitioning powers).

Among other duties, a *fideicommissum* or an entail manager, the latter also called *ordinatus* (Polish *ordynat*), was obliged to administer the real estate, maintain the military force, ensure financial support to particular members of the family, e.g. widows of the former *ordinatus*, his brothers or other persons named in the charter. Much attention was devoted to movable property referred to as: works of art, collections of art and monuments. Despite the absence of a formal statute that would provide for the differences in the meaning of the above terms, it is clear that differences among them existed and were recognised. The ownership of both institutions always remained private.

The ownership of a Polish *fideicommissum*, or an entail, has been widely researched, especially regarding the rights of the *ordinatus*, the 'expectators' (other members of the family), and the entire family. As the findings suggest, entail ownership could originally be shared by an *ordinatus* regarded as one with a right *in rem* to the property of another (ownership in use), and the expectators who were considered owners (supreme ownership). Some time later, the ownership right was vested in the *ordinatus*, but his right *in rem* was substantially limited. Under Austrian and Prussian law the view that eventually prevailed supported the shared ownership approach. This solution was also in line with the stipulation that the unity of a family should be secured.[360] It should be added though that while, according to the Austrian civil code, the right of use and utility (*dominium utile*) due to the *fideicommissum* manager (*ordinatus*) corresponded to the right of *dominium directum* due to the remaining members of the family, the Prussian civil code provided for the right of use and utility of the *ordinatus*, leaving the supreme ownership to the whole family, while a family constituted a separate legal entity. In the 20th century it was believed that the construction of the ownership in use of an *ordinatus* is closer to the limited right *in rem*.[361]

358 Ibid. p. 33.

359 Draft of the Gołuchów Entail founding charter, BPP, ms. 845, sheet 19.

360 K. Sójka-Zielińska, op. cit., pp. 72–79.

361 *Encyklopedia podręczna prawa prywatnego…*, p. 1226.

The legal status of an entail had its practical aspect as well. For example the Revenue Office in Jarosław, when determining income tax due from taxpayers, treated an entail as a legal person. At the same time it stated that "throughout all legislation applicable in the Republic of Poland this institution demonstrated common fundamental features".[362] The earlier legal structures of an entail never quite fell into any category of tax. Following the *per analogiam* reasoning, it was claimed that an entail family had very similar characteristics to those of a university which "acquires the 'character' of a legal person when it acts as an independent legal entity, but in all other cases it is a constituent element of the State Treasury".[363] In the case of the Sieniawa entail (also called the Sieniawa *fideicommissum*) its property belonged to the family, while the use of the property always belonged to its *ordinatus* (i.e. an individual). It was then deemed that for tax purposes the entail will be regarded as a legal person generating income and with organs such as a council, a manager (*ordinatus*) or a curator, although there are no reasons why the same entail could not be treated in all other aspects as an item of property owned by the *ordinatus*. Similar discussions arose when the information of the owner of the entail or his property were to be entered in the land and mortgage register.[364]

When it comes to the purpose of entails, we notice a public aspect: their objects included a will to make the cultural heritage available to the public and to ensure the indivisibility of a collection. A *fideicommissum* whose creation underlay a plan that one day it be turned into a private museum most certainly had such a public character. An example may be Prince Władysław Czartoryski, founder of the Czartoryski Museum in Kraków and owner of the Lambert Hotel in Paris, whose efforts to create an entail came to a successful end after his death.[365] And then the press also played a role as numerous articles called for "securing the existence of collections that were known in and valuable for Galicia, and therefore Austria as well".[366] Similarly, the attempts commenced in 1883 to create the Izabela Czartoryska Gołuchów entail, ended successfully ten years

362 Letter of advocate Jerzy Łoziński of 12 July 1939, Czartoryski Library, ms. 7619.

363 Ibid.

364 *Encyklopedia podręczna prawa prywatnego...*, p. 1226.

365 A detailed background of the creation of the entail can be found in: J. Nowak, *Ordynacja sieniawska książąt Czartoryskich. Plany – zamierzenia – realizacja*, "Rocznik Biblioteki Naukowej PAU i PAN w Krakowie" 2000, p. 121–148.

366 *Ordynacja imienia książąt Czartoryskich* [Entail named after Princes Czartoryski], "Głos Narodu", 13 November 1896.

later.[367] And yet, these examples do not mean that conscious management of cultural heritage was the predominant concern of drafters of entail charters. These had to provide for many other important aspects of the operation of a museum, from settling its internal affairs, disposition of proceeds earned from the entail, the function of the curator and the duties of the council, the order of succession, forfeiture of the status of an *ordinatus* and appointment of a new one to acquire the former's rights, or the *ordinatus* obligation to continue the memory of the deceased of the family.

The principles governing the disposal of elements of a collection were of the essence from the point of view of the integrity of the collection and the security of privately owned objects. In the case of a German *fideicommissum*, the limitation period clause did not apply, while in the case of a Polish entail, the unauthorised disposal of some property could be deemed ineffective and the *ordinatus* could be called to return the sold elements to the estate.[368] The document containing a report on the preparatory work before the Sieniawa entail was created states that the legal effect of the inclusion of the collection in the entail property meant that the collection "may be kept in the city of Kraków or within the boundaries of our monarchy for ever" which further meant that when inherited, the collection could not be sold or taken abroad by any heir, as such an act would constitute an "irreparable loss".[369]

Entails guaranteed the surest and most efficient management of property that was available at the time of their creation. With the passage of time, however, the requirement of the inseparability of the property did not fit in with the market and the developing economy. This problem had already been noted in the 19th century when an entail could not take out a bank loan if not secured by its assets, e.g. real estate. Consequently, the investing capability of the entail manager was quite limited.[370] It may be worthwhile to quote here Adam Smith, a representative of economic liberalism who referred to this situation, saying that "ownership of contemporary generations has to be (now) [...] regulated in a way that it accounts for the caprice of those who died, maybe, 500 years ago".[371] The only changes in a property once set

367 See R. Kąsinowska, *Gołuchów. Rezydencja magnacka w świetle źródeł*, Gołuchów 2006, pp. 112–114.
368 A. Mełeń, op. cit., p. 38.
369 Summary of the work on the entail, following the submission of documents required by the law 1891, Czartoryski Library, 7294.
370 Quoted after K. Sójka-Zielińska, op. cit., pp. 122–123.
371 A. Smith, *Badania nad naturą i przyczynami bogactwa narodów*, Vol. 1, Warszawa 1954, p. 491 quoted after K. Sójka-Zielińska, op. cit., p. 136.

apart and made into an entail were possible by passing a new law, unless there were a change in state borders (due to e.g. warfare). These early solutions and resulting restrictions seemed anachronic and some suggested that a change was needed to meet the challenges of a developing economy.

As stated above, the primary purposes for which entails were created included the proper management of family land, efforts to protect it from being broken up and continuous additions to the collection. Later on these purposes included collecting objects of art and other elements of cultural heritage, with the same idea of preserving them from dispersal. This had to be accompanied by the development of legal solutions regulating ownership of landed property and objects of artistic value added to the original entail collection. The main objective of entails created in the 19th century, apart from the protection of family property, was the protection of art collections (e.g. The Princes Czartoryski entail in Gołuchów or the Sieniawa entail). The decision on which objects of cultural heritage should be included in the two entails was conscious and not accidental. The same objects were later listed in the Schedule to the Act on the liquidation of family entails (1939) as those important for the national culture or as having value as archives, library and museum collections. What is more, their history, although influenced by different legal systems (Prussian in the case of the Czartoryski entail in Gołuchów later transformed into the Gołuchów entail, and Austrian in the case of the Sieniawa entail of Princes Czartoryski, later transformed into the Sieniawa entail) were in the interwar period (1919–1939) administered by Adam Ludwik and Maria Ludwika Czartoryski, since the former took over management of the entail after the death of his brother, Witold Czartoryski, the first Gołuchów *ordinatus*.[372]

As can be seen from the above, the determination of which movable property should be included in an entail property was of key importance. Article 2 of the Princes Czartoryski Museum charter provided for the main task of each *ordinatus* to "preserve and maintain" the integrity of the entail, whereas Article 7 of the same charter determined the way in which the collection was to be specified, and provided a relevant list of objects. This list was to constitute an integral part of the main inventory of the entail. Other items of the entail property were to be listed in a court inventory kept for the entail. The Gołuchów Entail charter in § 1 clause 7 makes reference to constituent elements of the entail, which include all pieces of furniture, objects of art, paintings, engravings, silverware and porcelain housed in the Gołuchów Castle and listed in an appendix entitled

372 J. Nowak, op. cit., p. 152.

"Collections of art objects of Countess Izabela Działyńska nee (Princess) Czartoryska, at Gołuchów Castle",[373] except for the library which was to remain as allodial property.

The provisions in the Czartoryski entail charter regarding the prohibition of the alienation of its movable property are worthy of note. The inalienable objects were those gathered in the Princes Czartoryski Museum in Kraków.[374] Article VIII of the entail charter provided that none of the *ordinatus* was allowed to deplete the collection left in his care. In the event of damage or loss to the property, each subsequent *ordinatus* was obliged to seek to obtain appropriate compensation for the missing part of the collection from the *ordinatus* responsible for the depletion. Every five years after the first *ordinatus* took up management of the entail, the existing *ordinatus* was obliged, at his own cost, to order an inventory of all the movable and immovable property, and note down all losses or damage identified. The integrity of the Gołuchów entail property as a whole was provided for in § 4 of its charter in which reference was made to that property as being indivisible and left for the sole use of each subsequently appointed *ordinatus*. In a similar way as in the case of the Sieniawa entail, every five years a review of the entail property was to be carried out, and a relevant report submitted to its committee. The committee was vested with the task of restoring the property to its original state either by implementing direct measures or taking legal action.

Additions to the property were also envisaged. In the case of the Princes Czartoryski Museum, a revenue of 200, 000 marks (as specified in the charter) was to be devoted to enlarging the Museum collection and to activities supporting learning and liberal arts.[375] What is interesting is that the charter of the Gołuchów entail was silent on the obligation to add new objects to the collection and only provided for its maintenance (§ 13 clause 4). Although a special requirement to that end was considered, it was eventually decided to leave the wording of § 12 clause 2 of the draft charter which provided that the *ordinatus* was obliged to "use at least 2% of the net profit for protecting, making up for losses, and maintaining and administering the museum". At least 4% of the revenues generated by the entail, i.e approx. 4 000 marks was therefore to be assigned for the needs of the museum and

---

373 Charter of the entail (family *fideicommissum*) of Princes Czartoryski in Gołuchów, Fast printing house, J. Szczeciński, Kalisz 1933, Archiwum MNP.

374 K. Zalasińska, op. cit., p. 39.

375 Errichtungsurkunde des Furstlich Czartoryski'chen Familien-Fideicommisses. Ustanowa Ordynacyi rodzinnej Książąt Czartoryskich, Kraków, printed by W. L. Anczyc i Sp., Kraków 1898; K. Kościński, *Polskie ordynacye i związki rodzinne ze szczególnem uwzględnieniem ordynacyi książąt Sułkowskich*, Poznań 1906, p. 41.

was believed to be sufficient for maintaining its resources.[376] The above shows how from the very beginning there had been varying concerns underlying the creation of an entail: while the former (Sieniawa) was meant to initiate a national collection, the latter (Gołuchów) was meant to make accessible the existing collection of national heritage, the composition of which was specifically determined by the founder. Thus the Gołuchów collection was perceived as a collection constituting a whole and tied to the person of the collector while the Czartoryski Museum was from the start meant to function as a living organism, attempting to be independent of its founder. What happened in practice though was that new elements were also added to the existing collection but at no extra cost, using only the funds assigned in the charter for its maintenance.

Pursuant to the draft charter of the Gołuchów entail and the provision of its § 12 clause 1, an *ordinatus* was to insure Gołuchów castle, the Museum and the immovable. In the event of there being no insurance company or of a refusal on the part of an insurer to insure the property, 2% of the net profit of the entail was to be transferred annually to an entail insurance fund specifically created. It is noteworthy that in the first drafts of the charter, the obligations towards the property of historic importance were mentioned as of first and foremost importance, whereas concern for the welfare for the members of the family came second.[377] This provision was absent from the final draft of the charter, though. Today, insurance of the national heritage collection and securing it from theft are among the main responsibilities of the state when it comes to the protection of the national cultural heritage.[378] Each owner of an item of national heritage is obliged by statute to take measures to protect and secure the objects owned. In the case of a public collection it is the state and in the case of a private collection, private owners.

Each of the entails discussed above had an audit system appointed to control the state of the property and, indirectly, the activity of an *ordinatus* towards the entail. The Sieniawa entail had a Council composed of three members whose deputies or replacements were to be appointed following a procedure provided for in the entail charter. The Council was to be convened for annual ordinary meetings or more frequently, when need be.[379] Its tasks included among other

376 Draft of the Gołuchów Entail founding charter, BPP, ms. 845, 30/II.

377 Draft of the Gołuchów Entail founding charter, BPP, ms. 845, sheet 30–32.

378 For more on the origin of monument insurance see I. Gredka, *Ubezpieczenia dóbr kultury w muzeach i zbiorach prywatnych*, Kraków 2013, pp. 103–105 and literature reports quoted therein.

379 If a meeting of the entail council were difficult to convene, a decision could be taken by circulation by sending letters to members of the Council who would approve

things making sure that the *ordinatus* has "duly performed his obligations towards the Princes Czartoryski Museum". The Entail Council had a right to participate in the making of inventories. Where discrepancies were found, it was its duty to inform the court with proper jurisdiction over it and pass a motion for taking remedies to rectify the situation. The Gołuchów entail had two audit organs: the entail committee and the curator. While the composition of the former was recommended in the charter, the following compositions were made pursuant to the choice made by the descendants of the entail, in the order as provided for in § 17 of the charter. The curator was appointed by the entail committee whose members were representatives of the family. The curator, being a supervising entity, received regular remuneration and shared his observations and opinions with the entail committee. In this way the entail founder's intention to separate the actual and professional control from the control of the 'family' represented by members of the committee was achieved. This approach was reflected in the wording of the entail charter that "a certain curator is needed, who could attend to the technicalities of the work performed by the entail Council and who could also supervise the activities of the *ordinatus*".[380] Members of the entail Council, likewise the members of the committee had to be persons of unblemished character, and additionally, those sitting on the Council had to be at least thirty years of age, able to prove their ability to manage their own property, while members of the committee were required to enjoy full civic rights and reside in Europe.

The principles according to which museums were to be managed were clearly specified in the charters of entails. Sometimes they restricted the *ordinatus's* competences and required the formal approval of the entail council.[381] An interesting situation occurred when there were plans to move the collection from the Gołuchów Museum to the Działyński Palace in Poznań. One of the justifications for the decision was the fact that "the museum treasures kept in Gołuchów were intended by the founder to be freely accessible to the public but "because of poor communications failed to fulfil that requirement".[382] Whereas, it was claimed,

---

their contents. An example here being Letter of 15 November 1938 to the Chairman of the Entail Council of the Princes Czartoryski Entail in Sieniawa, Prince Witold Czartoryski, requesting release from the entail of certain plots of land, Czartoryski Library, ms. 7619, IV.

380 Draft of the Gołuchów Entail founding charter, BPP, ms. 845, sheet 36.

381 To the high entail council of the Princes Czartoryski Entail in Gołuchów of 30 January 1904 (copy), BPP, ms. 902, sheet 120.

382 Ibid.

"having a *pied-à-terre* in Poznań, the Count *ordinatus* will have more opportunities of staying in the Duchy (of Posen) and getting closer to our society thus building up Public life in Poznań".[383] After an analysis of the removal project it was decided that "the charter and the will of the founding countess was not an obstacle hindering the transfer of the collection to another entail palace".[384] This decision and the removal procedure needed, however, to be endorsed by the entail council and were also subject to the opinion of the curator of the entail.

The collection was moved to Poznań and occupied the some floors and the attic of the palace. Apart from the space offered for the collection of objects of arts moved from Gołuchów, there was another exhibition hall available and adjacent to it two reading rooms, one for scholars and one for the general public. The collection of the Kórnik Library was put into a building nearby.[385] Thus two cultural institutions, a museum and a library, were to be combined, their operations to be put under joint management, including the management of their financial affairs.[386] This was an idea conceived in the first years of the 20th century, but very close to the model desired today, when the common management of different forms of cultural activity is believed to be the answer to better cost efficiency. The "Common Budget of the Museum and the Library"[387] envisaged one director common for both institutions, two specialist staff, a museum conservator, a librarian and their assistants. The expenses projected in the budget were 8000 marks for each institution whereas their common budget totalled 150 000 marks. It was decided to assign 32% of the budget for the purchase of objects of art, the organisation of exhibitions, lectures, preparation of catalogues (the Museum) as well as for books, periodicals, and the publication of its own journals (the Library). This part of the project is very interesting and valuable as it provides accurate information on the allocation of costs and expenditure, broken up into

383 Ibid.

384 Project to remove the Gołuchów Museum to the Działyński Palace in Poznań as presented to me, Brussels 21.02.1908, BPP, ms. 906, sheet 117.

385 Ibid.

386 A. Jagielska-Burduk, W. Szafrański, *Sektor kultury…*, p. 18.

387 Project to remove the Gołuchów Museum…, sheet 118/II. The Author proposed to resign as the main director and initially to commence collaboration with Feliks Jasiński, and to make available an exhibition hall in which he would be able to exhibit his own collection of contemporary Japanese art, in consideration of 3000 marks per year to use for the maintenance of the museum. This collection, shown together with the Gołuchów collection would give the museum a universal and unique character in Poland.

maintenance of the estate, personnel and current running costs. The budget of the following year was accepted for a total of 30 000 marks to be spent on the running of the Museum. Unlike the previous budget, however, this one lacked detailed recommendations on how the funds ought to be spent.[388] What must be emphasised though, is the will expressed by Count Władysław Zamoyski and Prince Witold Czartoryski likewise, to participate to a similar extent in the financing of new objects.[389] And although the plan to combine the two institutions never materialised, the very fact that such advanced negotiations to that end did take place is the best proof that noble and aristocratic families were seriously and positively interested in ensuring the public character of the collections they had built.[390] Some charters, for example the charter of the Sieniawa entail, apart from appointing persons obliged to supervise the entire entail, appointed a curator with the specific duty of looking after the museum collection. In that, the curator's function was similar to that played by the *fideicommissum* court.[391]

In the event a hereditary line ending, the continuity of the entail management was bound to be broken. Envisaging such options, founders provided for remedies and appointed in charters other persons to whom management of the entail estate would pass. In the case of the Sułkowski entail, upon the end of the Sałkowski family line, the management of all the estate, and all the movable and immovable property as well as the revenues they generated were to be passed on to the Commission of National Education with a view to supporting its activities.[392]

An example of 20th century legislative interference in the regime of an existing entail was the Act of 13 July 1939 on the liquidation of family entails. However, the liquidation of entails that were related to institutions of significance to national culture was quite complicated and their liquidation required the consent of the Council of Ministers. The Decree of 8 October 1944 introducing a new tax law[393]

---

388 Project to remove the Gołuchów Museum…, sheet 178.

389 Proof that still, almost within the scope of Project No. 2 is a budget for the joint removal of the Gołuchów Museum to the Działyński Palace next to the Kórnicka Library, BPP, ms. 906, sheet 176.

390 S. K. Potocki, *Miejsce Biblioteki w Koncepcjach Fundacji Kórnickiej*, "Pamiętnik Biblioteki Kórnickiej" 1978, Issue 14, pp. 151–153.

391 Document: Legal opinion prepared by attorney Dr Józef Skąpski of 6 September 1949, Czartoryski Library, ms. 13224.

392 A. Meleń, op. cit., p. 59, K. Kościński, op. cit., p. 24. In the absence of a relevant provision the property was to pass on to the legal heirs of the last ordinatus.

393 Dekret z dnia 8 października 1946 r. Przepisy wprowadzające prawo spadkowe [Decree of 8 October 1946. Provisions implementing succession law], Dz. U. 1946, No. 60, item 329.

repealed the Act on the liquidation of family entails with the exclusion, however, of those listed in Article IV point 4, again with some exceptions. According to the legislator, leaving those exceptions did not, violate "the provisions of the Decree of 6 September 1944 on the acquisition of certain forests by the State Treasury, or the provisions of the Act of 3 January 1946 on the State Treasury taking over ownership of the fundamental sectors of the national economy, or any other legal regulations pursuant to which the State may expropriate property, impose enforced management or introduce other restrictions of ownership or the right of possession".[394] At the same time Article XXIII § 1 liquidated family entails of all types: family trusts, *maioratus*, family *fideicommissum*, *primogeniture* as well as *ultimogeniture* and the like. Where an entail was related to a foundation, the foundation authorities could alter in the founding charter of the foundation those provisions which applied to the liquidation of the entail. The legal opinion on that regulation prepared by Dr Józef Skąpski in 1949 read that "all the property passes to the unrestricted ownership of the minor heirs of the last *ordinatus*".[395]

Museums established within an entail fulfilled their public function by opening to the general public and exhibiting their collections. By making their collections widely accessible, museums, supported in this by members of entail families, realised a policy aimed at ensuring public access to cultural property, which in the 20th century became a constitutional norm. However, running a museum was only one of the many activities of a broader cultural institution, and from the economic point of view it was not necessarily beneficial to the other elements of the institution, apart from those involved in managing cultural heritage. Thus the above quoted view expressed by Adam Smith may once again be recalled, and we may say that, looking at it today and having regard to the particular significance of national heritage objects owned by contemporary generations who inherited them, these objects may continue to be regulated in accordance with the will of a previous generation. What is more, such stability of regulation would indeed be very advantageous in certain fields. The introduction of a *fideicommissum* was the beginning of a road taken to find the best legal regulations for property management and for serving a public purpose. Choices of legal regulations were determined by the laws binding at a given time, and were also influenced by the political situation. For example, in the mid 19th century, when the process of Germanisation in the Duchy of Poznań intensified, Tytus Działyński decided that the private status of his collection

394 Ibid.
395 Document: Legal opinion prepared by attorney Dr Józef Skąpski…

would be a better and safer solution. Therefore he did not support the creation of a collection by the Poznań Society of the Friends of Science, regarding it an uncertain undertaking, and a possible object of annexation by the Prussian authorities.[396] The complicated procedures for creating an entail and changing attitudes to such Polish initiatives in the Austrian-Hungarian Empire and Prussian Empire,[397] plus the fact that the economic conditions in those lands were not favourable, caused Polish noble families who owned items of cultural hertitage to establish family based entities, or look for other ways of protecting their collections. Unlike Tytus Działyński, the Mielżyński family wished to collaborate with the Poznań Society of the Friends of Science in finding the best way to protect their collection. However, because the Society needed to procure a permit to acquire real property to organise a museum, Mielżyński's heirs decided to set up a company under the name Mielżyński, Kurnatowski & Co, make the necessary investment and then collaborate with the Poznań Society of the Friends of Science. The museum was opened in a building that the company purchased in its name. This arrangement with the Society allowed the Mielżyński heirs to realise their business plans (purchasing a building) and plans to support a cultural project based on organising a museum in which the collection could be exhibited.[398]

There were other attempts at collaboration with public bodies in the process of creating institutions with a public dimension, but remaining private as a part of an entail. In 1847 the Kraków authorities granted a plot of land situated in the centre of the city to Prince Władysław Czartoryski for museum purposes. It is interesting from today's point of view to learn what Kraków expected from the Prince in return. And so, Prince Czartoryski was obliged to restore a fragment of the city wall, investing in the work a certain specified sum, although he was not obliged to maintain that wall in the future. After a longish process of negotiation, the real estate for a museum was eventually included in the entail property[399] which finally could develop further. The good will on the part of the Kraków authorities to collaborate on a cultural heritage project initiated by Prince Czartoryski is worth noting. This and other similar examples of

396 S. K. Potocki, op. cit., p. 146.

397 K. Maliszewski, op. cit., p. 291.

398 A. Jagielska-Burduk, W. Szafrański, M. A. Górska, op. cit., pp. 24–25.

399 J. Nowak, op. cit., p. 135. Copy of a land and mortgage book, 60 documents, Czartoryski Library, ms. 7147 IV, Contract entered into by the Kraków Municiplity and JO Władysław Czartoryski, Czartoryski Library, ms. 7147 IV, "Czas" [Time] 17 October 1887, Czartoryski Library, ms. 7147.

public-private collaboration, such as supporting private initiatives with public funds, are exceptionally important today. It is a shame that the existing legal regulations do not always permit such collaboration, or prevent it from being successful. Similar private-public projects could also be conducted with partial financing from the budget, e.g. local authorities (in Poland, territorial units of self-government). Nowadays, public-private projects do not always end in success. As an example can be given a never realised proposal made by Grażyna Kulczyk, to set up a museum in the vaults of Stary Browar in Poznań, which upon its completion would be maintained in the future by the city.[400]

The following Table contains a summary of the pros and cons of an entail as a legal form of institution operating in the field of cultural heritage management. A similar assessment, although of global character, was made in the past, before the Gołuchów entail was created.

Negative aspects of an entail	**Detailed problem, Possible solution**
Financial issue, formation costs – court fee (stamp duty)	4%
Fear that a childless *ordinatus* might not be much concerned about the future of the entail	This could be regulated in the charter
Political conditions	Contingent upon procurement of permits from public authorities
Concerns related to the financial situation of the family of an *ordinatus* (siblings, mother and the widow of the former *ordinatus*)	Provisions to that end could be made in the charter
Requirement to tie the *ordinatus* to Gołuchów	This requirement was eventually not included in the charter. It was suggested that the *ordinatus* should stay 3 months each year on the Gołuchów estate, and if he failed to do so, 10% of the net profit was to be paid to the '*minorat*' fund

Source: own analysis (A. J.-B.) based on the draft charter and founding act of the Gołuchów Entail. Outline information on the formation of the Princes Czartoryski family entail, BPP, RKP 845, sheet 14–17, Draft document of the formation of the Gołuchów Entail, BPP, RKP 845, sheet 18–36.

400 J. Miliszkiewicz, *Interview with Grażyna Kulczyk*, "Santander Art and Culture Law Review" 2015.

As can be seen, the problematic areas included the rather high cost of stamp duty upon the founding of an entail and personal issues, as well as the political environment. Some of the risks were possible to eliminate by appropriate provisions written into the charter, others were beyond the control of the founders and entities collaborating with entails. All in all, it can be said that an entail chosen as one of the possible mechanisms of managing cultural heritage always had to operate in compliance with the legal regulation of its external environment, and was also subject to the conditions arising from the political environment.

Another reservation, at times quite burdensome, was the requirement of the integrity of a collection as a whole, which meant that its individual elements could not be traded in or otherwise disposed of, or exchanged for others. The experience gained when the Gołuchów collection was moved to Poznań, highlighted the importance of the charters and their provisions, and of making sure that they are so drafted that amendments will always be possible, should circumstances change. Many entails were created predominantly to ensure that the collections would remain property in Polish hands. Before WWI as well as in the interwar period, the political situation was uncertain and there was a fear that the partitioning powers or foreign governments might interfere with private property or property entrusted to foundations and societies. Hence attempts to find safer or more efficient solutions. Options were weighed whether to leave property totally in the private hands of families or perhaps as the property of a Society, but only such a Society that could not be taken over by a public authority of a different state as a result of a military action. What should be remembered is that an entail was frequently composed of real estate situated on the territory of different states, or different parts of Poland under different partitions, and subject to different legal regulations.

As can be read in certain source documents, when the collection of Princes Czartoryski was mentioned in the context of Prince Władysław Czartoryski's attempts to acquire Nicholas Copernicus's letters, it was referred to as "something like a *fideicommissum*",[401] while a reference to the Gołuchów entail as a fully fledged *fideicommissum* appeared in correspondence during the second world war when the transfer of a part of the collection from Poznań to Warszawa was considered. It was also then that the integrity of the collection provided for in

401 J. Nowak, op. cit., p. 132 source material referred to in footnote 30 (*non vidi*).

the entail charter was used as one of the arguments advanced by the German authorities in Poznań.[402]

Fideicommissum type entities and Polish entails were institutions of private law, but definitely with a strong public character noticeable from the very beginning. Apart from the family, property, or formal factors attributable to entails, the public aspect of their operations, the museums or libraries which prospective entails sought to open, certainly helped them to procure the permits necessary to establish themselves. The requirement that their founding act and charter had to be formally endorsed by public bodies added to the public-private character of an entail, and this duality is also present in their operations in the sphere of cultural heritage protection. Additionally, an entail was an institution influencing private property while at the same time providing access to and protection of collections and museum objects, and this already influenced the public sphere. What is more, entails were perceived as institutions with a social role.[403] The institution of a *fideicommissum* reflects a differentiation between the spiritual and tangible sphere, even if the difference between the two is almost negligible. The spiritual aspect may be considered as related to the memory of the family and continuation of its social role and contribution to the development of Polish culture, while the tangible aspect is reflected in regulations providing for the share of individual family members of the revenues generated by the property covered by the entail and the political role the family played in the building of a powerbase upon the country's landed property.

In the light of other legal mechanisms available today, it seems rather pointless to reactivate an institution that would be an accurate equivalent of a *fideicommissum* in its most narrow sense and form (as has been mentioned earlier, although the term was also used in Poland, frequently in reference to an entail, and

402 M. Kuhnke, *"Dworzanin" i "Dama" Jana Mostaerta. Historia dwóch obrazów ze zbiorów Muzeum w Gołuchowie*, "Muzealnictwo" 2006, No. 47, p. 201 source material referred to in footnote 33 (AMN in Poznań. Wartime correspondence. Gotfried Reiner's letter of 6 December 1943 (on behalf of Dr Vosse) to head of Kaiser Friedrich Museum in Poznań, Dr S. Ruhle (AMN, Poznań).

403 *Ordynacya książąt Czartoryskich*, "Czas" [Time], 6 May 1894. However, it was not only for family reasons or respect but also because of the need to act in a higher interest, that an entail is recommended to be formed. The entail ought to provide for the maintenance and development of the famous Princes Czartoryski Museum in Kraków. **The common benefit will thus be ensured with no burden or cost for the country** (authors' emphasis) arising from the maintenance of the enterprise, since all burdens will be borne by the entail".

sometimes these two names were used interchangeably, despite slight differences between them). What is more, since it plays a similar function to that contemporarily played by trusts and funds operating in countries with an Anglo-Saxon legal system, it would not stand the test of time. However, the theoretical concept of a *fideicommissum* could be used in discussions on new solutions in which the emphasis would be placed on new 'entitled' subjects – future generations.

Owing to the fact that while the property in a *fideicommissum* is set apart from the owner, or ownership, continues to be of concern. Hence this construction could be an interesting subject of discussion in debates on cultural heritage and the cultural rights of the international community. An example here could be a debate on the right to cultural property. As the perception of heritage diminishes, the new role of communities as an entity entitled to tangible cultural heritage has been growing and becomes the subject of legal regulation. Thus the protection of cultural heritage both nationally and internationally is becoming one of the elements necessary to ensure human rights[404] and such a new context needs regulation as well. The way a *fideicommissum* determines the owner in the relationships it creates is open to challenge.

404 Compare: results of the research by A. Jakubowski, *State Succession in Cultural Property*, Oxford 2015.

III. A new *image* of heritage: protection or management

Each element of heritage enjoys a history and existence of its own. Together, however, they form an entity which is essential for the recognition of its value and the assimilation into its structures of private and public property. Recently a new type of interdisciplinary study has evolved, called *heritology*.[405] In the specialist literature concepts such as *heritigisation processes*[406] have now appeared, in which an essential part is played by current cultural heritage protection undertaken for the sake of the values embodied by the subject, irrespective of other issues such as questions of ownership or history. For many authors *heritigisation* is perceived as a universal process which demands, in the light of global processes, a comprehensive analysis at a global and regional level.[407]

More and more frequently in international discussions concerning movable elements of heritage there appears a need to introduce a *lex culturalis* which indirectly indicates that the study of the legal regulation of cultural heritage has evolved onto a new stage. One of the recurring themes of international discussion of movable heritage is the question of claims and the return of objects to their respective countries of origin and that of establishing the relation between the object and a country as well as legal and non-legal justifications for such actions.[408] The developments in theory and practice in the field of cultural heritage have also contributed to the growing awareness of the importance of cultural heritage among members of the public. Thus, as a consequence of the development of the Polish legal system, and like environmental protection legislation,

405 J. Purchla, *Europa wobec dziedzictwa*, in: *Europa wobec dziedzictwa. Modele mecenatu na rzecz ochrony dziedzictwa kulturowego*, (ed.) Ł. Gałusek, Kraków 2005, pp. 31–36.

406 V. Vadi, H. Schneider, *Art, Cultural Heritage and the Market: Legal and Ethical Issues*, in: *Art, Cultural Heritage and the Market. Ethical and Legal Status*, (eds.) V. Vadi, H. Schneider, Berlin - Heidelberg 2014, pp. 16–17.

407 K. Kuutma, *Concepts and Contigencies in the Shaping of Heritage Regimes*, in: *Heritage Regimes and the State*, (eds.) E. F. Bendix, A. Eggert, A. Peselmann, Gotingen 2013, p. 32.

408 A. Eriksen, *From Antiquities to Heritage. Transformations of Cultural Memory*, New York - Oxford 2014, p. 133.

cultural heritage protection laws can be looked upon as a separate branch of the Polish legal system.[409]

This new image of cultural heritage is the result of the reinterpretation of the concept. It is the continually evolving outcome of a re-evaluation of the attitude towards the heritage and the search for a model of heritage management that is open to its current beneficiaries and to the use of heritage for social and economic development.

The new image of heritage also features in discussions concerning the legal framework of heritage, which must constantly be adapted to changes within it. The "National Programme of the Protection and Guardianship of Monuments of 2014–2017" defines the reinterpretation as a "process which is the result of social, economic, political, spatial and cultural processes and a consequence of constant social re-evaluations and transformations of cultural heritage wealth as well as of the definition of its modern, socially accepted meaning and use".[410] Frequently the reinterpretation of heritage will also be related to changes in the legal system which themselves are the consequence of social processes.[411] The axiomatic background for the new perception of heritage is analysed in the philosophy of heritage, focusing in particular on its existence as a common cultural good that joins the present and the future. Against the background of cultural heritage management the issue of the contextualisation of heritage features, also in relation to art and its place in the public domain[412]. In the case of heritage it will concern the history of its elements and its relationship with individual social groups and, in the system of monument legal protection, it will involve the contextualisation of decision making processes with respect to heritage.

In heritage management it is essential that its wealth is maintained while, at the same time, made optimal use of for the benefit of society. It is the consequence of treating heritage as a proportion of what is left when all its other components

---

409 K. Zeidler, *Prawo ochrony dziedzictwa kultury jako nowa gałąź prawa*, in: *Prawo ochrony zabytków*, (ed.) K. Zeidler, Warszawa – Gdańsk 2014, p. 23 et seq.

410 The National Programme of the Protection and Guardianship of Monuments 2014–2017, p. 36, http://bip.mkidn.gov.pl/media/download_gallery/20140818Krajowy_Program_Ochrony_Zabytkow_i_Opieki_nad_Zaby.pdf (accessed: 15.06.2015)

411 For example the change in perception of German heritage in Poland, or Polish cultural heritage in the Ukraine.

412 Programme Signs of Time and local collections of modern art, e.g. a collection created by the Wielkopolskie Towarzystwo/Society(of) Zachęty/Encouragement of the Fine Arts – sculpture in the Cytadela Park in Poznań.

have been destroyed.[413] Apart from the preservation of the wealth of heritage its management will be related to a series of actions whose aim is to popularise its value and create a data collection system. Once the identification of the heritage has been achieved, the need for its control automatically appears, and because of the ever- increasing wealth of cultural heritage there is undeniably a case for carrying out continuous identification work. All these activities should be centrally co-ordinated and should complement each other. In this context it is necessary to stress the importance of documents, and particularly their use in the planning of heritage protection. These documents are created at different levels and, in the case of the national system, they provide, to a large extent, details of tasks specified in documents approved at a higher level with reference to the individual and particular conditions of a given region.

Cultural heritage management may be compared to a mosaic of activities occurring at a national, European Union and international level. Although these activities share a common goal, i.e. the preservation of cultural heritage, they also differ in many respects. One of them is the extent, scope and intensity of cultural heritage policies. Also legislation applicable to the above-mentioned levels is not of equal weighting and in the case of soft law regulations even the application of its norms by its consumers will not be uniform either. Bearing this in mind it is feasible to talk of a phenomenon of different speeds of legal protection of cultural heritage both in terms of territory[414] and subject matter.[415] Legislative regulations in the form of international agreements, laws and executive acts as well as directives, orders and documents of trade organisations and associations define the limits and, when not legally binding, the desirable standards of heritage protection.

In anything to do with management it is essential to refer to the economic capacity of bodies managing heritage wealth and to the organisational potential and involvement of individuals. We can thus distinguish public bodies, which not only establish the organisational framework of policies and protection but actually implement it. Private bodies, apart from investing their own capital when dealing with elements of cultural heritage, also become involved in its management. It is not possible to overstate the involvement of state and public bodies in cultural heritage protection, as attested by relevant paragraphs of the

413 K. Kuutma, op. cit., p. 22.

414 National, European and international legislation, regional regulations.

415 Legal regulations about museums, archives, movable and non-movable monuments.

Constitution.[416] This involvement is closely tied to decisions about financing, or in some cases not financing, particular undertakings. Consequently, it is essential to acknowledge the importance not just of the criteria which define cultural property in need of protection, but also the criteria and mechanisms for allocating financial support for them. In the Anglo-Saxon model a good example of creating and using such evaluation tools is that of the British National Heritage Fund working together with Demos- a *think tank*.[417]

The institutional type of heritage management may take different forms, each working within its own legal framework and the tools for providing heritage protection may also acquire different forms. When discussing the criterion for financial support, direct and indirect support may be distinguished. Examples of indirect support would be tax incentives, lotteries and the system of allocating grants for specific projects. Financial support can also be incidental and permanent (subject related).[418] When range is a criterion, however, those activities will be undertaken on either a regional, national or international scale. Any state – led activity in support of cultural heritage will give rise to questions of the accessibility to the wider public of its elements as well as to the limits of the laws governing the obligations of private owners of heritage to conform to specified rules in the use of their own properties.[419] It is because of the complicated and varied types of heritage ownership that the appropriate heritage management strategies apply both to private and public bodies.

Many a time in the past the rationale for creating institutionalised culture frameworks has been questioned. Zygmunt Bauman proclaimed that culture should be free of management and politics and exist in its own right. According to him the concept itself is ambiguous and its attribute is permanent. Cultural products are created as goods in their own right and are beyond any control.[420] Tony Bennett considers the importance of the legal regulation of cultural

416 These questions will be tackled comprehensively in the chapter on ownership of heritage and forms of monument protection.

417 D. O'Brien, *Cultural Policy. Management, value, modernity in the creative industries*, London – New York 2014, p. 125.

418 A. Klamer, A. Mognosa, L. Petrova, *Cultural heritage policies: a comparative perspective*, in: *Economics of Cultural Heritage*, (eds.) I. Rizzo, A. Mognosa, Massachusetts 2013, p. 45.

419 F. Benhamou, *Public intervention for cultural heritage: normative issues and tools*, in: *Handbook on the Economics of Cultural Heritage*, (eds.) I. Rizzo, A. Mognosa, Massachusetts 2013, p. 6.

420 More in Z. Bauman, *Kultura jako praxis*, Warszawa 2012, pp. 23–30.

phenomena as necessary to create correct cultural ties based on intercultural understanding.[421] In the light of the above reasoning to allow cultural products to be left alone and exposed to any type of treatment would be harmful for future generations. It is for the benefit of future inheritors of cultural heritage that state cultural policies are the result of endeavours and decision making at different levels.

Cultural policy can be implemented with differing structural support by public governing bodies. Their organisation can be centralised or decentralised and will involve different grades of participation at the regional level. The type of organisation will in each case be the result of the administrative division of a country and of the legal principles defining the role of the state. In the case of Poland these regulations are included in the laws specifying the duties of Local Government in the Constitution of the Polish Republic. Within the framework of international cultural policies global (UNESCO documents and conventions) and European policies may be distinguished. The extent of European policies can additionally be analysed by checking the legislative work of the European Council and European Union laws. A careful scrutiny of legislative documents and their application allows us to see how varied the realisation of the same objective of cultural heritage protection can be.

It would be appropriate here to mention 'The Explanatory Report of The Council of Europe Framework Convention on the Value of Cultural Heritage for Society' (Faro Convention)[422] which states that on signing up to the Convention each state is free to choose the most suitable means appropriate to its national legal tradition, politics and common practice. Preparation for the ratification of the Framework Convention on the Value of Cultural Heritage for Society features also in "The National Programme of the Protection and Guardianship of Monuments for years 2014–2017".[423] In the opinion of the report's authors "the ratification of the Convention recommendations will result, on the one hand, in greater awareness of the use of cultural heritage wealth in socio-economic development, and on the other hand, it will improve social responsibility for the condition of monuments." The development and level of social responsibility play

421 After K. Kuutma, op. cit., p. 31.

422 Preparation for the ratification of the Framework Convention on the Value of Cultural Heritage for Society features also as one of the objectives in The National Programme of the Protection and Guardianship of Monuments 2014–2017, http://bip.mkidn.gov.pl/media/download_gallery/20140818Krajowy_Program_Ochrony_Zabytkow_i_Opieki_nad_Zaby.pdf (accessed: 15.06.2015).

423 Ibid. p. 60.

a key role in seeing the cultural heritage as a common good which needs to be managed over a long period of time.

The Framework Convention does not oblige the states to undertake specific actions, instead, it defines the objectives, assuming that each state will strive to use means and methods in common with those adopted by other states.[424] The emphasis placed on each state's individual way to achieve the common social goal is meant to reflect the recognition of the uniqueness not only of the legal systems. The objective of the Framework Convention, with its new perception of the European cultural heritage, has been compared to the direction and destination of an unspecified journey through Europe or to a detailed road map or even a timetable. Article 11 of the Convention specifies the role of legislation in cultural heritage management. According to the Convention directives the state establishes and develops a framework of laws enabling co-operation between public and private institutions and their representatives in their task of protecting cultural heritage and by allowing them the freedom to choose the legal tools also reinforces this co-operation. Two objectives included in Article 1 of the Convention deserve special mention here: the first is that of a collective and individual responsibility towards cultural heritage and taking the necessary steps towards the synergy of competencies among all the public, institutional and private actors. In the Convention for the first time an exhaustive definition of cultural heritage has been used,[425] at the centre of which there is man and his basic rights as well as sustainable development and the quality of life of constantly evolving societies.[426]

Some authors hold the opinion that too much state freedom in applying international solutions to cultural heritage conservation actually weakens the objective. They point out that, in certain circumstances, to allow for discretion in state realisation of its objectives out of respect for its cultural, legal and *organisational* diversity may hinder co-operation in cultural heritage preservation.[427] The type of cultural policy to be practised depends also on the level at which it is applied. Thus, in the case of regions and countries there will be a need for

---

424 Council of Europe Framework Convention on the Value of Cultural Heritage for Society: Explanatory report, 27.10.2005, http://conventions.coe.int/Treaty/EN/Reports/Html/199.htm (accessed: 15.06.2015).

425 Taking into account tangible and non-tangible heritage.

426 F. von Saint André von-Armin, *Der Wert des Kulturerbes für die Gesellschaft. Genesis und Gegenstand der Europarats-Rahmenkonvention von 2005*, Hamburg 2007, p. 73.

427 Compare R. F. Bendix, A. Eggert, *A. Peselman, Introduction: Heritage regimes and the State*, in: *Heritage Regimes and the State…*, p. 11.

greater participation of private and non-governmental bodies, whereas at the international level we will see increased involvement of public actors and their experts.[428] In the context of intangible heritage and the Convention on the Preservation of Intangible Heritage this is the stance adopted by Lucas Lixinski in his analysis of political participation and the involvement of different entities.[429]

An analysis of current mechanisms of cultural heritage management needs to happen within a specified framework, all the more so as cultural heritage regulations are aimed at individual elements of the heritage.[430] This lack of complexity of regulations is the result of the need to create detailed regulations. Unfortunately, owing to the wide scope of regulations individual legal acts do not form a cohesive system. Moreover, in the case of some laws one can see the influence of the interests of some professional groups while at the same time the role of the subject requiring protection is diminished, a good example of which are Act on Museums and Act on the National Archival Resource and State Archives. Undeniably the structure and organisation of heritage conservation requires some in-depth analysis by lawmakers, but when the focus has not been applied accurately then it misses its objective, i.e. an item of cultural heritage.

It appears that each regulation ought to consider what is valuable culturally, including items which "emerge irrespective of conservation principles and directives, or on the good advice of self-appointed experts, and whose emergence is affected by the passing of time and the special talents of their creators".[431] Thus our perception of heritage and the elements that comprise it and subsequently its management tools constantly have to adapt not only to social development and changes but also to new forms of cultural phenomena in ever increasing numbers. At the same time all the solutions ought to aim at the universal goal of passing the heritage on to future generations. This is a very difficult task to carry out in practice, limited, among other things by the different stages of development of societies, different regulations to do with artistic freedom and by

---

428 A. Klamer, A. Mognosa, L. Petrova, op. cit., p. 39.

429 L. Lixinski, *Heritage for Whom? Individuals' and Communities' Roles in International Cultural Heritage Role*, in: *International law for common goods. Normative perspective on Human Rights, Culture and Nature*, (eds.) F. Lenzerini, A. Vrdoljak, Oxford 2014, p. 196 et seq.

430 St. F. King, *Cultural resource laws and practice*, New York – Toronto – Plymouth UK 2013, pp. 4–8.

431 T. Chrzanowski, *Czy Polakom potrzebne zabytki?*, in: *Spotkania w Willi Struvego 1998–2001. Wykłady o dziedzictwie kultury*, (ed.) K. J. Kwiecińska, Warszawa 2001, p. 15.

the economic potential of cultural development sponsors. Action supporting the growth of heritage assets should be considered on two levels. On the one level, the support ought to be directed at owners of works of art some of which might be conferred the status of a monument in the future. The other level would concern primarily those monuments that are included in the national heritage conservation and related legislation. Heritage protection will thus entail all actions to do with the creation and popularisation of objects of cultural importance and then subsequently, in relation to some of those monuments, the application of a form of legal protection.

More and more in museology and discussions about museum pieces and collecting policies there arises the question of the evaluation of museum items in the context of the beliefs and customs of specific social groups and the way they protect human dignity and basic human rights.[432] That is why nowadays many museums stress the quality and importance of their collections whose variety is also considered an added value. This type of approach to public collections is expressed in the *Declaration on the Importance and Value of Universal Museums*,[433] in which the largest museums are considered not as, *sensu stricto*, guardians but rather as teachers of heritage interpretation.[434] The *Declaration* is also used as an argument in support of refusals of claims for the return of items from American and European museums to their respective countries of origin.[435] When considering countries that have a wealth of cultural heritage and those that import such cultural heritage objects we can see how vital export regulations in heritage management are as they establish not just historic and cultural but also formal links between the object and a given country. *The Declaration*, although not binding in itself, recognises the primacy of the law of accessibility to international collections representing universal human achievement over the importance of the

---

432 See Zbiory Muzeum Branly, A. Jagielska-Burduk, *Zabytek ruchomy*, Warszawa 2011, p. 267.

433 Declaration on the Importance and Value of Universal Museums, reprinted ICOM News, 2004, No. 1, p. 4, http://icom.museum/fileadmin/user_upload/pdf/ICOM_News/2004-1/ENG/p4_2004-1.pdf (accessed: 10.06.2015).

434 J. Cuno, *View from the universal museum*, in: *Imperialism, art and restitution*, (ed.) H. Merryman, Cambridge 2006, pp. 15–16.

435 C. Forrest, *International Law and the Protection of Cultural Heritage*, London – New York 2010, p. 165, "Museums are agents in the development of culture, whose mission is to foster knowledge by a continuous process of reinterpretation. Each object contributes to that process. To narrow the focus of museums whose collections are diverse and multifaceted would therefore be a disservice to all visitors."

link between a given object and its country of origin, and in the case of objects of outstanding value, of their importance for the whole cultural heritage of the country of origin.[436] It therefore follows that the work of European Museums (*encyclopaedic museums*) which at different stages in history have amassed collections reflecting the diversity of human achievement as well striven constantly to enlarge those collections is in itself a contradiction of the concept of national cultural heritage protection so vital for the countries with a cultural heritage.[437]

Jacek Purchla, a Polish specialist in the field of cultural heritage management has suggested turning the famous historical phrase "the past of the future", coined in connection with Countess Isabella Czartoryska, founder of the Puławy Museum into the question "What is the future of our past". He defines heritage very broadly as encompassing simultaneously knowledge, cultural product and political resource. Heritage, in his view, should be perceived as "omnipresent and limitless" as opposed to the countable number of cultural artefacts and monuments.[438] Cultural heritage is to do, apart from tangible cultural property, with utilising the past for current purposes.[439] The fundamental question in heritage protection is who the owner of the heritage is and their rights in relation to it. In order to find the answer to this we need to establish to what extent we are dealing with either a global or regional heritage and at what stage we can treat it as a national heritage. In the case of Polish heritage ownership law, ownership rights to an object are very limited during the period of actual ownership, allowing for incidental protective measures, including that of stripping of the right of ownership or the legal right to ownership.[440] In the context of relations between current heritage and its owners it is possible to talk of heritage without inheritors and the heritage of the disinherited.[441] Cultural heritage needs to be treated as a resource

---

436 A. Jakubowski, *Territoriality and State Succession in Cultural Heritage*, "International Journal of Cultural Property" 2014, No. 21, Vol. 4, p. 383.

437 D. A. Scott, *Modern Antiquities: the Looted and the Faked*, "International Journal of Cultural Property" 2013, No. 1, p. 52.

438 J. Purchla's lecture in the Trybunal Konstytucyjny (Constitional Tribunal Court) "Naród–Dziedzictwo–Pamięć"(Nation–Heritage–Memory), 14 May 2013, http://tkonst.linuxpl.info/video/narod-dziedzictwo-pamiec-wyklad-prof-jacka-purchli-w-trybunale-konstytucyjnym-14-maja-2013-r/ (accessed: 1.06.2015).

439 J. Purchla, *Naród – Dziedzictwo – Pamięć*, "Zagadnienia Sądownictwa Konstytucyjnego" 2012, No. 2, p. 63.

440 A. Jagielska-Burduk, op. cit., p. 175.

441 J. Purchli's lecture in the Trybunal Konstytucyjny…, J. Purchla, *Naród – Dziedzictwo – Pamięć…*, p. 66.

of common responsibility, assuming that public entities will share this responsibility and formulate its legal and financial framework.

A good example of the role private entities can play in heritage management is the case of the Ossolinski Enterprise (Zakład Ossolinskich) and its history after WWI – "estates have been largely devastated and, as land without actual owners, have not had the capacity for regeneration typical of private property".[442] This statement, irrespective of circumstances such as wartime operations or socio-political changes, could also be applied to other forms of management which has originated through private initiative. Frequently private entities unhindered in their actions stand a greater chance of protecting heritage resources than the institutions whose very objective is heritage protection. Hence those who protect heritage or who support "future heritage" creators ought to be aware that the planning of a sound system of heritage protection ought to allow for private and public entities acting in parallel or in co-operation.

On the national as well as the international level the legal system of heritage protection forms a kind of network of complementary legal norms. Even assuming the concept of a rational legislator and his rationality as to the completeness of the legal system, any analysis of current legislature should be undertaken with great caution and in each case should try to verify if a specific legal norm achieves its basic aim, i.e. that of heritage protection. This kind of interpretation is particularly important because of its subject whose rightful owner, understood in the widest sense, are the future generations. In this part of the legal system public law, including international and administrative law co-applies to and co-regulates cultural heritage with private law. For example, in the case of the return of cultural property we must take into account international law, conventions relating to the return of cultural property removed illegally from the country of origin, the civil law of the country in possession of the object and the civil law of the country of its origin.[443]

One could ask why it is that cultural property should be treated differently from other property in regulations concerning handling and transport. Why do they stand out among other property? It appears that a natural answer to this has its origin in people's love of beautiful objects and the emergence of artists in societies as well as the demand for their services. Art in its different forms has gradually gained in importance in the way societies function. Successive

---

442 M. Gębarowicz, *Zbiory muzealne w Zakładzie Narodowym im. Ossolińskich*, in: *Ossolineum. Księga pamiątkowa w 150-lecie Zakładu Narodowego imienia Ossolińskich*, (ed.) B. Olszewicz, Wrocław 1967, p. 138.

443 V. Vadi, H. Schneider, op. cit., pp. 1 and 10.

generations have created objects enriching an already existing collection. On the global scale a collection will have been undergoing changes to do with its shrinking or growth. Frequently the size of the collection has not changed but it is only that its items have changed their location, sometimes with and sometimes without the owner's permission. Recently cultural heritage has become the means of expressing not only memory and artistic values but also it has become the carrier of material value. This type of value is particularly essential in the case of the heritage management of movable objects. Restrictions in the national law concerning the trade and transfer of cultural property do, however, reflect the protection of not the whole entity of the cultural heritage but only of the items of national cultural heritage.[444]

The starting point for the analysis of available mechanisms, apart from the actual "heritage" value of monuments and objects will be their economic value which determines many solutions to do with, for example, the security aspect of the item. The economic value will, on the other hand, be of lesser importance from the point of view of its protection than its universal value which can also differ in relation to different social groups. In recent times, apart from the values inherent in the Polish definition of a cultural heritage, i.e. artistic, historic, scientific ones, there has been a lot more importance attached to the values closely connected to basic human rights and dignity.[445] It would be possible to acknowledge that the degree of complexity of protection increases depending on the demands of the present day and social developments. On the other hand, an analysis of phenomena such as donation agreements, lending, or *fideicommissum* convinces us that private law solutions do not pass the test of time which, in the case of the cultural heritage, should be considered one of the most important issues.

In this case it would be better to keep away from the syndrome of the reduced and poor Polish heritage and, instead, with the help of private sector entities, concentrate on the creation of a new one. Assuming that in the Polish legislation a distinction has been made between the protection and care of monuments (APGM) this kind of distinction is not without significance for the heritage. Following the German or British model the distinction is made on the basis of whether an activity is of a legal or factual type. Polish law has accepted a double criterion, the first one relating to the entity or owner responsible for the care of the monument and the public body implementing its protection, and only in the

444 Compare W. Kowalski, *Kolizyjnoprawne problemy restytucji dóbr kultury*, in: *Rozprawy prawnicze. Księga pamiątkowa profesora Maksymiliana Pazdana*, (eds.), L. Ogiegło, W. Popiołek, M. Szpunar, Kraków 2005, pp. 125–126.

445 V. Vadi, H. Schneider, op. cit., p. 6.

second place a distinction has been made between factual and legal activity. The first mistake which makes it difficult to implement cultural heritage management based on the participation model enabling long term and constant heritage enrichment is made by placing the trustee of a monument as an entity subordinate to the cultural heritage bodies.

Cultural heritage planning makes it possible to assess the objectives and establish the difficulties involved in the implementation process. The conditions essential for cultural heritage protection and care of monuments in Poland are specified in the National Programme of Protection and Guardianship of Monuments. In accordance with the provisions of Article 84 of the APGM the competent Minister of Culture and National Heritage, with the help of the General Inspector of Monuments, initiates and works out a national programme of protection and guardianship of monuments. The national programme is then passed by the Cabinet on the advice of the Minister of Culture and National Heritage. Following that at different levels of local government, voivodeship (*wojewodztwo*), county (*powiat*) and community (*gmina*) the respective plans of protection and guardianship of monuments are then worked out. The national plan and the plans at the local government level last for four years, with a two-year review period. The report on the implementation of the programme is submitted by the Minister to the Cabinet, by the voivodeship administrations to the voivodeship parliament (*sejmik*), by the commune (*powiat*) administration to the county council and by *wójt* (head of a commune) to the commune council (*rada powiatu*). The provisions of the protection and guardianship of monuments programmes at the local government level are to some extent imposed by the national policy as specified in the national programme. Examples of programme aims have been defined in Article 87 clause 2 of the APGM[446] There

---

446 They comprise: including monument protection issues within the system of strategic tasks of spatial management of the country, considering monument protection, cultural landscape and archaeological heritage together with nature protection and ecological balance, halting the process of degradation of monuments and improving their condition, displaying particular monuments and the values of the cultural landscape, undertaking actions to increase the attractiveness of monuments for social, tourist and educational needs, supporting initiatives that increase financial support for monument protection, defining terms of co-operation with monument owners, which eliminate conflicts in the use of the monuments, undertaking steps to create jobs in monument protection.

are no similar guidelines for the national programme which in itself might be considered a risk for legal national heritage protection.[447]

The first document which was based on the statute was "*Tezy do opracowania krajowego programu ochrony zabytkow i opieki nad zabytkami zatwierdzone przez Ministra Kultury Waldemara Dąbrowskiego.*"[448] This document was published as an introduction to studies of the national heritage protection and care of monuments and did not aim to replace it. The original document, i.e. the National Programme of Protection and Guardianship of Monuments which was voted through by the Council of Ministers on 24 June 2014, puts great emphasis on legal safeguards. The National Programme will be implemented under the guidance and control of the General Inspector of Monuments in strict co-operation with the voivodeship inspector of monuments, the office of the Minister of Culture, voivodeship local governments, the National Heritage Board of Poland and the National Institute for Museums and Public Collection. It allows for drawing on the advice of the National Heritage Protection Council, whose role as an advisory body is to co-operate both with the Minister and the Team overseeing the Programme in the National Heritage Department. The programme has appropriately allocated tasks and actions both on the national and regional level. The role of the voivodeship inspector of monuments will be of particular importance when proposals for the new structure of heritage protection bodies are made. In the light of the studies with the representatives of voivodeship conservation officers it would appear that the proposal for change should emerge from each level and a new model for co-operation would then eliminate communication barriers between particular levels.[449] The implementation of the National Programme has been delegated to the respective competency centres of state cultural institutes, i.e. the National Institute for Museums and Public Collection and the National Heritage Board of Poland. The National Programme work is carried out in parallel by the specialists employed by those centres and by the co-operating bodies.

---

447 On the negative influence on the protection regulations cf. K. Zalasińska, *Prawna ochrona zabytków nieruchomych w Polsce*, Warszawa 2010, p. 182.

448 Thesis for the development of the national programme of monument protection and guardianship approved by the Minister of Culture Waldemar Dąbrowski, http://www.kobidz.home.pl/pliki/tezy.pdf (accessed: 15.06.2015).

449 These barriers have also been mentioned by the participants in the studies of the Focused group survey carried out on 27 May 2015 within the scope of the project. There is more information in the report to be published in the Annex of the "Santander Art and Culture Law Review" 2016, No. 3 [in print].

The combination of the projected approach to the plan, the establishment of specific phases for concrete tasks together with the appointment of co-ordinators allow for the effective inclusion of entities representing regions and experts. It appears that the basic assumptions of the National Programme, at least to some extent, achieve the aim of transforming the system of national heritage protection into a model of effective heritage management, and consequently, the adoption of a new image of cultural heritage and its protection in the national policy. Making use of cultural heritage for today's society derives from the new image of cultural heritage while simultaneously maintaining the basic objective of passing on cultural heritage to future generations. This type of model should have the confidence of local communities which, together with owners and users of monuments, are the key link in heritage management.[450]

The new image of heritage has become a catalyst for changes in the approaches to its protection and management that have been suggested by, among others, art historians, sociologists, economists and lawyers, closely followed by decision-makers responsible for cultural policies. For these bodies the new image is of vital importance. Culture and heritage as its product has become fashionable again for the development of creativity, use of resources and the consequent growth of the GDP. The need to build a new relationship with heritage has already been signalled in the cited below Report on the protection of the national cultural heritage in Poland after 1989. Heritage protection should be perceived as a departure from static protection in favour of using a dynamic formula of "creative management of inherited cultural heritage carried out by means of technical achievements, the natural inventiveness of individuals, the economic situation as well as the scientific resources of the theories of conservation".[451] The new image of heritage at the international and national level has an influence on the way it is perceived, in the form of new programmes and protection plans and new searches for effective heritage management within cultural policy.

Theory of Cultural Heritage Knots

In the second part of this publication the following legal institutions related to heritage management are presented: ownership law, *res extra commercium*, forms of monument protection and legal separation of monuments from an estate. In

---

450 A. Böhm, P. Dobosz, P. Jaskanis, J. Purchla, B. Szmygin, *Raport na temat funkcjonowania systemu ochrony dziedzictwa kulturowego w Polsce po roku 1989*, (ed.) J. Purchla, Kraków 2008, p. 73.

451 Ibid. p. 36.

each of these legal institutions as well as in agreements (donations, lending for use and deposits) there exists a dominant specific knot between cultural heritage and groups of entities representing different interests. In colloquial language a knot is understood as a thickening in the place of tying or a loop.[452] The most famous ancient knot is the Gordian knot, which could only be undone by the combination in one blow of an imperial power and the sword. Similarly in the case of the legal management of cultural heritage, although it is impossible to undo the smaller fragmentary knots, in the process of untying the main one it is possible to distinguish weaker and stronger knots within cultural management processes. In Roman law a form of legal knot was expressed by the term *vinculum iuris* in which a debtor and a creditor were tied into a kind of knot of obligation.[453] However, this kind of legal relationship did not appear in the relationship between an owner, a possessor, a third party and an object.

In the represented theory a knot means a relationship between an object and a specified subject or a group of subjects. This relationship is a consequence of applying a specific legal mechanism of heritage management and follows on from "the spirit of a given institution", taking into account the specific character of cultural heritage to which it is applied. An emerging knot radiates out into its basic function at the same time positioning it in a certain way in relation to the other integral knots of a given legal institution. In each knot a mechanism of heritage management appears whose aim of is to preserve the elements of cultural heritage for future generations. The particular knots that appear in a given legal mechanism have to form a universal knot, which eventually functions as a form of bracket and coupling for all the others. Accepting an inheritance is like a mainstay of relations with future generations. Despite numerous attempts over the years at defining, deconstructing and redefining the concept of heritage the most secure element of heritage management is the relationship of passing on the heritage.

---

452 *Słownik języka polskiego*, (eds.) J. Karłowicz, A. Kryński, W. Niedźwiedzki, Vol. 7: *T-Y*, Warszawa 1919, p. 527.

453 For more information see W. Dajczak, T. Giaro, F. Longchamps de Bérier, *Prawo rzymskie. U podstaw prawa prywatnego*, Warszawa 2009, pp. 427–428 and W. Dajczak, *The Nature of the Contract in Reasoning of Civilian Jurists*, Poznań 2012, pp. 17–50.

This universal knot is closely linked to the concept of the defence of the interests of successors[454] or the Eternal Rhombus,[455] it links cultural heritage elements to future generations and the main objective for its creation is the preservation of cultural heritage. In view of the concept of the defence of the interests of successors those entitled to the heritage in the first place are the future generations and in the second place in this hierarchy is the current society. A change in the perception of monuments and the new image of cultural heritage seem to justify this change of emphasis of the target. In order to avoid the impermanence of heritage ownership laws and to secure it for future generations there is a need for constant work on legal regulations and maybe even for a change in the system of property rights.[456] Changes in the system of property rights might go in the direction of excluding certain objects from circulation, adopting additional regulations governing the acquisition of ownership rights to cultural goods or in the direction of looking for new legal solutions. The latter direction, in view of the constitutionality of heritage protection laws and in the context of proportionality, appears to be more feasible.

To begin with, it is important to point out that knots should not be looked upon as relations identical to legal relations modelled on Roman law because a knot links only an object and an entity, and of secondary importance is the legal relationship between the entity which remains in the closest relationship with objects tied to other entities, if such a one exists at all. Taking into account the special character of knots relating to cultural heritage or to cultural heritage together with objects (family estate) it is possible to distinguish knots permanently tied to their creator or initiator, knots separating themselves from him (depending on the content of acts of law which establish something, e.g. a foundation or an institution) or knots independent of the heritage trustee (e.g. forms of monument protection). In this sense one should not link knots with heritage stakeholders, as they are created through using specific legal institutions and not through the very fact of heritage existence and the need for its protection.

In this work particular knots that are based on a variety of legal institutions of private and public law have been analysed. It is impossible not to notice that

---

454 The idea of A. Jagielska-Burduk and W. Szafrański put forward for the first time in: A. Jagielska-Burduk, op. cit., pp. 281–286.

455 The idea of A. Jagielska-Burduk and W. Szafrański put forward for the first time in: W. Szafrański, *Mity i patologie obrotu dziełami sztuki*, "Santander Art and Culture Law Review" 2015, No. 1, pp. 161–168, and in greater detail in this publication.

456 The idea of A. Jagielska-Burduk and W. Szafrański put forward for the first time in: A. Jagielska-Burduk, op. cit., pp. 282–283.

the first detailed knots have appeared in private law, and only with the development of states has the public element of cultural heritage management gained in significance. Some of the knots have evolved naturally (rights of ownership, civil contracts) or artificially, through the involvement of legislators in the knot conceived by the entity which originally initiated it (institutions or enterprises). Some of these promising entities disappeared because of socio-political changes. Meanwhile the objective of each institution generating a knot ought to be considered as a common objective irrespective of the current political system, especially in a situation where we are evaluating only a particular knot and not the legal system that makes it.

In the case of *fideicomissum* the strongest knot is the family knot which stands out more clearly than the organisational knot. The family knot results in the formation of an estate which is independent of individual people and which constitutes an object of ownership of representatives of a family defined in a narrower or wider way. At the time of setting up a *fideicomissum* it was allowed to include as its elements cultural and scientific undertakings as well as those involved in popularising cultural heritage thus making it similar to a foundation. A specific knot in the context of enterprise is an organisational knot, which in itself is elastic and solely at the behest of the founder, which used to be confused with the *fideicomissum* because of its specific aim and the separation of the estate.[457] However, the basic aim of an enterprise, declared in the initial setup document, is to separate it from the estate of the founder. That does not mean that in each case it results in the separation from the person of the founder. Such a model of strict relationship with the founder happens at each phase in the working of a foundation which is so frequently used in the case of modern foundations in private law. In the case of foundations the organisational knot is the dominant one. The same can be said of a trust as a mechanism of heritage management. The search for the most sensible solution, free of emotional involvement[458] has been preceded by detailed comparison of legal institutions, and the financial and legal risks involved in it. A conscious management of cultural heritage for public benefit is most noticeable in modern foundations, less so in the policies of heritage protection.[459]

The strongest knot in the case of donations is that of enriching the public cultural heritage resource. Simultaneously with the transfer of ownership rights

457 C. chapter on enterprises.

458 The founders were led by emotions at the time of making a decision to manage the resource in the public interest (the moment when the universal knot has germinated), but not when choosing the tools to implement this decision.

459 The analysis of the cost effectiveness of Lists of National Treasures.

to an object a donor gives it a new, usually public legal status, or when the private ownership status is retained, hands it to a body whose aims are to popularise and protects cultural heritage (donation to a private museum, enterprise, foundation). In the case of giving in use there appears an even stronger knot of popularisation, which is a natural consequence of a contract when something is given to use for free as in the case of donation contracts.[460] In the case of deposit contracts the strongest is the knot of security, also present but to a lesser degree, in donation and giving in use contracts. The knots in question that have been present in donation, deposit and giving in use contracts, have often not passed the test of time. The civil law foundations of these knots have not assured their initiators as to the safety of collections or guaranteed the respect for decisions made over the years involving collections and their future. Hence the need to refer to the idea of the Eternal Rhombus of the Law which on the private level imposes a new entity for the relation with an object while at the same time accepting the existence of private bodies. Taking into account the economic and legal status of entities the aspect of justice, itself an offshoot of the limitations of cultural heritage, plays an important part in The Eternal Rhombus of the Law.

The knot of exclusion which appears in *res extra commercium* is a sign of the strongest type of intervention on the part of a legislator into objects of law and their division. To exclude an object from commercial circulation deprives it of its essential quality, i.e. its verifiable economic and commercial value. Hence this type of knot is not often used, and if it is, it is only with reference to specific and clearly defined goods. Exercising great caution in using this knot follows from the need to respect basic laws and freedoms, including the law to protect private property. In the public sphere *res extra commercium* could be considered compatible with the knots of popularising and enriching current resources which are present in donation contracts made in favour of public entities or entities which realise public objectives. For example, under French law museum pieces in the public domain are excluded from commercial circulation. Unfortunately, even this type of law does not guarantee full safety in the face of almost professionally organised illegal export, theft and forum shopping. The knot of exclusion constitutes the next stage in the slow pursuance, which has already appeared in the scientific discussions, to focus states on the joint international protection of monuments of exceptional value. Gradually the legal regulations to do with *res extra commercium* will be respected at an international level, forming a common regime of protection.

460 Directions in donation contracts referring to making gifted objects accessible.

The knot based on the right of ownership of cultural heritage comes into existence independently of others. After all, despite the very poor actual condition and provenance of an object it is always possible to establish the owner of a particular item of heritage.[461] The of methods of establishing the ownership status or the legal regulations employed for this purpose will not be discussed here because the main aim of this chapter is the law of ownership of cultural heritage as such, not the way in which it is acquired or managed. The knot of ownership anchored in the broadly understood right *in rem* does not fit in with the law of ownership. In this respect this knot is closer to the proposed relation similar to the right *in rem* with the participation of a new entity, i.e. future generations. The placing of an object at the centre of the legislators' interest has for many years been the subject of discussions to do with interference into owners' privileges and their situation with respect to ownership rights.

The knot of ownership is at the moment the basic knot round which particular knots should be placed. If we were to imagine an ownership knot at the very centre of a spider's web, the more the initiator of a knot interferes in the rights of ownership or even controls them, the nearer it is on the web. The further knots will on the other hand be for example knots transferring the possession and a right to use (contract of lending for use). When it comes to the relations with the universal knot, we could compare it to two parallel spider's webs where the universal knot is above the basic and particular knots. Transferring particular knots onto the web of the universal knot will immediately change their position in relation to it. On this level they are perceived as more or less effective in heritage protection through the prisms of the realisation of objectives and not through the prism of owner entity and its limitations. In this way civil law solutions compete with administrative solutions or they can provide support for each other. Undoubtedly the historic knot to be analysed in further sections of this publication does not enter into relation with the administrative knots, however that would be possible in the case of organisational, popularising and safety knots. The knot of ownership and knots anchored in civil law will be overlapped by the public knots as forms of monument protection. Concluding, the universal knot covers the ownership knot and particular knots matched thereto.

In the process of analysing chosen legal mechanisms several knots have been identified. They appear in different degrees in many legal mechanisms. Usually the legal construction adopted by the initiators has aimed at or will aim at carrying out their intentions as to the elements of heritage. In the search for the most

461 Cf. ideas as to the primacy of law in cultural heritage protection.

favourable management mechanisms, and consequently for the knots, questions of form, management, finance, cost-effectiveness of the mechanisms and possibilities for future self-financing will be of vital importance. The theory of knots with the universal knot that links the present with the past can also be used for analysing other legal institutions. Perhaps if the spider's web woven round the ownership knot were to be rejected in favour of the web formed round the universal knot, it would make it possible to build a legal institution that would make use of the full potential of a particular knot, while at the same time taking into consideration the new image of culture. Thus maximum use would then be made of the indestructability of the universal knot, which in its character should be free of the external factors so far threatening the knots, i.e. the passage of time and changes in the legal and political system. The model, if presented in further studies, could form a basis of national and international solutions with reference to objects of outstanding value, maintaining the supremacy of the universal knot over the ownership knot.

<table>
<tr><td>KNOT</td><td>LEGAL INSTITUTION</td><td rowspan="8">BASIC KNOT

(OWNERSHIP RIGHT)</td><td rowspan="8">NEW IMAGE OF CULTURAL HERITAGE</td><td rowspan="8">UNIVERSAL KNOT</td></tr>
<tr><td>FAMILY</td><td>FIDEICOMMISUM</td></tr>
<tr><td>ORGANISATIONAL</td><td>ENTERPRISE
TRUST
FOUNDATION</td></tr>
<tr><td>CULTURAL HERITAGE ENRICHMENT</td><td>DONATION</td></tr>
<tr><td>POPULARISATION</td><td>GIVING IN USE</td></tr>
<tr><td>SECURITY</td><td>DEPOSIT</td></tr>
<tr><td>ADMINISTRATIVE POWERS</td><td>FORMS OF HERITAGE PROTECTION</td></tr>
<tr><td>EXCLUSION</td><td>RES EXTRA COMMERCIUM</td></tr>
</table>

Source: author's description (A. J.-B.)

Bibliography

[rom], *Archiwum Herberta zostaje w Warszawie*, "Gazeta Wyborcza", 29 December 2004, http://wiadomosci.gazeta.pl/wiadomosci/1,114873,2469418.html (accessed: 1.08.2015).

[Mm], *Co z archiwum Herberta?*, "Gazeta Wyborcza" 3 November 2004, http://wyborcza.pl/1,75475,2373893.html (accessed: 1.08.2015).

Annex of the "Santander Art and Culture Law Review" 2016, No. 3, in print.

Anton M., *Zivilrecht - Guter Glaube im internationalen Kunsthandel*, Berlin 2010.

Antoniak P., Cherka M., in: *Ustawa o ochronie zabytków i opiece nad zabytkami. Komentarz*, (ed.) M. Cherka, Warszawa 2010.

Baslar K., *The Concept of the Common Heritage of Mankind in International Law*, Martinus Nijhoff, The Netherlands 1998.

Bauman Z., *Kultura jako praxis*, Warszawa 2012.

Bendix R. F., Eggert A., *A. Peselman, Introduction: Heritage regimes and the State*, in: *Heritage Regimes and the State*, (eds.) E. F. Bendix, A. Eggert, A. Peselmann, Gotingen 2013.

Bendixen P., *Wprowadzenie do ekonomiki kultury i sztuki*, Kraków 2001.

Benhamou F., *Public intervention for cultural heritage: normative issues and tools*, in: *Handbook on the Economics of Cultural Heritage*, (eds.) I. Rizzo, A. Mognosa, Massachusetts 2013.

Bieniek G., Matusik G., in: *Ustawa o gospodarce nieruchomościami. Komentarz*, (ed.) S. Kalus, Warszawa 2012.

Böhm A., Dobosz P., Jaskanis P., Purchla J., Szmygin B., *Raport na temat funkcjonowania systemu ochrony dziedzictwa kulturowego w Polsce po roku 1989*, (ed.) J. Purchla, Kraków 2008.

Bończak-Kucharczyk E., *Ustawa o gospodarce nieruchomościami. Komentarz*, Warszawa 2014.

Bończa-Szabłowski J., *Lista Skarbów*, interview with P. Żuchowski, "Rzeczpospolita", 21 August 2015.

Bruchnalski W., *Zakładu Narodowego im. Ossolińskich Ustawy, przywileje i rzeczy jego dziejów dotyczące*, Lwów 1927.

Cemka F., *Informacja o pracach związanych z ustawą o reprywatyzacji muzealiów w Polsce*, in: *Zbiory publiczne a kolekcjonerstwo prywatne. Problematyka ochrony dziedzictwa kulturowego w przeszłości i dzisiaj*, (ed.) J. Lipińska, Warszawa 2000.

Chrzanowski T., *Czy Polakom potrzebne zabytki?*, in: *Spotkania w Willi Struvego 1998–2001. Wykłady o dziedzictwie kultury*, (ed.) K. J. Kwiecińska, Warszawa 2001.

Cioch H., *Prawo fundacyjne*, Warszawa 2011.

Cioch H., *Wpływ orzecznictwa na rozwój prawa fundacyjnego*, in: *Aurea praxis, aurea theoria. Księga pamiątkowa ku czci Profesora Tadeusza Erecińskiego*, (eds.) J. Gudowski, K. Weitz, Vol. 2, Warszawa 2011.

Cisek A., Górska K., in: *Kodeks cywilny. Komentarz*, (eds.) E. Gniewek, P. Machnikowski, Warszawa 2014.

Cogliati-Bantz V., Forrest C., *Consistent: The Convention on the Protection of the Underwater Cultural Heritage and the United Nations Convention on the Law of the Sea*, "Cambridge Journal of International and Comparative Law" 2013, No. 2.

Crewdson R., *Cultural Property – a Fourth Estate?*, "The Law Society Gazette" 1984, No. 18.

Criteria of the procedure of recognising object as a Monument of History adopted by the Monument Protection Council of 6 October 2005 www.nid.pl/pl/Dla_wlascicieli_i_zarzadcow/opieka-nad-zabytkami/dobre-praktyk/Kryteria_procedury_uznawania_obiektu_za_pomnik_historii.pdf (accessed: 1.06.2015).

Cuno J., *View from the universal museum*, in: *Imperialism, art and restitution*, (ed.) H. Merryman, Cambridge 2006.

Dajczak W., Giaro T., Longchamps de Bérier F., *Prawo rzymskie. U podstaw prawa prywatnego*, Warszawa 2009.

Dajczak W., *The Nature of the Contract in Reasoning of Civilian Jurists*, Poznań 2012.

Dąbkowski P., *Prawo prywatne polskie*, Vol. I, Lwów 1910.

Decision of 14 November 2013 on permission to delete the collection of the Poznań Society of Friends of Sciences from the inventory of museum objects.

Dembska R., *Problemy dziedziczenia kolekcji w świetle polskiego prawa spadkowego*, in: *Wokół problematyki prawnej zabytków i dzieł sztuki*, (ed.) W. Szafrański, Poznań 2007.

Dobosz P., *Ewoluujące prawne formy ochrony zabytków w Polsce*, in: *Prawo ochrony zabytków*, (ed.) K. Zeidler, Warszawa – Gdańsk 2014.

Dobosz P., *Formy i sposoby ochrony zabytków*, in: *Prawo ochrony zabytków*, (ed.) K. Zeidler, Warszawa – Gdańsk 2014.

Dobosz P., *Koncepcja Listy Skarbów Dziedzictwa w systemie prawa ochrony zabytków w Polsce*, in: *Kultura w praktyce. Zagadnienia prawne*, Vol. 2: *Wokół problematyki prawnej zabytków i rynku sztuki*, (ed.) A. Jagielska-Burduk, W. Szafrański, Poznań 2013.

Dobosz P., *Ponadczasowe wartości Dekretu Rady Regencyjnej z dnia 31 października 1918 r. o opiece nad zabytkami sztuki i kultury*, in: *Prawna ochrona dziedzictwa kulturowego. Wokół problematyki prawnej zabytków i dzieł sztuki*, Vol. 3, (eds.) W. Szafrański, K. Zalasińska, Poznań 2009.

Drela M., *Formy ochrony zabytków a wyrównanie szkody doznanej przez właściciela nieruchomości*, in: *Prawna ochrona zabytków*, (eds.) T. Gardocka, J. Sobczak, Toruń 2010.

Drela M., *Glosa do wyroku TK z dnia 8 października 2007 r. K 20/07*, "Państwo i Prawo" 2008, Issue 11.

Drela M., *Własność zabytków*, Warszawa 2006.

Drela M., *Własność zabytku*, in: *Leksykon prawa ochrony zabytków. 100 podstawowych pojęć*, (ed.) K. Zeidler, Warszawa 2010.

Drela M., *Z orzecznictwa Trybunału Konstytucyjnego (obowiązek finansowania prac archeologicznych przez inwestora), Glosa do wyroku z 8 X 2007, K 20/07*, "Państwo i Prawo" 2008, Issue 11.

Einhorn T., *Israel*, in: *Handbook on the Law of Cultural Heritage and International Trade*, (ed.) J. A. R. Nafziger, R. K. Paterson, London 2014.

Encyklopedia podręczna prawa prywatnego, założona przez H. Konica, [Reference Encyclopaedia of Private Law by H. Konic], (eds.) F. Zoll, J. Wasilkowski, Vol. 2, Warszawa 1936.

Eriksen A., *From Antiquities to Heritage. Transformations of Cultural Memory*, New York - Oxford 2014.

Errichtungsurkunde des Furstlich Czartoryski'chen Familien-Fideicommisses. Ustanowa Ordynacyi rodzinnej Książąt Czartoryskich, Kraków, printed by W. L. Anczyc i Sp., Kraków 1898

Findlay M., *Calague raisonné*, in: *Ekspert kontra dzieło sztuki. Rozpoznanie falsyfikatów oraz fałszywych atrybucji w sztukach plastycznych*, (ed.) R. D. Spencer, Warszawa 2009.

Fischer A., *Zakład Narodowy imienia Ossolińskich (Ossolineum), 1817–1917*, Lwów 1917.

Forrest C., *International Law and the Protection of Cultural Heritage*, London – New York 2010.

Francioni F. F., *The evolving Framework for the Protection of Cultural Heritage in International Law*, in: *Cultural Heritage, Cultural Rights, Cultural Diversity. New Developments in International Law*, (eds.) S. Borelli, F. Lenzerini, Leiden – Boston 2012.

Fyderek N., Szafrański W., *Sprzedaż muzealiów – niewykorzystana szansa czy brak konieczności*, w: *Kultura w praktyce. Zagadnienia prawne*, Vol. 3: *Muzea a rynek sztuki. Aspekty prawne*, (eds.) A. Jagielska-Burduk, W. Szafrański, Poznań 2014.

Gadecki B., *Ochrona podwodnego dziedzictwa kultury – aspekty prawnokarne i kryminologiczne*, Warszawa 2014.

Gai, *Institutiones*, text and translation W. Rozwadowski, Poznań 2003.

Gałyga M., *Status Zakładu Narodowego im. Ossolińskich w okresie zaborów i w latach międzywojennych*, "Czasopismo Zakładu Narodowego imienia Ossolińskich" 1992, Issue 1.

Gardocka T., *Cmentarze jako dobra kultury*, in: *Prawna ochrona dóbr kultury*, (eds.) T. Gardocka, J. Sobczak, Toruń 2009.

Gazur Ł., *Dama z łasiczką i ministrem* "Dziennik Polski", 21 January 2014, http://www.dziennikpolski24.pl/artykul/3304068,dama-z-lasiczka-i-ministrem,id,t.html?cookie=1 (accessed: 15.06.2015).

Gębarowicz M., *Zbiory muzealne w Zakładzie Narodowym im. Ossolińskich*, in: *Ossolineum. Księga pamiątkowa w 150-lecie Zakładu Narodowego imienia Ossolińskich*, (ed.) B. Olszewicz, Wrocław 1967.

Gillman D., *The Idea of Cultural Heritage*, Cambridge University Press, Cambrigde 2011.

Gniewek E., in: *Prawo rzeczowe. System Prawa* Prywatnego, Vol. 3, (ed.) T. Dybowski, Warszawa 2013.

Golat R., *Ustawa o ochronie zabytków i opiece nad zabytkami. Komentarz*, Kraków 2004.

Gotfried Reiner's letter of 6 December 1943 (on behalf of Dr Vosse) to head of Kaiser Friedrich Museum in Poznań, Dr S. Ruhle).

Górski M., *Commentary to the ECHR judgment of 29th March 2011 r.*, 33949/05, LEX/el. 2011.

Grabowski J., *Wywłaszczenie jako środek ochrony zabytków*, "Państwo i Prawo" 1967, Vol. 3.

Gredka I., *Ubezpieczenia dóbr kultury w muzeach i zbiorach prywatnych*, Kraków 2013.

Gromski W., entry: *Instytucja prawna*, in: *Wprowadzenie do nauk prawnych. Leksykon tematyczny*, (ed.) A. Bator, Warszawa 2012.

Gutowska K., Kobyliński Z., *Zarządzanie dziedzictwem kulturowym – nowa dziedzina nauczania akademickiego i badań naukowych*, "Mazowsze. Studia Regionalne" 2011, No. 6.

Gutowska K., Kobyliński Z., Wysocki J., *Nauczanie zarządzania dziedzictwem kulturowym w ramach różnych kierunków studiów wyższych*, in: *Nauczanie i popularyzacja ochrony dziedzictwa*, (ed.) B. Szmygin, Warszawa 2014.

Howard P., Ashworth G. J., *European Heritage, Planning and Management*, Intellect, Exeter 1999.

http://www.unesco.org/eri/la/convention.asp?KO=13520&language=E&order=alpha (accessed: 1.09.2015).

Ilczuk D., *Ekonomika kultury*, Warszawa 2012.

Instytucje Justyniana, translated by C. Kunderewicz, Warszawa 1986.

J. Purchla's lecture in the Trybunal Konstytucyjny (Constitional Tribunal) "Naród – Dziedzictwo – Pamięć" (Nation – Heritage – Memory), 14 May 2013, http://tkonst.linuxpl.info/video/narod-dziedzictwo-pamiec-wyklad-prof-jacka-purchli-w-trybunale-konstytucyjnym-14-maja-2013-r/ (accessed: 1.06.2015).

Jabłońska W., *Ustawy fundacyjne Józefa Maksymiliana Ossolińskiego*, "Ze Skarbca Kultury" 1977, Issue 28.

Jagielska-Burduk A., *Koncepcja świadomego dysponenta zabytków w polskim prawie ochrony zabytków*, in: *Prawo ochrony zabytków*, (ed.) K. Zeidler, Warszawa – Gdańsk 2014.

Jagielska-Burduk A., *Nabycie własności dobra kultury od nieuprawnionego. Wybrane zagadnienia*, "Santander Art and Culture Law Review" 2015, No. 1.

Jagielska-Burduk A., *Własność zabytków w świetle wyroku Trybunału Konstytucyjnego z dnia 8 października 2007 r.*, in: *Prawo wobec wyzwań współczesności*, Vol. 6, (eds.) B. Guzik, N. Buchowska, P. Wiliński, Poznań 2010.

Jagielska-Burduk A., *Zabytek ruchomy*, Warszawa 2011.

Jagielska-Burduk A., Mularski K., *Problematyka reprywatyzacji zabytków ruchomych. Uwagi na marginesie wyroku Sądu Najwyższego z dnia 16 lutego 2012 r. (III CSK 208/11)*, in: *Kolekcje i zbiory muzealne: problematyka prawna*, (eds.) P. Stec, P. P. Maniurka, Opole 2016.

Jagielska-Burduk A., Szafrański W., *Sektor kultury – działalność kulturalna. Wokół problematyki prawnej*, in: *Kultura w praktyce. Zagadnienia Prawne*, Vol. 1, (eds.) A. Jagielska-Burduk, W. Szafrański, Poznań 2012.

Jagielska-Burduk A., Szafrański W., Górska M. A., *Wirtualna Galeria im. Mielżyńskich. Historia – idea – prawo*, Poznań 2013.

Jakubowski A., Jakubowski O., *Pierwokup przy wywozie dóbr kultury za granicę – analiza kierunkowych zmian w prawie polskim*, in: *Kultura w praktyce. Zagadnienia prawne*, Vol. 3: *Muzea a rynek sztuki. Aspekt prawny*, (eds.) A. Jagielska-Burduk, W. Szafrański, Poznań 2014.

Jakubowski A., *State Succession in Cultural Property*, Oxford 2015.

Jakubowski A., *Territoriality and State Succession in Cultural Heritage*, "International Journal of Cultural Property" 2014, No. 21, Vol. 4.

Kadłuczka I., *"Rozbitek" Siemiradzkiego sprzedany. "To wielka strata dla Polski"*, "Gazeta Wyborcza", 28 November 2013, http://wyborcza.biz/biznes/1,100896,15035897,_Rozbitek__Siemiradzkiego_sprzedany___To_wielka_strata.html (accessed: 1.08.2015).

Kalinowski K., *Fundacja im. Raczyńskich przy Muzeum Narodowym w Poznaniu - model nowej własności historycznej kolekcji*, in: *Zbiory publiczne a kolekcjonerstwo prywatne. Problematyka ochrony dziedzictwa kulturowego w przeszłości i dzisiaj*, (ed.) J. Lipińska, Warszawa 2000.

Kąsinowska R., *Gołuchów. Rezydencja magnacka w świetle źródeł*, Gołuchów 2006.

King St. F., *Cultural resource laws and practice*, New York - Toronto - Plymouth UK 2013.

Klamer A., Mognosa A., Petrova L., *Cultural heritage policies: a comparative perspective*, in: *Economics of Cultural Heritage*, (eds.) I. Rizzo, A. Mognosa, Massachusetts 2013.

Kopff A., *Własność dóbr kultury*, "Studia Cywilistyczne" 1969, Vol. XIII–XIV.

Kosiewski P., *Własność a zbiory publiczne*, in: *Własność a dobra kultury*, (eds.) G. Czubek, P. Kosiewski, Warszawa 2006.

Kościński K., *Polskie ordynacye i związki rodzinne ze szczególnem uzględnieniem ordynacyi książąt Sułkowskich*, Poznań 1906.

Kowalski W., *Droga do Konwencji UNIDROIT z 1995 roku oraz jej podstawowe rozwiązania*, "Santander Art and Culture Law Review" 2015, No. 1.

Kowalski W., *Kolizyjnoprawne problemy restytucji dóbr kultury*, in: *Rozprawy prawnicze. Księga pamiątkowa profesora Maksymiliana Pazdana*, (eds.), L. Ogiegło, W. Popiołek, M. Szpunar, Kraków 2005.

Kowalski W., *Konwencja UNESCO o ochronie podwodnego dziedzictwa kulturowego z 2001 r.*, "Cenne, Bezcenne, Utracone" 2014, No. 3–4.

Kowalski W., *Nabycie własności dzieła sztuki od nieuprawnionego*, Kraków 2004.

Kowalski W., *Ochrona integralności zespołów zabytkowych w Polsce - podstawy prawne i praktyka*, "Ochrona Zabytków" 1995, No. 3.

Kowalski W., *Prawna ochrona zabytków w świetle aktualnych problemów zachowania dziedzictwa kulturowego Polski*, in: *Prawna ochrona dziedzictwa kulturowego. Wokół problematyki prawnej zabytków i dzieł sztuki*, Vol. 3, (eds.) W. Szafrański, K. Zalasińska, Poznań 2009.

Kowalski W., *Problematyka prawa obrotu dobrami kultury*, in: *Rynek sztuki. Aspekty prawne*, (eds.) W. Kowalski, K. Zalasińska, Warszawa 2011.

Kowalski W., *Trust and res extra commercium in search of legal instruments to strengthen the protection of cultural heritage*, in: *Ius est ars boni et aequi: festschrift für Stanisława Kalus*, red. M. Hadbas, A. Wudarski, Frankfurt 2010.

Kowalski W., Piotrowska-Nosek K., Schreiber H., Zalasińska K., *Konwencje UNESCO w dziedzinie kultury. Komentarz*, (ed.) K. Zalasińska, Warszawa 2014.

Kowalski W., Zalasińska K., *Prawo ochrony dziedzictwa kulturowego w Polsce – próba oceny i wnioski*, in: *System ochrony zabytków w Polsce – analiza, diagnoza, propozycje*, (ed.) B. Szmygin, Lublin – Warszawa 2011.

Krzyżanowska A., *Resort nie przyznaje się do wad w ewidencji zabytków*, "Gazeta Prawna", 3 July 2015.

Kuhnke M., *"Dworzanin" i "Dama" Jana Mostaerta. Historia dwóch obrazów ze zbiorów Muzeum w Gołuchowie*, "Muzealnictwo" 2006, No. 47.

Kuutma K., *Concepts and Contigencies in the Shaping of Heritage Regimes*, in: *Heritage Regimes and the State*, (eds.) E. F. Bendix, A. Eggert, A. Peselmann, Gotingen 2013.

Letter of 14th November 2012, RPO-706860-IV/12/JP, http://www.sprawy-generalne.brpo.gov.pl/pdf/2012/06/706860/1682077.pdf (accessed: 29.06.2015).

Lixinski L., *Heritage for Whom? Individuals' and Communities' Roles in International Cultural Heritage Role*, in: *International law for common goods. Normative perspective on Human Rights, Culture and Nature*, (eds.) F. Lenzerini, A. Vrdoljak, Oxfodr 2014.

Loewe R., *Preliminary Draft Convention on the Restitution of Cultural Property*, UNIDROIT, 1988, Study LXX – Doc. 3.

Maliszewski E., *Ordynacye polskie (Dokończenie)*, "Ziemia. Tygodnik Krajoznawczy Ilustrowany", 7 May 1910.

Mautner M., *"The Eternal Triangles of the Law": Toward a Theory of Priorities in Conflicts Involving Remote Parties*, "Michigan Law Review" 1991, No. 10.

Mełeń A., *Ordynacje w dawnej Polsce*, Lwów 1929.

Merryman J. H., *Thinking about Elgin Marbles: Critical Essays on Cultural Property. Art and Law*, The Hague – London – Boston 2000

Merryman J., *The Nation and the Object*, "International Journal of Cultural Property" 1994, Vol. 3, Issue 1.

Mikiciuk I., *Gminna ewidencja zabytków w świetle zmian wprowadzonych ustawą o zmianie ustawy o ochronie zabytków i opiece nad zabytkami oraz zmianie niektórych innych ustaw*, "Kurier Konserwatorski" 2010, No. 9.

Miliszkiewicz J., *Interview with Grażyna Kulczyk*, "Santander Art and Culture Law Review" 2015, No. 2.

Monaco R., *Outlines for a Private Law Convention on the International Protection of Cultural Property*, UNIDROIT, 1988, Study LXX – Doc. 2.

Morisset L. K., *Des régimes d'authenticité. Essai sur la mémoire patrimoniale*, Rennes 2009.

Motion put to the Constitutional Tribunal Court by Poland's President requesting examination of the compliance with the Constitution of the Act amending the act on the protection and guardianship of museums of 31 July 2015, http://www.prezydent.pl/download/gfx/prezydent/pl/defaultaktualnosci/2073/16/1/20150731_wniosek_do_tk_ws_ustawy_o_ochronie_zabytkow.pdf (dostęp 15.06.2015).

Moustaira E., *Art, Collections, Private and Public: A Comparative Legal Study*, Cham – Heidelberg – New York – Dordrecht – London 2015.

Mrówczyński M., *Uwarunkowania prawne tworzenia instytucji kultury oraz stowarzyszeń i fundacji prowadzących działalność kulturalną*, in: *Kultura w praktyce. Zagadnienia prawne*, Vol. 2: *Wokół problematyki prawnej zabytków i rynku sztuki*, (eds.) A. Jagielska-Burduk, W. Szafrański, Poznań 2013.

Nahlik S., *Grabież dzieł sztuki. Rodowód zbrodni międzynarodowej*, Wrocław – Kraków 1958.

Nieć H., *Ojczyzna dzieła sztuki. Międzynarodowa ochrona integralności narodowej spuścizny kulturalnej*, Warszawa – Kraków 1980.

Noga M., *Kultura a ekonomia*, Warszawa 2014.

Nowak J., *Ordynacja sieniawska książąt Czartoryskich. Plany – zamierzenia – realizacja*, "Rocznik Biblioteki Naukowej PAU i PAN w Krakowie" 2000.

O'Brien D., *Cultural Policy. Management, value, modernity in the creative industries*, London – New York 2014.

Ochendowski E., *Zakład administracyjny jako podmiot administracji państwowej*, Poznań 1969.

Ogrodzki P., *Rola baz danych w zwalczaniu przestępczości przeciwko dziedzictwu narodowemu*, in: *Prawna ochrona dziedzictwa kulturowego. Wokół problematyki prawnej zabytków i dzieł sztuki*, Vol. 3, (eds.) W. Szafrański, K. Zalasińska, Poznań 2009.

Ordynacja imienia książąt Czartoryskich [Entail named after Princes Czartoryski], "Głos Narodu", 13 November 1896.

Ordynacya książąt Czartoryskich, "Czas" [Time], 6 May 1894.

Paczuski W., *Handel dziełami sztuki w Unii Europejskiej*, Kraków 2005.

Pietraszak-Dmowski M., *Fundacja im. Raczyńskich przy Muzeum Narodowym w Poznaniu*, "Kronika Wielkopolski" 1993, No. 1.

Piotrowska K., *Aspekty prawne zarządzania dziedzictwem na przykładzie pomników historii i miejsc światowego dziedzictwa*, in: *Prawo ochrony zabytków*, (ed.) K. Zeidler, Warszawa – Gdańsk 2014.

Piotrowska-Nosek K., *Konwencja w sprawie ochrony światowego dziedzictwa kulturalnego i naturalnego*, in: W. Kowalski. K. Piotrowska-Nosek, H. Schreiber, K. Zalasińska, *Konwencje UNESCO w dziedzinie kultury. Komentarz*, (ed.) K. Zalasińska, Warszawa 2014.

The management plan for the World Cultural Heritage, http://www.unesco.pl/kultura/dziedzictwo-kulturowe/swiatowe-dziedzictwo/procedura-wpisu/plan-zarzadzania/ (accessed: 10.08.2015).

Po 75 latach obrazy z Muzeum Lubomirskich wracają do zbiorów Ossolineum, http://ossolineum.pl/index.php/po-75-latach-obrazy-z-muzeum-lubomirskich-wracaja-do-zbiorow-ossolineum/ (accessed: 10.06.2015).

Pomian K., *Dlaczego chronimy zabytki*, in: *Spotkania w Willi Struvego 2001–2003. Wykłady o dziedzictwie kultury*, (eds.) D. Królak-Merska, K. J. Kwiecińska, Warszawa 2004.

Potocki S. K., *Miejsce Biblioteki w Koncepcjach Fundacji Kórnickiej*, "Pamiętnik Biblioteki Kórnickiej" 1978, Issue 14.

Poulios I., *Discussing strategy in heritage conservation: Living heritage approach as an example of strategic innovation*, "Journal of Cultural Heritage Management and Sustainable Development" 2011, Vol. 4, No. 1.

Poulios I., *Is every heritage site a 'living' one?: linking conservation to communities' association with sites*, "The Historic Environment: Policy and Practice" 2011, Vol. 2, No. 2.

Principles underlying the establishment of a cultural park, its management and the preparation of its protection plan. Guidelines for commune self-governing units, authors of protection plans and voivodeship and commune inspectors of monuments, http://www.nid.pl/pl/Informacje_ogolne/Zabytki_w_Polsce/Parki_kulturowe/Zasady%20tworzenia%20Parku%20Kulturowego,%20zarz%C4%85dzania%20nim%20oraz%20sporz%C4%85dzania%20planu%20jego%20ochrony.pdf In these documents the legal aspects permeate the managerial issues (accessed: 15.06.2015).

Prott L. V., O'Keefe P., *Cultural Heritage or Cultural Property*, "International Journal of Cultural Property" 1992, No. 1.

Prott L. V., O'Keefe P., *Law and Cultural Heritage*, Vol. 1: *Discovery and Excavation*, London 1984.

Prott L. V., O'Keefe P., *Law and Cultural Heritage*, Vol. 3: *Movement*, London 1989.

Prott L. V., *Strengths and Weaknesses of the 1970 Convention: An Evaluation 40 years after its adoption*, 2nd edition, 2012, pp. 1–12. http://www.unesco.org/new/fileadmin/MULTIMEDIA/HQ/CLT/pdf/Prott_2_en.pdf (accessed: 15.06.2015).

Pruszyński J. P., *Dziedzictwo kultury i ochrona zabytków w Polsce. Perspektywa na najbliższe dziesięciolecie*, in: *Spotkania w Willi Struvego 2001–2003. Wykłady o dziedzictwie kultury*, (eds.) D. Królak-Merska, K. J. Kwiecińska, Warszawa 2004.

Pruszyński J. P., *Regulacja ustawowa ochrony zabytków*, "Ochrona Zabytków" 1985, No. 1.

Pruszyński J., *Dziedzictwo kultury Polski. Jego straty i ochrona prawna*, Vol. 1, Kraków 2001.

Purchla J., *Europa wobec dziedzictwa*, in: *Europa wobec dziedzictwa. Modele mecenatu na rzecz ochrony dziedzictwa kulturowego*, (ed.) Ł. Gałusek, Kraków 2005.

Purchla J., *Naród – Dziedzictwo – Pamięć*, "Zagadnienia Sądownictwa Konstytucyjnego" 2012, No. 2.

Raczyński E., *Rogalin i jego mieszkańcy*, Poznań 1991.

Reichelt G., *The International Protection of Cultural Property*, UNIDROIT, 1988, Study LXX – Doc. 4.

Reichelt G., *The Protection of Cultural Property*, UNIDROIT, 1986, Study LXX-Doc. 1.

Resolution No. 4 adopted at the "First Congress of Polish Museologists", http://kongresmuzealnikow.pl/projekty-uchwal/ (accessed: 14.06.2015).

Romainville C., *Le statut des collections publiques muséales en droit domanial*, in: *L'inaliénabilité des collections de musée en question. Actes du colloque tenu au Musée royal de Mariemont le 28 avril 2009*, Morlanwelz 2010.

Saint André von-Armin F. von, *Der Wert des Kulturerbes für die Gesellschaft. Genesis und Gegenstand der Europarats-Rahmenkonvention von 2005*, Hamburg 2007.

Sax L., *Playing Darts with Rembrandt. Public and Private Rights in Cultural Treasures*, Ann Arbor 2001.

Scott D. A., *Modern Antiquities: the Looted and the Faked*, "International Journal of Cultural Property" 2013, No. 1.

Scovazii T., *The definition of Intangible Cultural Heritage*, in: *Cultural Heritage, Cultural Rights, Cultural Diversity. New Developments in International Law*, (eds.) S. Borelli, F. Lenzerini, Leiden – Boston 2012.

Sienkiewicz T., *Umowa o oddanie gruntu w użytkowanie wieczyste jako nienazwana forma ochrony zabytków*, in: *Kultura w praktyce. Zagadnienia prawne*,

Vol. 3: *Muzea a rynek sztuki. Aspekty prawne*, (ed.) A. Jagielska-Burduk, W. Szafrański, Poznań 2014.

Słownik języka polskiego, (eds.) J. Karłowicz, A. Kryński, W. Niedźwiedzki, Vol. 7: *T-Y*, Warszawa 1919.

Smith A., *Badania nad naturą i przyczynami bogactwa narodów*, Vol. 1, Warszawa 1954.

Soldani A., Jankowski D., *Zabytki. Ochrona i opieka. Praktyczny komentarz do nowej ustawy. Tekst ustawy z dnia 23 lipca 2003 r.*, Zielona Góra 2004.

Sójka-Zielińska K., *Fideikomisy familijne w prawie pruskim (w. XIX i pocz. w. XX)*, Warszawa 1962.

Stahl M., *Przyrzeczenie publiczne (administracyjne)*, in: *Prawo administracyjne. Pojęcia, instytucje, zasady w teorii i orzecznictwie*, (ed.) M. Stahl, Warszawa 2013.

Standing G., *Prekariat. Nowa niebezpieczna klasa*, Warszawa 2014.

Statement by P. Żuchowski, Secretary of the State at the Ministry of Culture and National Heritage responding to a question posed by a deputy in the parliament in 2013 regarding the status of a public, http://www.sejm.gov.pl/sejm7.nsf/InterpelacjaTresc.xsp?key=34230811 (accessed: 15.06.2015).

Stawecki T., Winczorek P., *Wstęp do prawoznawstwa*, Warszawa 2003.

Stec P., *Dyrektywa 93/7 EWG z perspektywy dwóch dekad funkcjonowania*, "Santander Art and Culture Law Review" 2015, No. 1.

Stelmach J., *Uporczywe upodobanie. Zapiski kolekcjonera*, Olszanica 2012.

Suchocki W., *Fundacja im. Raczyńskich przy Muzeum Narodowym w Poznaniu*, in: *Własność a dobra kultury*, (eds.) G. Czubek, P. Kosiewski, Warszawa 2006.

Suski P., *Stowarzyszenia i fundacje*, Warszawa 2011.

Szafrański W., "*Dama*" *na liście skarbów*, "Rzeczpospolita", 8 January 2014, http://prawo.rp.pl/artykul/1077063.html (accessed: 15.06.2015).

Szafrański W., *Dekret o rejestracji i zakazie wywozu dzieł sztuki z 1946 r. – czy praktyka rozmijała się z celami regulacji prawnej?*, "Studia Iuridica Toruniensia" 2012, Vol. 10.

Szafrański W., *Mity i patologie obrotu dziełami sztuki*, "Santander Art and Culture Law Review" 2015, No. 1.

Szafrański W., *Publiczne aspekty prywatnych kolekcji*, in: *Kultura w praktyce. Zagadnienia prawne*, Vol. 1, (eds.) A. Jagielska-Burduk, W. Szafrański, Poznań 2012.

Szydło W., in: *Kodeks cywilny. Komentarz*, (eds.) E. Gniewek, P. Machnikowski, Warszawa 2014.

Szymaniak P., *Dzieło sztuki będzie można znacjonalizować*, "Gazeta Prawna", 15 June 2015, http://prawo.gazetaprawna.pl/artykuly/877250,dzielo-sztuki-bedzie-mozna-znacjonalizowac.html (accessed: 7.08.2015).

The Act that was on 31 July 2015 referred to the Constitutional Tribunal Court by President of the Republic of Poland to review its compliance with the Constitution, http://www.prezydent.pl/download/gfx/prezydent/pl/defaultaktualnosci/2073/16/1/20150731_wniosek_do_tk_ws_ustawy_o_ochronie_zabytkow.pdf (accessed: 15.06.2015).

The fate of Lubomirski Dürers. Recovering the Treasures of the Ossoliński National Institute, (eds.) A. Juzwenko, T. Mirecki, Wrocław 2004.

The Impact of Culture on Creativity z 2009 r. http://www.keanet.eu/docs/execsum_creativity_english%20.pdf?4f4eb7 (accessed: 10.07.2015).

The International Protection of Cultural Property. Observations L. Prott, UNIDROIT, 1988, Study LXX – Doc. 7.

The National Programme of the Protection and Guardianship of Monuments 2014–2017, (appendix to resolution No. 125/2014 RM of 24 VI 2014), http://bip.mkidn.gov.pl/media/download_gallery/20140818Krajowy_Program_Ochrony_Zabytkow_i_Opieki_nad_Zaby.pdf (accessed: 15.06.2015)

Thesis for the development of the national programme of monument protection and guardianship approved by the Minister of Culture Waldemar Dąbrowski, http://www.kobidz.home.pl/pliki/tezy.pdf (accessed: 15.06.2015).

Thorsby D., *Ekonomia i kultura*, Warszawa 2010.

Towse R., *Ekonomia kultury. Kompendium*, Warszawa 2011.

Tronchetti F., *The Exploitation of Natural Resources of the Moon and Other Celestial Bodies. A Proposal for a Legal Regime*, Leiden 2009.

Truszkiewicz Z., *Użytkowanie wieczyste. Zagadnienia konstrukcyjne*, Kraków 2006.

Trzciński M., *Definicja zabytku archeologicznego – problemy i kontrowersje wokół stosowania prawa*, in: *Prawo ochrony zabytków*, (ed.) K. Zeidler, Warszawa – Gdańsk 2014.

Trzciński M., *Glosa do wyroku TK (sygn. akt K 20/07)*, "Zeszyty Naukowe Sądownictwa Administracyjnego" 2008, No. 2.

Trzynadlowski J., *Zakład Narodowy imienia Ossolińskich 1817–1967. Zarys dziejów*, Wrocław – Warszawa – Kraków 1967.

Tułodziecki A., in: J. Jaworski, A. Prusaczyk, A. Tułodziecki, M. Wolanin, *Ustawa o gospodarce nieruchomościami. Komentarz*, Warszawa 2013.

Vadi V., *Cultural heritage in international investment law and arbitration*, Cambridge 2014.

Vadi V., *Culture, Development and International Law: The Linkage between Investment Rules and the Protection of Cultural Heritage*, in: *Cultural Heritage, Cultural Rights, Cultural Diversity. New Developments in International Law*, (eds.) S. Borelli, F. Lenzerini, Leiden – Boston 2012.

Vadi V., Schneider H., *Art, Cultural Heritage and the Market: Legal and Ethical Issues*, in: *Art, Cultural Heritage and the Market. Ethical and Legal Status*, (eds.) V. Vadi, H. Schneider, Berlin – Heidelberg 2014.

Vigneron S., *Protecting cultural objects: Enforcing the Illicit Export of Foreign Cultural Goods*, in: *Art, Cultural Heritage and the Market Ethical and Legal Issues*, (eds.) V. Vadi, H. Schneider, Berlin – Heidelberg 2014.

Vrdoljak A. F., *Human rights and Illicit Trade in Cultural Objects*, in: *Cultural Heritage, Cultural Rights, Cultural Diversity. New Developments in International Law*, (eds.) S. Borelli, F. Lenzerini, Leiden – Boston 2012.

Waltoś S., *Prawna ochrona dóbr kultury w Europie (Tezy)*, in: *Spotkania w Willi Struvego 1998–2001. Wykłady o dziedzictwie kultury*, (ed.) K. J. Kwiecińska, Warszawa 2001.

Wasilkowski J., *Pojęcie własności we współczesnym prawie polskim*, Warszawa 1972.

Weber M., *New Swiss Law on Cultural Property*, "International Journal of Cultural Property" 2006, No. 13.

Weidner A., *Kulturgüter als res extra commercium im internationalen Sachenrecht*, Berlin – New York 2001.

Wijesuriya G., *The past is in the present: perspectives in caring for Buddhist heritage sites in Sri Lanka*, in: *Conservation of Living Religious Heritage: Papers from the ICCROM 2003 Forum on Living Religious Heritage: Conserving the Sacred*, (eds.) H. Stovel, N. Stanley-Price, R. Killick, ICCROM, Rome 2005.

Williams S., *The International and National Protection of Movable Cultural Property. A Comparative Study*, Dobbs Ferry – New York 1978.

Wittgenstein L., *Uwagi o barwach*, Warszawa 2014.

Worthing D., Bond S., *Managing Built Heritage. The role if cultural significance*, Oxford 2008.

Zalasińska K., *Glosa do wyroku Trybunału Konstytucyjnego z dnia 8 października 2007 r., K 20/07*, "Przegląd Orzecznictwa" 2008, No. 2.

Zalasińska K., *Muzea publiczne. Studium administracyjnoprawne*, Warszawa 2013.

Zalasińska K., *Ochrona ruchomego dziedzictwa kulturowego w Polsce – wybrane zagadnienia*, "Opolskie Studia Administracyjno-Prawne" 2011, Vol. 8.

Zalasińska K., *Ochrona zabytków. Orzecznictwo z komentarzem*, Warszawa 2010.

Zalasińska K., *Prawna ochrona zabytków nieruchomych w Polsce*, Warszawa 2010.

Zalasińska K., *Wpływ zmiany przepisów dotyczących wywozu zabytków za granicę na rynek sztuki w Polsce*, in: *Rynek sztuki. Aspekty prawne*, (eds.) W. Kowalski, K. Zalasińska, Warszawa 2011.

Zeidler K., *O dobre prawo dla zabytków – rozważania na gruncie ustawy z 2003 roku o ochronie zabytków i opiece nad zabytkami*, "Gdańskie Studia Prawnicze" 2010, Vol. XXIV.

Zeidler K., *Pomniki historii*, "Spotkania z Zabytkami" 2006, No. 8.

Zeidler K., *Prawo ochrony dziedzictwa kultury jako nowa gałąź prawa*, in: *Prawo ochrony zabytków*, (ed.) K. Zeidler, Warszawa – Gdańsk 2014.

Zeidler K., *Prawo ochrony dziedzictwa kultury*, Warszawa 2007.

Zielniewicz T., statement found in: "Biuletyn Forum Debaty Publicznej. Pomniki historii – źródło dziedzictwa kultury. Twórczość, dziedzictwo kulturowe i przyrodnicze bogactwem Polski" 2012, No. 10.

Ziembiński Z., *Podstawowe problemy prawoznawstwa*, Warszawa 1980.

Zoll F., *Pandecta czyli nauka rzymskiego prawa prywatnego*, Vol. I: *Część ogólna*, Kraków 1914.

Zoll F., *Prawo prywatne w zarysie przedstawione na podstawie ustaw austriackich*, Kraków 1910.

Legal acts

Bundesgesetz über den internationalen Kulturgütertransfer (KGTG or CPTA) of 20 June 2003 (in force as of 1 June 2005).

Convention concerning the Protection of the World Cultural and Natural Heritage adopted on 16th November 1972 by the General Conference of the United Nations Educational, Scientific and Cultural Organization meeting in Paris at its seventeenth session, http://portal.unesco.org/en/ev.php-URL_ID=13055&URL_DO=DO_TOPIC&URL_SECTION=201.html (accessed: 18.01.2016).

Council of Europe Framework Convention on the Value of Cultural Heritage for Society: Explanatory report, 27.10.2005, http://conventions.coe.int/Treaty/EN/Reports/Html/199.htm (accessed: 15.06.2015).

Cour de Cassation, 10 VI 1872, in: *Pasicrisie Belge*, 1872, I, p. 352.

Cour de Cassation, 11 XI 1886, in: *Pasicrisie Belge*, 1886, p. 401.

Declaration on the Importance and Value of Universal Museums, reprinted ICOM News, 2004, No. 1, http://icom.museum/fileadmin/user_upload/pdf/ICOM_News/2004-1/ENG/p4_2004-1.pdf (accessed: 10.06.2015).

Declaration UNESCO on the Responsibilities of the Present Generations Towards Future Generations, adopted on 12 November 1997, http://portal.unesco.org/en/ev.php-URL_ID=13178&URL_DO=DO_TOPIC&URL_SECTION=201.html (accessed: 10.06.2015).

EU Directive 2014/60, OJ L 159, 28.05.2014.

Ordinance of the Council (EC) No. 116/2009 of 18 December 2008 on the export of cultural property, OJ L 39, 10.02.2009.

Protocol no. 1 to the Convention for the Protection of Human Rights and Fundamental Freedoms of 11th November 1950. Dz. U. 1995, No. 36, item 175; Poland ratified Protocol no. 1 on 10th October 1994.

UNIDROIT Convention on Stolen or Illegally Exported Cultural Objects (of 24 June 1995), http://www.unidroit.org/english/conventions/1995culturalproperty/1995culturalproperty-e.pdf (accessed: 10.06.2015).

Ustawa z dnia 13 lipca 1939 r. o znoszeniu ordynacji rodowych [Act of 13 July 1939 on the liquidation of family entails], Dz. U. 1939, No. 63, item 417.

Ustawa z dnia 15 lutego 1962 r. o ochronie dóbr kultury [Act of 15 February 1962 on the Protection of Cultural Property and Museums], Dz. U. 1962, No. 10, item 46 as amended.

Ustawa z dnia 14 lipca 1983 r. o narodowym zasobie archiwalnym i archiwach [Act of 14 July 1983 on the National Archival Resource and State Archives], Dz. U. 2011, No. 123, item 698 as later amended.

Ustawa z dnia 6 kwietnia 1984 r. o fundacjach *[Act of 6 April 1984 on Foundations]*, Dz. U. 1984 No. 21 item 97 as later amended.

Ustawa z dnia 6 kwietnia 1984 r. o fundacjach [Act of 6 April 1984 on Foundations], uniform text Dz. U. 1991, No. 46, item 203 as later amended.

Ustawa z dnia 19 lipca 1990 r. o zmianie ustawy o ochronie dóbr kultury i o muzeach [Act of 19 July 1990 amending the Act on the protection of cultural property and on museums], Dz. U. 1990, No. 56, item 322.

Ustawa z dnia 5 stycznia 1995 r. o fundacji – Zakład Narodowy imienia Ossolińskich [Act of 5 January 1995 on the Foundation – the Ossoliński National Enterprise], Dz. U. No. 23, item 121 and of 2002 No. 153, item 1271.

Ustawa z dnia 21 listopada 1996 r. o muzeach [Act of 21 November 1996 on Museums], Dz. U. 1997, No. 5, item 24 as amended.

Ustawa z dnia 21 sierpnia 1997 r. o gospodarce nieruchomościami [Immovable Property Management Act of 21st August 1997], consolidated text Dz. U. 2010, No. 102, item 651 as amended.

Ustawa z dnia 27 marca 2003 r. o planowaniu i zagospodarowaniu przestrzennym [Act of 27 March 2003 on spatial planning and development], uniform text, Dz. U. 2015, No. 199.

Ustawa z dnia 23 lipca 2003 r. o ochronie zabytków i opiece nad zabytkami [Act on the Protection and Guardianship of Monuments, currently in force], Dz. U. 2003, No. 162, item 1568 as amended.

Ustawa z dnia 5 lipca 2007 r. o zmianie ustawy o fundacji – Zakład Narodowy imienia Ossolińskich [Act of 5 July 2007 amending the Act on the Foundation – Zakład Narodowy imienia Ossolińskich], Dz. U. 2007, No. 147, item 1029.

Ustawa z dnia 18 marca 2010 r. o zmianie ustawy o ochronie zabytków i opiece nad zabytkami i zmianie niektórych innych ustaw [Act of 18 March 2010 amending the APGM and some other Acts], Dz. U. 2010, No. 75, item 474.

Ustawa z dnia 20 lutego 2015 r. o rzeczach znalezionych [Unclaimed Property Act], Dz. U. 2015, item 397.

Ustawa z dnia 10 lipca 2015 r. o zmianie ustawy o ochronie zabytków i opiece nad zabytkami oraz ustawy o muzeach [Act to amend the APGM and the Act on Museums], the text of the Act available from http://orka.sejm.gov.pl/proc7.nsf/ustawy/3112_u.htm (accessed: 20.07.2015).

Rozporządzenie Prezydenta Rzeczypospolitej Polskiej z dnia 6 marca 1928 r. o opiece nad zabytkami [Regulation by the President of the Republic of Poland of 6 March 1928 on the Care for Monuments], Dz. U. RP No. 29, item 265 as later amended, repealed in 1962.

Rozporządzenie Ministra Rolnictwa i Reform Rolnych z dnia 1 marca 1945 r. w sprawie wykonania dekretu Polskiego Komitetu Wyzwolenia Narodowego z dnia 6 września 1944 r. o przeprowadzeniu reformy rolnej [Decision of the Minister of Agriculture and Agricultural Reform of 1 March 1945 on the execution of the Decree of the Polish National Liberation Committee of 6 September 1944 on the enforcement of an agricultural reform], Dz. U. 1945, No. 10, item 51 as later amended.

Rozporządzenie Prezydenta Rzeczypospolitej Polskiej z dnia 4 lipca 2014 r. w sprawie uznania za pomnik historii "Trzebnica – zespół dawnego opactwa cysterek" [Regulation by the President of the Republic of Poland of 4 July 2014 on the conferral of the status of a Monument of History" to "Trzebnica – the former Cistercian nuns Abbey complex"], Dz. U. 2014, No. 957.

Rozporządzenie Prezydenta Rzeczypospolitej Polskiej z dnia 16 lutego 2015 r. w sprawie uznania za pomnik historii "Łódź – wielokulturowy krajobraz miasta przemysłowego" [Regulation by the President of the Republic of Poland of 4 July 2014 on the conferral of the status of a monument of history" to "Łódź – a multi-cultural landscape of an industrial town"], Dz. U. 2015, No. 315.

Rozporządzenie Prezydenta Rzeczypospolitej Polskiej z dnia 23 lutego 2015 r. w sprawie uznania za pomnik historii "Gdynia – historyczny układ urbanistyczny śródmieścia" [Regulation by the President of the Republic of Poland of 4 July 2014 on the conferral of the status of a monument of history" to "Gdynia, a historic layout of the city centre"], Dz. U. 2015, No. 356.

Dekret Rady Regencyjnej o opiece nad zabytkami sztuki i kultury z dnia 31 października 1918 r. [Decree of 31 October 1918 of the Regency Council on the Guardianship of Monuments of Art and Culture], Dz. U. 1918, No. 16, item 36.

Dekret PKWN z dnia 6 września 1944 r. o przeprowadzeniu reformy rolnej [Decree of the Polish National Liberation Committee of 6 September 1944 on the enforcement of the agricultural reform], Dz. U. 1945, No. 3, item 13 as later amended.

Dekret z dnia 1 marca 1946 r. o rejestracji i zakazie wywozu dzieł sztuki plastycznej oraz przedmiotów o wartości artystycznej, historycznej lub kulturalnej [Decree of 1st March 1946 on the Registration and Export Prohibition of Works of Fine Art and Objects of Artistic, Historical and Cultural Value], Dz. U. 1946, No. 14, item 99.

Dekret z dnia 8 października 1946 r. Przepisy wprowadzające prawo spadkowe [Decree of 8 October 1946. Provisions implementing succession law], Dz. U. 1946, No. 60, item 329.

Dekret z dnia 24 kwietnia 1952 r. o zniesieniu fundacji [Decree of 24 April 1952 on the liquidation of foundations], Dz. U. 1952, No. 25, item 170 and 171.

Dekret z dnia 31 grudnia 1956 r. o uzupełnieniu przepisów o zniesieniu fundacji [Decree of 31 December 1956 on the completion of the provisions liquidating foundations], Dz. U. 1957, No. 1, item 3.

Lex et Res Publica
Polish Legal and Political Studies

Edited by
Anna Jarón

Vol. 1 Anna Jarón: Socio-Economic Constitutional Rights in Democratisation Processes. An Account of the Constitutional Dialogue Theory. 2012.

Vol. 2 Stanisław Filipowicz: Democracy – The Power of Illusion. 2013.

Vol. 3 Teresa Dukiet-Nagórska (ed.): The Postulates of Restorative Justice and the Continental Model of Criminal Law. As Illustrated by Polish Criminal Law 2014.

Vol. 4 Agnieszka Kupzok: Enforcement of Patents on Geographically Divisible Inventions. An Inquiry into the Standard of Substantive Patent Law Infringement in Cross-Border Constellations. 2015.

Vol. 5 Alicja Jagielska-Burduk / Wojciech Szafrański: Legal Issues in Cultural Heritage Management. A Polish Perspective. 2016.

www.peterlang.com

www.ingramcontent.com/pod-product-compliance
Ingram Content Group UK Ltd.
Pitfield, Milton Keynes, MK11 3LW, UK
UKHW020836290926
15470UKWH00004B/1373

9 783631 670330